Hitler's Secret Bankers

The Myth of Swiss Neutrality During the Holocaust

Adam LeBor

A BIRCH LANE PRESS BOOK
Published by Carol Publishing Group

A Birch Lane Press Book
Published by Carol Publishing Group
Birch Lane Press is a registered trademark of Carol Communications, inc.

Editorial, sales and distribution, rights and permissions inquiries should be
addressed to Carol Publishing Group, 120 Enterprise Avenue, Secaucus,
N.J. 07094

In Canada: Canadian Manda Group, One Atlantic Avenue, Suite 105,
Toronto, Ontario M6K 3E7

Carol Publishing Group books may be purchased in bulk at special
discounts for sales promotion, fund-raising, or educational purposes. Special
editions can be created to specifications. For details, contact Special Sales
Department, Carol Publishing Group, 120 Enterprise Avenue, Secaucus,
N.J. 07094.

Manufactured in the United States of America
10 9 8 7 6 5 4 3 2 1

Cataloging data for this publication can be obtained from the Library of
Congress.

In memory of my beloved grandparents:
Benjamin and Luba LeBor, who left in time

"For six days a week Switzerland works for Nazi Germany, while on the seventh it prays for an Allied victory."

Wartime saying

CONTENTS

ACKNOWLEDGMENTS

This book is a carefully compiled jigsaw, its constituent parts formerly scattered across archives, libraries, and wartime survivors' memories around the world. It took an international team of dedicated researchers, friends, and colleagues to help me put the jigsaw together, working in London, Washington, D.C., Bern, and Jerusalem. We trawled through dusty boxes of declassified intelligence files, sifted through reams of wartime diplomatic correspondence, tracked down out-of-print history books, interviewed Holocaust survivors and their descendants, and compiled an ever-growing library of contemporary newspaper and magazine cuttings as, during the second half of 1996, every week brought new revelations about Swiss economic collaboration with the Third Reich. Every member of this investigative network deserves to be acknowledged.

Foremost among these is my chief researcher, Barbara Wyllie, a tenacious historical investigator with a needle-sharp eye for detail, whose detective skills turned up a small mountain of historical jewels. A large part of the core material of *Hitler's Secret Bankers* is based on her invaluable work. I am also especially indebted to historian Marc Masurovsky, in Washington, D.C., whose invaluable advice and encyclopedic knowledge of Operation Safehaven and Allied economic intelligence operations in wartime Switzerland helped keep me on track. Thanks also to Cathy Starllings of the *Times* bureau in Washington, D.C., for her assistance. In Budapest I was aided by a team of researchers and translators: the indomitable Dora Czuk, Judit and Janos Zegnal, Kati Csepi, Nora Milotay, and Gaby Komar. In Bern historian

Guido Koller illuminated Switzerland's dark record of turning away Jewish refugees, while in Jerusalem author Tom Segev provided me with several valuable leads.

I am grateful also to the staff of the following archives and libraries for their assistance in locating documents and providing valuable advice: in London, the British Public Records Office, the Imperial War Museum, the Wiener Library, and the Jewish Chronicle Library; in Washington, D.C., the U.S. National Archives; in Bern, the Swiss Federal Archives; and in Jerusalem, the Central Zionist Archives and the Yad Vashem Holocaust Museum.

Thanks also to the following for their help: Elan Steinberg at the World Jewish Congress in New York; Greg Rickman at Senator Alfonse D'Amato's office in Washington, D.C.; Janice Lopatkin at the Holocaust Educational Trust in London; Ernest David at the Association of Jewish Refugees; and the staff of the Bank for International Settlements in Bern, particularly general manager Andrew Crockett and historian Piet Clement, who readily answered all of my questions about the BIS's compromising wartime activities. The Internet Holocaust Mailing List (h-holocaust@h-net.msu.edu), moderated by Jim Mott, also provided some valuable contacts. Still in cyberspace, Dr. Janos Muth, of Compuserve Hungary, provided me with an invaluable complimentary account that allowed me access to Compuserve's many databases and information services.

At the *Times* I am grateful to Colette Forder and Nicholas Wapshott of the *Saturday Magazine,* who first commissioned me to write the article that would be the genesis of this book, and especially to Lisette Felix, of the foreign desk, for all her help over the past six years. Thanks also to my colleagues Matthew Valencia at the *Economist,* Joe Cook at *Business Central Europe,* and Jenni Frazer of the *Jewish Chronicle.* My gratitude extends also to all the individuals who sat down with me for many hours and related what happened to their families during the Holocaust, a process of remembering that caused them some emotional pain, particularly Isabelle Silberg in London and Yvonne and Ron Singer in Toronto. I am also grateful to Edward Reichmann, who flew to Budapest to meet me and outline his family's wartime history.

Fulsome thanks also to my agent, Jennifer Kavanagh, whose faith in this project helped greatly to bring it to fruition, Helen Gummer and

Ingrid Connell at Simon and Schuster for their valuable editorial advice, and Andrew Armitage for his copy editing skills. All of which also holds true for Hillel Black, Donald J. Davidson, and India Cooper at Birch Lane Press in New York, whose unrelenting enthusiasm for *Hitler's Secret Bankers* was always a source of inspiration.

Many friends too helped, some with support, hospitality, and late-night whiskies, others just by being there: in Washington, D.C., Charles and Katerina Lane and Peter Maass; in New York, Sam Loewenberg; in Budapest, Chris Condon, Simon Evans, John Nadler, Rob Scott, Colin Woodard, Laszlo Petrovics-Ofner, Dora Szalai, Tony Stearns, Steve Carlson, Emmanuelle Richard, Matt Welch, and, especially, for laughter and inspiration, Agnes Csonka; in London, Justin Leighton and, of course, my parents. In Zurich, Mike Shields and Alison Langley provided me with lengthy hospitality, while in Tel Aviv, Andy Goldberg was a fine host. Thanks also to Gisela Blau.

I would also like to acknowledge here a small historical debt: to Mrs. Jo Wagerman, formerly of the Jewish Free School in London, and to Dr. Roy Bridge of Leeds University, two teachers of history who first taught me how to think analytically and question accepted wisdoms.

Finally, I must mention three books that have inspired and instructed me during the writing of *Hitler's Secret Bankers: The Rise and Fall of the Third Reich,* by William L. Shirer, a phenomenal work of history by a contemporary observer of the Nazi regime; Professor Yehuda Bauer's pioneering examination of wartime Jewish–Nazi negotiations, *Jews for Sale?;* and David Kahn's *Hitler's Spies,* an encyclopedic account of the Nazis' secret intelligence networks.

Doubtless there are some who aided me whose names I have unintentionally omitted; to all I say thank you.

INTRODUCTION

Traveling in December 1996 on a pristine Swiss train to Bern, site of the Swiss Federal Archives, I met an American expatriate who, fifteen years earlier, had relocated to Zürich. Our conversation soon turned to the question of Holocaust victims' dormant accounts and the revelations about Swiss-Nazi economic links that had dominated the international headlines from the spring of that year.

Why, I asked, had the Swiss bankers responded in such a clumsy and ham-fisted manner to the revelations that for decades they had sat on money owed to the descendants of Holocaust victims, even demanding that claimants produce death certificates for their parents who had been killed in Auschwitz? "The problem with the Swiss bankers and Holocaust victims' accounts," he said, "is that the bankers have a concept deficit about this." A concept deficit. It was a telling, two-word summation of a complicated issue. This phrase, suggestive of a moral rather than financial shortfall, I thought, encapsulated a lot more than the bankers' refusal to hand over monies deposited by Jews who died in the gas chambers or were shot into mass graves by SS Einsatzgruppen troops.

Insulated by decades of political neutrality and historical isolationism, buttressed by the massive amounts of the world's questionably acquired wealth that still lies in the Swiss banks' vaults, the bankers didn't understand why they should have to answer questions from anybody, let alone from claimants without the proper paperwork. Rules were rules; that was how Swiss banks had always operated and that is how they always would, they believed. Swiss banks, and by extension Switzerland itself, were unaccountable. Perhaps the best example of this was the furor that erupted in January 1997 when outgoing Swiss president Jean-Pascal Delamuraz described as "extortion and blackmail" demands by Jewish organizations that the Swiss banks, who made so much money by trading with the Nazis, set up a Holocaust compensation fund. This too was part of the "concept deficit," with Swiss government leaders failing to realize that the world has changed, and no nation, not even a neutral one, is an island. But even Switzerland must adjust to changing realities of global realpolitik, and Delamuraz later apologized for his remarks.

The concept, if you will, of the "concept deficit" aptly sums up all the key strands in the network of connections that bound the wartime Swiss economy into the Nazi war machine and anointed the ever-discreet financial mandarins of Zürich, Basel, and Bern as Hitler's Secret Bankers. For the monies deposited in good faith by Holocaust victims and sat on for over fifty years by stonewalling bank clerks are just the opening shot of the case against the Swiss banks. Swiss officials claim that their policies toward the Allied and Axis powers were those of balanced neutrality, but the scales were heavily tipped in favor of the Nazis, at least on economic matters.

Declassified intelligence reports reveal that Swiss banks, particularly the Swiss National Bank, accepted gold looted from the national treasuries of Nazi-occupied countries and from dead Jews alike, gold they either bought outright or laundered for the Nazis before sending it on to other neutral countries. Swiss banks supplied the foreign currency that the Third Reich needed to buy vital war material. Swiss banks were the vital financial conduit that allowed Nazi economic officials to channel their loot to a safe haven in Switzerland. Swiss banks financed Nazi foreign intelligence operations by providing funds for German front companies in Spain and Portugal. At the Basel-based Bank for International Settlements, Nazi and Allied nationals even worked together all through the war as their compatriots were slaughtering each other on Europe's battlefields.

There is a powerful argument that, without the considerable efforts of Swiss bankers to help keep the Nazi war machine sufficiently funded, the Second World War could have ended several years earlier, especially after the Wehrmacht's massive defeats at the battles of Stalingrad and Kursk, which were the final spasms of Operation Barbarossa, the invasion of the Soviet Union that cost many millions of Reichsmarks and hundreds of thousands of German lives. Certainly, other neutral countries also traded with and aided the Third Reich. Spain and Portugal supplied tungsten, Turkey chrome, and Sweden steel. But Turkey eventually severed diplomatic relations with the Nazis, and Sweden, together with Denmark, organized a mass rescue of thousands of Danish Jews by boat in the autumn of 1943, hid them, and gave them all sanctuary.

No other neutral country played as crucial a role in keeping the Nazi war machine rolling as Switzerland. Where did the money come from that allowed the Nazis to purchase these vital war materials? Swiss banks, for nobody in Madrid, Lisbon, Ankara, or Stockholm would accept Reichsmarks. True, there were banks in Lisbon and Stockholm too, but the Portuguese escudo and the Swedish krona were not a serious medium of international finance. The Nazis' trading partners wanted hard currency, Swiss francs, and those they got, supplied by Swiss bankers.

Switzerland's policy of neutrality, enshrined in international treaties, demanded that it avoid joining either side during the Second World War and pursue policies toward both the Allies and the Axis that were nondiscriminatory and impartial. For the Swiss, a people of four languages and cultures—German, French, Romansch, and Italian—neutrality is more than a way of avoiding neighboring wars. Neutrality is the glue that helps bind the country together, says Peter Burkhard of the Swiss government task force set up in the autumn of 1996 to examine Switzerland's wartime relationship with Nazi Germany. "Neutrality is part of the Swiss identity; it is like a myth. Every country and every people needs a common myth, especially Switzerland, where there is no such thing as a Swiss nation in cultural terms. Swiss identity is based on a common history, values, and experience, but not a common culture or language. Neutrality is one of the few things we have in common."

Even though there is no such thing as a Swiss nation in cultural terms, the various linguistic communities do share some common political and diplomatic history. By the early sixteenth century Switzerland had defended its independence—first declared in 1291—by repelling takeover attempts by the Austrians and Burgundians. In 1648 Swiss independence was recognized by the Holy Roman Empire, which then ruled much of western Europe. That lasted until 1798, when the

French revolutionary armies invaded and established a republic. At the Congress of Vienna in 1815, which followed the defeat of Napoleon, leader of the French armies, Swiss independence was once again restored, and Switzerland's neutrality was guaranteed by the European powers. As well as being enshrined in international treaty, Swiss neutrality is also based on a well-armed citizens' army that is ready to fight off any would-be invader. A universal conscription is mandatory for men aged between twenty and fifty, who undergo extensive military training. Just as in Israel, the army also helps cement different ethnic groups, French-, German-, Romansch-, and Italian-speaking, into a common nation.

Switzerland is composed of twenty-three local cantons, roughly corresponding to American states. These cantons were established by the 1848 constitution, which also established civil liberties and rudimentary parliamentary democracy. The franchise was not extended to women until 1971. The government is divided into two branches: the seven-member Federal Council, including the president, who holds the post for one year on a rotating basis; and a two-chamber parliament. Members of the council are chosen by the two houses of Parliament. They are usually, but not always, members of parliament and are drawn from the ruling coalition parties.

Switzerland has for decades been governed by a coalition of parties, which can be described as center-right. During the Second World War these parties were the Christian Conservatives, Social Democrats, Liberals, and the Farmers and Artisans Party; the coalition still rules now, although some party names have changed. Major political issues, such as whether to join the European Union, are decided by referendum. Switzerland is not currently a member of the European Union, NATO, or even the United Nations.

It was the Federal Council that, ruling with extra wartime dictatorial powers, set the policy of economic collaboration with the Nazis and decided in August 1942 to close the borders to Jewish refugees. While some bankers and much of the political and financial elite collaborated economically with the Nazis, much of the Swiss general public had little sympathy for the Third Reich. Few wished their country to actually be subsumed into the Third Reich. Both the press and some churchmen, in particular, pushed hard for the restrictions on Jewish immigration to be lifted. The liberal press was motivated by humanitarian considerations and the traditional desire of journalists to expose government wrongdoings while battling against wartime censorship. The churchmen, mostly Protestant together with some Catholic, emphasized Switzerland's tradition of giving sanctuary to fleeing refugees.

During the war, unlike in all of Switzerland's neighbors, there were no anti-Jewish laws passed affecting the status of Jews on Swiss territory proper, as opposed to rules governing Jewish immigration. But then Switzerland remained free and independent. Even so, in Switzerland, as in most European countries, there ran a current of anti-Semitism, which some authorities argue increased during the war, partly because of a spillover effect from the neighboring Third Reich and the strong economic links between Switzerland and Nazi Germany. During the war Swiss Jews were refused jobs manufacturing military equipment because of their religion. But at the same time, the Federal Council expended much effort on restricting Nazi and anti-Semitic propaganda.

Jews have been settled in Switzerland since the Middle Ages, although they suffered several expulsions and were not fully emancipated until 1874. Even now Jews do not enjoy full civil rights in that the kosher slaughter of beef is banned in Switzerland, forcing Orthodox Jews to import kosher beef, at much higher prices. Kosher slaughter of poultry is permitted, although at the end of 1996 Swiss Jews successfully fought off an attempt to extend the ban to poultry. The ban on kosher slaughter of beef was introduced in the last century after laws were passed that allowed any Swiss citizen to launch an initiative to pass a new law or amend the constitution.

Just as Switzerland itself veered between cooperating with the Allies and the Axis, the community of about 18,000 Swiss Jews (about the same number as today), too was pulled in two different directions. While a vocal minority supported organizing demonstrations and publicity to allow in more Jewish refugees, much of the communal leadership, led by Saly Mayer, took the traditional line of Jewish communities in an uncertain environment, a strategy that can be crudely, but not inaccurately, summed up as "don't make trouble." Specifically, Mayer agreed with the government that a massive influx of Jewish refugees would increase anti-Semitism. Mayer even wrote to Heinrich Rothmund, head of the Foreigner Police, who was a driving force behind the policy of keeping out Jewish refugees, thanking him for his work.

That said, there are two faces to Mayer's wartime activities. By negotiating with senior SS officers in 1944, as outlined in more detail in chapter 9, Mayer helped slow down the final stages of the Holocaust, playing a complicated game of bluff and delaying tactics against Nazi leaders, with very little to offer in return for Jewish lives. Swiss Jews, who during the war raised SF10 million ($2.2 million) themselves to support Jewish refugees, later set up a memorial fund for Mayer in recognition of his work. Just like Swiss neutrality, the record of the wartime Swiss Jewish leadership is ambiguous.

Just how neutral was wartime Switzerland? Not very, when it came to frontier controls, for example. After August 1942, when Switzerland's borders were almost hermetically sealed against fleeing Jewish refugees, Nazi financial officials such as Emil Puhl, Reichsbank vice-president and director of the Bank for International Settlements, could freely come and go. So could Allied diplomats, but when U.S. Treasury Department officials refused to release the Swiss gold held in the United States for fear that the Swiss would make it available to Nazi Germany, the supply of coal to the American embassy was cut off, all through the freezing winter of 1941. Their German occupation counterparts were warm enough, but then it was German coal that helped keep Swiss industry going during the war.

Certainly in active military terms Switzerland was truly neutral—no Swiss units fought with the British army or the Wehrmacht. In passive military terms there is room for debate. Swiss machine guns were fitted into Luftwaffe airplanes, and Swiss timing devices helped explode Luftwaffe bombs, although the Allies' armed forces too made use of the latter. Had the Nazis invaded Switzerland they would have had a tough fight on their hands, for military reasons, certainly—as subduing a nation with a well-armed and trained civilian army that was ready to blow up bridges and mountain passes and battle it out for months would have been a different matter from rolling waves of Panzer tanks into Belgium or Holland—but also for political and cultural reasons. There was little love for the Third Reich among much of the Swiss population, and the policy of economic appeasement toward the Third Reich followed by the Swiss Federal Council and many Swiss bankers did not enjoy the overall support of the Swiss general public. Only a tiny minority supported the pro-Nazi extreme right, and much of the Swiss press was fervently anti-Nazi during the war.

Switzerland does have several wartime heroes of whom it can be proud, particularly Charles Lutz, wartime diplomat in Budapest, and former police chief Paul Grueninger. Lutz initiated the policy of placing Budapest Jews under Swiss diplomatic protection as the Holocaust entered its final phase, a policy that was later followed by his Swedish counterpart, Raoul Wallenberg, as well as Spanish diplomats and the International Red Cross. The mutterings in Bern at the Swiss foreign ministry about his unconventional work did not prevent Lutz from putting 50,000 Jewish lives under Swiss protection. Six years before Lutz issued his first protection papers, Paul Grueninger, a local police chief, saved 3,600 Jews from being returned to Germany by altering their passports during the summer and winter of 1938. His reward was to be fired, lose all his pension rights, and be denied suitable employment in the private sector. Grueninger died in poverty in 1971, and he was not legally rehabilitated until 1995, after four attempts by his family to restore his good name.

It is true that there are also anti-Nazi credits as well as the many pro-Nazi debts, mainly economic, on the balance-sheet of Swiss wartime history. Switzerland tolerated Allied espionage operations, such as those run by the Office of Strategic Services, forerunner of the CIA, in Bern. Many Allied intelligence operations that involved tapping telephones and intercepting letters and telegrams were quite illegal, but Swiss authorities generally turned a blind eye toward them, as part of the country's wartime balancing act. Switzerland allowed Jewish and refugee organizations such as the World Jewish Congress and the U.S. War Refugee Board to operate freely, rescuing and aiding Jewish refugees escaping from the Nazis. Switzerland was the site of clandestine negotiations during 1944 between senior Nazis and Jewish officials that almost certainly slowed down the last stages of the Holocaust. And just as the Third Reich needed Swiss banks to keep the Nazi economy functioning, the Allies needed Switzerland as a place where diplomats could meet, an oasis of peace in the heart of wartime Europe. The Allies too sold gold to Swiss banks—over SF3 billion worth, almost twice as much as the Nazis' total of SF1.64 billion—although, unlike much of the German gold, that sold by the Allies to the Swiss National Bank was not stolen.

Switzerland was also home to the International Red Cross, which performed valuable humanitarian work throughout the war, though many Jewish organizations are critical of its lackluster response to the Holocaust. Almost a quarter of a million refugees passed through Switzerland during the Second World War, many staying for years, albeit often in camps behind barbed wire, guarded by armed police. Jewish refugees too found sanctuary in the land that had once given asylum to Lenin, about 22,000 in number, although as many were turned back into the arms of Nazi or Vichy France officials.

Switzerland was neutral, but it was an ambiguous, expedient kind of neutrality, which like most foreign policies was ultimately based far more on national self-interest than adherence to any abstract, let alone moral, principle. The J-stamp, the mark of shame in Jews' passports that the Nazis introduced in 1938—a full year before the war started— after pressure from Swiss officials wanting to dam the tide of Jewish refugees, is perhaps the best indication of how realpolitik generally won out over the country's humanitarian tradition.

That triumph of cynicism over the principles of neutrality, or the beginning of the governing Swiss Federal Council's pro-Nazi bias, depending on your point of view, can be dated back to a speech by Dr. Marcel Pilet-Golaz, Swiss foreign minister for most of the war. It was he who in large part steered Switzerland toward a policy of accommodation, if not active cooperation, with Berlin. Speaking after the Nazi invasion of France in May 1940, Pilet-Golaz addressed the nation on how Switzerland had then to face and adapt to the new political realities of Europe. "After that speech Pilet-Golaz was known as the man who would alter Swiss policy along the lines defined by Germany. He wasn't the only one, but he was the most famous," says historian Guido Koller.

Pilet-Golaz gave the green light for the bankers to expand and develop their relationship with Nazi Germany. For the "new reality" in wartime Europe meant that there was lots of money to be made in accepting and laundering Nazi gold. "There is a relation between policy in its narrow sense and economic policy. One reinforced the other," says Koller. In fact, the foreign minister was out of tune with the rest of the population, and Pilet-Golaz's speech was greeted with public protests. But Swiss neutrality was a many-headed beast that lurched in several directions, and as the Allies advanced across the former territories of the Third Reich, appeasing the Nazis was suddenly less popular than opposing them. Pilet-Golaz was sacked in 1944, just as the Swiss borders were gradually becoming more porous to Jewish refugees, and just as the Allied armies moved ever nearer to Berlin.

The Swiss-Nazi economic connection permeated virtually every layer of Swiss society, compromising more than the bankers of Zürich's Bahnhofstrasse. If any one relationship summarizes the web of compromise and concession between Bern and Berlin, it is the murky connection between Colonel Roger Masson and SS General Walter Schellenberg, head of Nazi foreign intelligence. Like other Nazi officials Schellenberg needed Swiss banks as a source of foreign currency, in his case to finance Nazi secret agents abroad. Like the Allies, he also needed Switzerland as a base to spy on Germany's enemies, as well as on the Swiss themselves. The card he held to play against Masson was the possibility of a Nazi invasion. Together with Swiss army chief General Guisan, Masson met Schellenberg in March 1943, but by then it was apparent that, with the Wehrmacht bogged down in the Soviet Union, Germany was completely incapable of opening a fresh offensive against Switzerland. Whether rightly or wrongly, the Nazis believed that the Swiss chief of military intelligence was in their pocket. "We have Masson," one senior German agent, based in Geneva, is quoted as saying in an American intelligence document.

Swiss banks laundering Nazi gold, Swiss banks providing foreign currency to the Nazis, Swiss border guards turning away refugees, Swiss intelligence and military chiefs trading information with their Nazi counterparts: all this happened over fifty years ago. So why has this episode in Switzerland's wartime history suddenly been thrust into the international media spotlight?

Three major factors combined to expose the story of Swiss economic collaboration with the Third Reich: the end of the Cold War and the fiftieth anniversary of the Allied victory in Europe, America's freedom of information policy, and the marriage of political and electoral convenience between the World Jewish Congress (WJC) in New York and Senator Alfonse D'Amato.

The V-E day anniversary celebrations triggered a bout of national soul-searching in Switzerland's neighbors France and Germany about their wartime history, and particularly the fate of their Jewish communities. Even neutral, isolationist Switzerland was not immune to these

currents and in May 1995 then Swiss President Kaspar Villiger apologized for the introduction of the J-stamp and Switzerland's wartime
record of turning away tens of thousands of Jewish refugees. At the
same time, the end of the Cold War meant that the borders of Eastern
Europe were once again open, in fact had been for several years. Jewish
Holocaust survivors and Jewish organizations were negotiating with the
new democracies in power in Poland, Hungary, Slovakia, and the Czech
Republic for the return of their property. From Eastern Europe it was
but a short hop to Switzerland, where for decades stories had been circulating about Swiss banks still sitting on Holocaust victims' money and
refusing to return it to account holders' surviving descendants.

But where to get adequate information about the notoriously secretive Swiss bankers? In the U.S. National Archives, where the comprehensive records of Operation Safehaven, the U.S. State and Treasury
departments' operation that monitored the flow of looted Nazi assets
into Switzerland, were both extant and readily available under the U.S.
Freedom of Information Act. As the WJC's researchers burrowed
through the archives, they discovered more than information about dormant accounts, and uncovered the whole international web of Swiss-
Nazi economic connections. Where once a few Swiss bankers stood in
the dock, charged with holding onto dead Jews' money, suddenly a
whole nation was on trial, charged with systematic economic collaboration with the Third Reich.

Ever alert to a hot topic, Senator Alfonse D'Amato, powerful chairman of the Senate Banking Committee, jumped on the bandwagon and
began holding hearings, at which tearful Holocaust survivors would testify how implacable Swiss bankers had refused to return their families'
monies. All that was enough to trigger a feeding frenzy by the world's
media, who knew the ingredients of a fabulous story—Jews and Nazis,
stone-faced bankers, smug Swiss functionaries, looted gold—when they
saw them. The trickle of documents turned into a torrent, and so the
pressure built, in Bern, Washington, D.C., and London.

Finally, by the autumn of 1996, the dam of Swiss obduracy, both
government and financial, broke. The WJC and the Swiss bankers set
up a joint commission to examine the question of dormant accounts,
while the Swiss government set up a commission of experts, with a
mandate to report back in five years on its investigation into the whole
Swiss-Nazi economic relationship.

Slowly, gradually, Switzerland's "concept deficit" about these dark chapters in its history is being reduced, in part by the Swiss themselves. This book, written during 1996 and early 1997, as the story broke about Swiss-Nazi economic collaboration, is part of the process of discovering how the Swiss were, indeed, Hitler's secret bankers.

A SHORT NOTE ON METHODOLOGY

Hitler's Secret Bankers is based on extensive research using several types of sources. These include declassified intelligence documents, wartime and postwar diplomatic correspondence, contemporary interviews with Holocaust survivors, previously published works of history, and discussions with historians and other analysts. This book also draws on the mountain of newspaper and magazine reports that were published in 1996 about Switzerland's wartime record of economic collaboration with the Third Reich.

Many of the intelligence documents upon which I have heavily drawn have only just been made available to the public and are still being examined by historians. They may not all be 100 percent accurate, distorted, like every account, by misinterpretation, inaccuracies, the writer's prejudices, and the simple need of a spy to justify his existence to his bosses by sending regular reports. Some of the wilder "revelations"—those supposedly detailing the movements of millions of dollars belonging to Nazi leaders via Swiss diplomatic pouches to South America, for example—I have not used in this book. That said, none of these caveats should detract from the documents' relevance as a primary historical source but merely should color our perceptions of the information contained within them.

Just as effective, thorough journalism should be, this book is a first, rough draft of history. Its contents are wide open to debate, argument, even contradiction. It does not contain the whole historical truth; nor, indeed, can any single work. But this book is certainly a part of the truth about Switzerland's economic collaboration with the Nazis. Whatever the reader's opinion of the conclusions drawn and the analyses made here, they are, at least, a starting point and a base on which others may build.

William Shirer, in the introduction to his seminal work *The Rise and Fall of the Third Reich,* says it best: "My interpretations, I have no doubt, will be disputed by many. That is inevitable, since no man's opinions are infallible. Those that I have ventured here in order to add clarity and depth to this narrative are merely the best I could come by from the evidence and from what knowledge and experience I have gained."

CURRENCY TABLE OF WARTIME VALUES:

One pound sterling = $4

One Hungarian pengö = twenty cents, i.e., $1 = 5 pengö

One Reichsmark = 40 cents, i.e., $1 = 2.5 Reichsmark

One Swiss Franc = 22 cents, i.e., $1 = SF4.5

Hitler's Secret Bankers

1

A Trust Betrayed

Money is the god of Swiss bankers.
> Katalin Csillag, Hungarian Auschwitz survivor, seeking restitution
> for her family wealth, deposited in a Swiss bank

*If this happened we are certainly very sorry, but we are not able to
verify this after fifty years.*
> Spokeswoman for Credit Suisse, responding to accusations that the
> bank demanded relatives of Holocaust victims produce death cer-
> tificates before providing access to their accounts

Even in the midst of the Second World War, Zoltan Csillag's letters to his young wife, Katalin, found their way home to her from the carnage of the eastern front. Csillag, then serving as a doctor with the Hungarian army, wrote frequently to Katalin, who he believed was relatively safe from the fighting, back at home in the small town of Tapolca, in western Hungary—until the summer of 1944, when they were returned unopened and stamped "sent to an unknown place." But the place where she had been sent was not unknown: it was called Auschwitz.

The couple had married in 1942, with a traditional Jewish wedding. It was a happy affair, attended by many relatives, to mark the union for life between the wealthy young woman, whose father, Adolf, ran the Lessner wine company, based in Vienna, which had been founded in 1703, and the successful young doctor, who, although Jewish, had been drafted to serve in the Hungarian army in its futile campaign against the Soviets. Even now the Csillags have copies of centuries-old bills of sale for the wine the Lessners sold to the Austro-Hungarian nobility.

With homes in Vienna and Tapolca, the Lessners were part of Hungary's burgeoning Jewish middle class, who were the country's economic mainstay. Like many Jews across Eastern Europe, they banked the family's wealth in Switzerland. Katalin knew that her dowry, deposited in a Swiss bank by her father, was unreachable, at least while the war continued. But like thousands of other Holocaust survivors, she had faith in the probity and rectitude of the bankers who had turned Switzerland into a byword for financial security; she believed that, when the war was over, she would get her money.

Centuries of persecution and pogroms in countries such as Poland and Russia, and institutionalized anti-Semitism in Hungary, had already persuaded Eastern Europe's Jews that their assets were far safer deposited in Switzerland, out of reach of the region's unstable regimes, which might at any moment appropriate them. And who knew when they might have to suddenly flee, with no time to deal with banking bureaucracy? Now Switzerland appeared to be an island of sanctuary in a continent at war. Its borders were far out of reach, and in any case all but closed to Jewish refugees. But if physical sanctuary was impossible for them, they were convinced the Swiss would at least provide financial security for their assets. They frantically transferred cash to banks in Zürich, Bern, and Geneva as the rule of the swastika advanced across the continent.

The Jews were wrong. Now, over fifty years later, those events are returning to haunt both Eastern Europe's Holocaust survivors and the bankers who have guarded their family assets—guarded them so zealously, in fact, that for decades they have refused to hand them back, obstructing and stonewalling, all the while profiting from a free injection of capital into their banks, capital deposited in good faith by Jews who feared they might perish but who hoped that their relatives, at least, might survive and inherit their wealth. The secrecy laws that were introduced in 1934—in part to protect Jews who were depositing money in Swiss banks—have, in a macabre twist, been turned against account holders' surviving relatives to prevent the return of Holocaust victims' assets. There were no death certificates issued at Auschwitz, but, in the most heartless twist yet of the Swiss bankers' bureaucratic mentality, their clerks even demanded written proof of death from the relatives of Holocaust victims who tried to reclaim their fathers' and grandfathers' wealth.

But money was the least of Katalin Csillag's concerns that summer morning in 1944 when the Germans came for her and her parents. Together with the rest of her family she was herded into a train and transported to Auschwitz. The town of Tapolca came under Zone Five of the annihilation plan, which covered western Hungary. The Holocaust came late to Hungary, which had joined the war in the spring of 1941, its ruler, Admiral Miklos Horthy, believing that, by aligning itself with the Nazis, Hungary could recover its ancient lands of southern Slovakia, and Transylvania, ceded to Romania in 1920. Horthy was a classic aristocratic anti-Semite, who sent fawning letters to Hitler thanking him for his birthday present of a yacht—although he would later balk at the wholesale extermination of his country's Jews. In fact, until the German invasion of March 1944, Hungary offered relatively safe haven for its Jews. True, stringent anti-Jewish laws had been passed in 1938, tightening up earlier legislation that limited Jewish entry into various professions and universities, but, unlike in Poland or Russia, Hungarian Jews were not slaughtered en masse until after the Germans invaded in 1944. Hungary even gave sanctuary to a few thousand Polish and Slovak Jews as they fled the Nazis.

About 50,000 Hungarian Jewish men had been deported in forced-labor battalions during the war years, mainly to Transylvania in Romania and to the front in the Ukraine. About 5,000 returned. But in towns like Tapolca and in the capital, Budapest, Jewish communal life continued. Then, in 1944, as Admiral Horthy dithered between surrendering to the Allies and remaining in the Axis, the Germans invaded while the admiral was out of the country, and the Hungarian Holocaust soon began in earnest, under the supervision of Adolf Eichmann, who installed himself at the Hotel Majestic in Budapest's Schwab Hill. The plans for the deportation of the Jews in Zone Five were finalized at a conference in late June 1944 at Siofok, a resort town at Lake Balaton. This was a Magyar mini-Wannsee, a Hungarian version of the meeting of the Nazi leadership on a lake outside Berlin where the plans for the final solution were completed on 20 January 1942.

Like the Wannsee conference, the Siofok meeting was a pleasant affair for those attending as they wined and dined, enjoying the view of Lake Balaton as it glittered in the summer sun. They included local police and administrative officials, all ready and enthusiastic to send their fellow Hungarian citizens to their deaths. Laszlo Endre, a key figure in the destruction of Hungarian Jewry, was vacationing there at the time, together with his fiancée, Countess Katalin. Endre, a fervent anti-Semite and secretary of state in the Horthy regime, became close friends with Adolf Eichmann and surely interrupted his holiday for a few hours to check on the plans for the Hungarian Holocaust. Eichmann was so impressed with Endre's anti-Semitism that he once claimed that "Endre wanted to eat the Jews with paprika." Endre's reward, like Eichmann's, was the noose: he was hanged in March 1946 as a war criminal.

The deportations were well organized, both by the Hungarians at the departure points and by the SS at the reception area in Auschwitz. At the height of the mass killings the camp, the largest extermination center in Nazi-occupied Europe, was receiving between 12,000 and 14,000 people a day. Randolph Braham, in *The Politics of Genocide: The Holocaust in Hungary*, describes Auschwitz in the summer of 1944 as its workers prepared for the final stage of the Holocaust, the eradication of Hungarian Jewry:

> The extermination machinery, which had lagged for months, was put into peak condition to assure smooth, effective continuous operation. The crematoria were renovated, the furnaces relined, the chimneys strengthened with iron bands, and large pits were dug in the immediate vicinity of the crematoria. A new railway line was laid between Auschwitz and Birkenau, and the debarkation point was advanced to within 200 yards of the crematoria. The strength of the two Jewish special Kommandos was increased from 224 to 860, and the Canada Kommando, which was in charge of sorting the loot, was increased to about 2,000.

Loot was always a primary concern for the Nazis. Teeth with gold fillings were pulled from the dead and piled up before the gold was extracted. Rings, jewelry, spectacle frames: it was all melted down eventually, before being molded into gold bars, the most gruesome dividend of the Holocaust Bonanza. As for the Allies, they well knew what was happening at Auschwitz but refused to precision-bomb either the railway lines or the gas chambers, claiming such a raid would divert vital resources from other war operations. There were plenty of partisan groups operating in the areas traversed by the trains of death as well, but there was not a single attempt to blow up the railway lines.

A letter from the chief secretary's office of the Government of Palestine, dated 12 July 1944 and stamped "Secret," to David Ben-Gurion, first prime minister of Israel, then working at the Jewish Agency in Jerusalem, shows the full extent of the Allies' knowledge of the Nazi extermination as it entered its final stage:

> Received fresh reports from Hungary stating that nearly one half total of 800,000 Jews in Hungary have already been deported at a rate of between 10,000 to 12,000 per diem. Most of these transports are sent to death camp of Birkenau near Osweicim [Auschwitz] in Upper Silesia, where in the course of the last year over 1,500,000 million Jews from all over Europe have been killed and have detailed reports about numbers and methods employed. . . . These facts which are confirmed by various letters and reports from reliable sources should be given widest publicity and present Hungarian government should again be warned that they will be held responsible because they are aiding Germans with their own police to arrest and deport and thus murder Jews.

Together with her parents and brother, Katalin Csillag spent several days packed into a freight train on the journey to Auschwitz. There were usually between seventy and ninety people jammed into each car, as well as two buckets. One was filled with water; the other was empty but was soon filled with excrement. The windows and doors were locked.

These unbearable conditions were all part of the master race's master plan. Many died on the way, particularly old people and infants, while those who survived were so desperate for water and air on their arrival at Auschwitz that they barely had the will to live, let alone resist being pushed down that 200-yard stretch from the train to the gas chambers. Auschwitz was operating at full capacity that summer, as one eyewitness describes:

> Even the primitive gas chambers which had been used before the crematoria were constructed had to be brought back into commission. Enormous heaps of corpses were cremated in recently prepared pits. The entire area was wreathed in smoke which at times completely blotted out the sun. A revolting stench of burning human bones and flesh pervaded the camp. Night and day, without a break, the murdering continued—in several shifts.

Ever ingenious, ever concerned with that favorite German trait—efficiency—the SS officers even worked out how to maximize the burning of the corpses in the crematoria pits. Trenches were dug around the piles of bodies, a primitive irrigation system along which ran not water but human fat, which, released from the burning bodies, was then returned onto them, so they would burn ever faster. Somewhere in the mass graves of Auschwitz lie the remains of Katalin Csillag's parents, together with those of about 400,000 other Hungarian Jews killed there in the summer of 1944.

Katalin Csillag is now seventy-five and lives with her husband, Zoltan, eighty-two, in a spacious flat in Budapest, under the historic castle where Admiral Horthy lived. The Csillags are elderly now, but they are still a bright and sprightly couple, ever ready with a supply of coffee for visitors. Mrs. Csillag, though, is bitter about the failure of the Swiss bankers to try to help her regain her family's assets.

"I have no papers about the money in the banks, because everything was destroyed in 1944. My parents were taken to Auschwitz and never came back; I was the only one to return. I don't like to talk about Auschwitz, because then I won't sleep for a month," she says, drawing on a cigarette as she speaks. "I knew for some time that there was a tradition that the women in our family would get a dowry paid into Swiss banks. My father had five sisters, and each one had a hundred thousand Swiss francs paid into a Swiss bank account. I also had some money. This was our family story, that my father talked about.

"I should have got the money in 1942, but you know how the world was then, and it would have been very dangerous to try and travel to Switzerland. We were a wealthy family, but most of it has gone, apart from a few paintings and some furniture. I haven't had any correspondence with the banks until now, because we didn't have any papers and so we couldn't do anything, and there is a law that we cannot have money in a foreign bank account."

The Austrians, at least, have returned some of the family assets. In 1986 Zoltan Csillag recognized a magnificent wooden chest, used for storing silver cutlery, in a list of looted goods published in Austrian newspapers. It had belonged to his family and was stolen by the Nazis from their home in Kapuvar. The Csillag family monogram still sits on its lid, and amazingly, over forty years after it was stolen, the family silver still sat inside. It took six years to prove his ownership, but eventually the Austrian authorities returned it to its rightful heir.

Zoltan Csillag smiles when I ask him how it felt when the box finally came home, but over fifty years after the Holocaust, the emotions still surge deep within him. "Don't ask me how I feel. I can't really tell you about it. If I was a poet I could talk to you about it, but I'm not."

Swiss officials, though, have been less cooperative. In the summer of 1996 the Csillags wrote to the ombudsman appointed by the Swiss Bankers' Association (SBA), asking for assistance in locating the family account, of which, admittedly, they have few details. The ombudsman's response was standard: pay SF100 ($44) and we might help you.

"I got a long form back and I have to pay a hundred Swiss francs, with the possibility of paying more," says Katalin Csillag. "I am outraged at this. This is a lot of money for us. We are pensioners. How can we pay it? Secondly, and perhaps this is the more important thing, the Swiss banks have a lot of money. They are making money from it and now they want more. This all happened a long time ago and they could have done something after the war. Money is the god of Swiss bankers."

Across the Danube from the Csillags' flat lies Wesselenyi Street, in downtown Pest. The Blue Danube ran red with blood that winter of 1944, when Hungarian Nazi Arrow Cross troops lined up Jews along its banks before shooting them into the river, and Wesselenyi Street is still a haunted place, a road that was once a main artery in Budapest's wartime Jewish ghetto, where history has laid its bloodied hand too heavily. The ghetto gate stood at the bottom, smashed aside by the troops of the Soviet Red Army as they fought their way through the wrecked city in January 1945, awed and horrified at the sight of the half-starved Jews who crawled out of the cellars to meet them. Dazed and terrified, the Jews had sheltered from the bombardment in the Great Synagogue, its adjoining graveyard even now crowded with rows of headstones dating from 1944, when the Hungarian Nazi Arrow Cross rampaged there, shooting and killing on sight.

FOR MANY children of Holocaust survivors, the defeat of the Third Reich marked the beginning of their battle to regain their families' wealth. Dr. Gyorgy Haraszti has his office at number 44 Wesselenyi Street, where he is principal of the American Endowment School for Jewish pupils. A scion of Hungary's now more or less vanished Jewish nobility, who lived in Hungary, banked in Switzerland, and were at home everywhere from Budapest to Berlin, Dr. Haraszti lost 160 relatives in the Holocaust. The Harasztis owned a large swathe of land, including forests and orchards, in Szabolc-Szatmar County, in the east of the country, an area once home to a thriving Jewish population, but their land was taken from them under communism. In compensation he recently received 2 million forints ($12,500), a substantial sum in a country where many earn less than 40,000 forints a month.

Dr. Haraszti's grandfather, like most Hungarian Holocaust victims, was killed in Auschwitz sometime in 1944. Before he died, says Dr. Haraszti, he sent 3 million pengös ($600,000) to Switzerland. "We were a well-to-do family. We had ten thousand acres taken away under the Communists, of forests, orchards. My grandfather told my father that he had deposited this money in Switzerland, in case something happened to him. I don't know how or where they sent it, and that is the problem, the heart of the matter."

But if Dr. Haraszti doesn't know where the money was deposited, he can prove it existed. "I have documents about the Hungarian properties that were taken by the Nazis and by the Communists. I can prove that my family was wealthy enough to be able to deposit three million pengös. Until the German occupation in March 1944 Hungarian Jews had the opportunity to send money to Switzerland—Hungarian Jews had contacts there. The Joint [a Jewish welfare organization] had a delegation in Switzerland. My parents and grandparents went there on holiday every year. I can show you postcards from Switzerland at the turn of the century."

By the summer of 1944 Europe was in chaos, especially Hungary. The deportation of the countryside Jews, from towns such as Tapolca, was under way. The Allies were advancing from the west, the Soviets from the east. Travel, communication, everything was virtually impossible. These were days of endless terror for Budapest's Jews: random roundups, sweeps, and deportations. There was no guarantee that if a Jew left home to buy a loaf of bread in the morning he would ever come home again, let alone possess the means to travel from the eastern border to the capital.

"My father had no chance to meet with his father in the summer of 1944, and so he didn't know the details, which bank account the money was in, or where it was," says Dr. Haraszti. "When he came back he heard that everybody was killed in the war, his father and mother. He took back what he could, such as the land, but everything was later taken by the Communists. I believe that the story of the three million pengös is true, because they were a really well-to-do family. I don't know if they used our original name, or a false name, when they opened the account. My father died nineteen years ago, but he couldn't go to Switzerland, or find somebody who knows the numbers, because he couldn't meet with his father before he was killed. I cannot document it, but the story is true."

That Dr. Haraszti can prove the extent of his family's former holdings substantially boosts his claim, says Sergio Karas, a Toronto-based lawyer acting for several relatives of Holocaust victims. "It helps establish that the people are not charlatans, that they do have reasonable grounds to believe that there is money there. Somebody who would have had property worth a couple of million dollars, even a couple of hundred thousand dollars, it stands to reason that they would have put some cash away. They would put it in Switzerland. There was nowhere else to put it then. In those days Switzerland was the only accessible place for these people."

Nobody knows how much unclaimed money is sitting in dormant Holocaust survivors' accounts in Switzerland, although some Jewish groups claim the figure, with fifty years' interest, could easily run into hundreds of millions, if not billions, of dollars. Under pressure from the New York–based World Jewish Congress (WJC) and Republican senator Alfonse D'Amato—the driving force behind the Whitewater hearings and chairman of the powerful Senate Banking Committee—the Swiss bankers finally buckled and agreed to start talking. That much of Senator D'Amato's constituency in New York is Jewish, and that there are few votes in supporting Swiss banks, only increased the senator's enthusiasm for blowing open the dormant-accounts issue. Subtle and not-so-subtle hints that the Senate Banking Committee might start discussing possible sanctions against Swiss banks—whose U.S.-based branches do millions of dollars' worth of business every year—also helped bring the bankers to the negotiating table.

An aide to Senator D'Amato, though, is keen to present his boss's crusade as a moral issue. "This is big money. A lot of very wealthy European Jews put their money into Switzerland—not by wire transfer: they came with suitcases. They wanted to know that it would be safe,

not just get a snotty answer. Now many of the claimants have a mentality that they are lucky they survived the war; they hit a stone wall
when they try and get their money, and so they say, 'Let's forget about
it.' But the facts show [Swiss-Nazi] cohabitation to the point of going
out of their way to hide assets and opening accounts on behalf of the
Germans. The Germans got paid, but when the Jews showed up the
Swiss said, 'Sorry, we don't have enough information.' Of course the
Swiss must see us as prying. For fifty years they've been saying, 'We'll
handle it,' or else, 'There's nothing there.' This is unfinished business.
It was not concluded at the end of the war, and not only for the Jews—
for anyone who didn't get paid back."

Until the spring of 1994 the Swiss bankers had for decades argued
that the matter was closed, settled for good by the 1962 law on the
question of assets held in Switzerland that had belonged to Holocaust
survivors, which registered approximately SF9.5 million ($2.1 million)
in dormant accounts. The 1962 law required that individuals and legal
entities register with the Swiss government any assets held with them
that met three criteria: that their last-known owners were not Swiss
nationals; that no information had been received from the owners since
9 May 1945; and that the owners were known or presumed to have
been victims of racial, religious, or political persecution. The 1962 law
also lifted professional and banking secrecy obligations that covered the
above and imposed criminal penalties for noncompliance.

By 1973 about three-quarters of the SF9.5 million had been
returned to its owners, and the rest was parceled out to Jewish organizations and the Swiss Refugee Aid Society. By then the matter was
closed, Swiss bankers believed. Relatives of Holocaust victims had
pleaded in the decades that followed for some flexibility to reclaim their
family assets but had been brushed off with terse letters and by bank
officials who refused to help.

But the issue would not go away. In 1994 the SBA decided to launch
a general study—i.e., one not specifically focused on Holocaust victims'
assets—of accounts that had been dormant for over ten years. It
appointed a banking ombudsman to act as a clearinghouse between
claimants and the banks. A year later, as the pressure increased from
the WJC to identify dormant Holocaust accounts, the SBA began a
second study, specifically targeted at identifying possible assets that
belonged to Holocaust victims.

In his testimony of 23 April 1996 to the Senate Banking Committee, Hans Baer, of Bank Julius Baer, explained the rationale behind this decision. The 1995 probe would have a wider mandate than the 1962 law, he explained. "This [1995] process was intended to be as inclusive as possible so that any assets of Holocaust victims that might still be held in Swiss banks and that might have escaped identification pursuant to the 1962 law would be identified. First, the SBA required that its members identify all assets that were deposited by non-Swiss nationals before the end of World War Two (9 May 1945), unless the banks had evidence of activity since that time."

The 1962 law had included a requirement of proof that the owner of the assets had been persecuted by the Nazis, or was presumed to have been, but the 1995 investigation did not require claimants to prove that the account holder had been persecuted. Baer said, "We recognize that it would be very difficult to prove or disprove whether an account identified today belonged or did not belong to a victim of the Holocaust."

Second, the banking ombudsman would also take on the work of liaising between claimants of Holocaust victims' accounts and the banks. Baer explained how this would work in practice. The rules for claimants would be laxer than in other countries, he said: "Specifically, the ombudsman has been charged with helping potential claimants (many of whom are elderly and who are not in possession of much information) prepare their claims and with transmitting information to the banks. The standard for submitting a claim is significantly more permissive than the general legal standard applicable in Switzerland or the United States. If a claimant can be matched with assets identified by a bank, the bank has the obligation to contact the claimant either directly or through the ombudsman."

Then, in January 1996, the SBA said it had unearthed SF38.74 million ($7.5 million) in 775 dormant accounts, although the funds had not necessarily been deposited by Jews. All of which begged the question, why had the bankers found SF9.5 million in 1962, and then, thirty-four years later, managed to locate another sum of over SF38 million? In his testimony to the Senate Banking Committee, Baer offered this explanation: "It is important to remember that the 1962 law required a determination that an asset belonged to a victim of Nazi persecution. In my personal opinion, that process was successful in identifying a large percentage of Holocaust victims' accounts. However, it is possible that the 1962 process did not identify absolutely all assets of Holocaust victims. For example, a Jewish person could have placed assets under an assumed non-Jewish name that would have given no clue to the owner's true ethnicity. In contrast the current process does not require a determination concerning the owners of the assets; it identifies all dormant accounts opened by any non-Swiss before the end of the war."

From the methodology of the SBA's investigation, Baer then moved on to the amounts involved. Jewish organizations claim that hundreds of millions of dollars or Swiss francs, deposited by Holocaust victims, could still be sitting in Swiss banks. The 1962 probe discovered SF9.5 million, the 1996 one SF38.74 million. So where had all the money gone? Much of it had never been there in the first place, while the rest had been moved on from Switzerland, said Baer. "Many people have asked why the amount identified is so small. This is the exact opposite of the previous question; on the one hand, we are being asked to explain why there are any assets left at all, and on the other hand, we are being asked why there are so little assets left. In any event we do not believe that, when considered in the appropriate context, the amount identified is small or should come as any surprise because, one, as I explained before, the initial amount of assets transferred to Switzerland was probably not as large as some have suggested; two, many of these assets were transferred out of Switzerland to other countries, especially the United States; three, a substantial amount of the remaining assets were claimed and distributed between 1945 and 1962; and, four, a large part of whatever was left was identified and distributed pursuant to the 1962 law."

Unclaimed funds that are identified as possibly belonging to Holocaust victims will be distributed to charities, said Baer. As for the press reports detailing the claimants that had been turned down, he argued that many lacked adequate information. "I can tell you from personal experience that, unfortunately, many claims are supported by almost no information. It is crucially important to treat all potential claims seriously and sensitively and to work with claimants to substantiate their claims, as the ombudsman is doing. However, a responsible institution cannot simply pay someone an indeterminate amount based on little more than a hope that there is an account somewhere in Switzerland belonging to some relative."

Jewish organizations and the SBA have now agreed to set up a joint commission, with three members appointed by each side, to find out just how much money remains. The barrage of international publicity over the dormant-accounts scandal was most unwelcome in the board-rooms of Bern and Zürich; but, unaccustomed to media attention, the bankers' PR machine lumbered into action only very slowly.

"We are doing the best we can" was the line spun to journalists by Jeffery Taufield, spokesman for the Swiss Bankers' Association. In cum-bersome bureaucratese, he said, "The Swiss banks have set up several procedures to respond to claims. The Swiss are trying to deal with it as sensitively as possible. They want to put this chapter in their history behind them."

In private, the bankers were less circumspect, grumbling about the supposed undue Jewish influence over the media and the way the WJC exploited each fresh batch of incriminating documents from the archives to keep the story running across the world's newspapers and television stations. But it will be easier said than done for the Swiss to put "this chapter in their history behind them." For many Swiss, includ-ing some in the government, are genuinely seeking to discover the truth about their country's record of economic collaboration with the Third Reich, and the Swiss government has set up another committee—of historians—to investigate the country's wartime history.

There is much to examine, says Sergio Karas, whose father was a Holocaust survivor. "This is the last great opportunity to clear this issue. Now a committee has been formed to appoint an independent auditor who perhaps will give us the real story. Why 'perhaps'? Because fifty years needs more than a day to do a forensic job. I don't care how com-plete or intact the records are, the passing of time alone is a factor.

"My biggest concern is that the people I am dealing with are very elderly, and I would like this thing to be resolved quickly. I don't know how long they will be around. I think they deserve some justice, once and for all. I always ask myself: what could their lives have been had the wealth deposited in their accounts been at their disposal?"

With interest alone, the amount of money in Holocaust victims' accounts could reach many millions of dollars, says Karas. "If you take compound interest into account, even if each person put ten thousand dollars into an account, the figure is staggering, enormous. The point also is that in those days people did not make a trip to Switzerland for ten thousand dollars. People made trips for substantial amounts of money. They had cash or gold. I will request interest for my clients, compounded at the going rate for whatever year it was. Otherwise this is a gross deprivation. If they don't pay you interest, basically they are paying you one-tenth of the money."

LIKE the Lessners and the Harasztis, Velvel Singer also had absolute faith that his money would be safe in Swiss banks. As one of the richest Jews in Lódz, Poland, Singer saw Switzerland as a natural haven for his considerable wealth. Born in Vzezein, a suburb of Lódz, in 1885, Singer had, by the time war broke out, built up a lucrative financial empire refurbishing Singer sewing machines. He was not related to the famous sewing-machine family of the same name—who even launched a lawsuit against him—although the coincidence of names certainly helped him expand his business.

Much of Singer's immediate family vanished in the maelstrom of the Holocaust, including his wife, Chaya, his eldest son, Itzik, who joined the Polish army in 1938 and disappeared, and his second son, Sruel Moishe, who also vanished in 1938. His sisters, Clara and Rivka, though, died peacefully in North America, as did his brothers, Moishe Leib, Hymie, and Philip.

A poignant photograph survives of Velvel, standing together with one of his sons, probably Sruel Moishe, outside a forest somewhere near Lódz. With his wooden cane, neatly trimmed beard, black frock coat, and shoes shined like a mirror, Singer is the picture of a well-off Jewish businessman. His tie is neatly knotted, his gaze confident as he looks out from underneath his small black hat.

Leaning against the same tree is his son, a Velvel in miniature, dressed in a junior version of his father's wardrobe, with a belted jacket. He too holds a cane as he stares seriously out at the camera from behind his wire-rimmed glasses. A note in Yiddish is inscribed on the side of the photograph. It says, "I wasn't feeling well for a while, now I'm better."

By the outbreak of the Second World War Lódz had Poland's second-largest Jewish population, after the capital, Warsaw. One-third of its 665,000 citizens were Jews. The city was a major center of Jewish life, home to Jewish schools, hospitals, social and welfare organizations, and every shade of political organization and party, from right-wing Zionists to Marxist revolutionaries, and some who somehow managed to combine both ideologies, Jews then, as now, being a disputatious bunch.

Jewish writers, artists, poets, and scientists all flourished there, including Ephraim Katzir, the fourth president of Israel. Over half of the Jewish population worked in industry, particularly textiles, sewing and manufacturing clothes, so Velvel Singer had a ready market for his refurbished machines. That all came to an end on 8 September 1939, when the Germans marched in, swastikas flying in the breeze as their knee-length black boots clicked a deadly path across the cobblestones. Lódz was annexed to the Warthegau, District Six of German-occupied Poland. The Holocaust there began.

Aided, as in every country occupied by the Nazis, by local Volkdeutsche (ethnic Germans) eager to prove their allegiance to Berlin, the troops of Einsatzgruppen 2 began the steady eradication of Jewish life in Lódz. The Jews had virtually no defenses against the massed forces of the Third Reich. German troops looted at will as the Nazi reign of terror began, a pattern that would soon be followed all over Europe. Jewish institutions were immediately closed, Jews' bank accounts blocked, and Jewish-owned businesses confiscated and given to Germans.

Just as in Hungary five years later, a stream of edicts were issued banning Jews from public life. The use of public transport was forbidden; the possession of cars and radios was outlawed. On 9 November Lódz was officially annexed to the Reich, and in the following fortnight the Germans blew up all the synagogues in the city. Apartments were confiscated, and the mass deportations to German concentration camps soon began, while other Jews fled to Warsaw and other cities.

The ghetto was established on 10 December 1939, and in February 1940 Jews were expelled from the rest of the city. On 30 April 1940 the ghetto was sealed off. About 164,000 Jews were forced into an area of just over 1.5 square miles, according to *The Encyclopedia of the Holocaust*. The Germans had two aims in establishing the Lódz ghetto: to concentrate the Jews in as small an area as possible, as a precursor to their ultimate elimination, and to make as much money as possible. In May 1940 the ghetto governor, Hans Biebow, ordered that factories be set up, where the workers would be paid in soup and bread. The Lódz ghetto turned a profit of about 350 million Reichsmarks ($140 million). It made so much money for the Germans that it survived the longest of the ghettos under direct German rule, for even the Nazis were some-times prepared to defer mass extermination of Jews as long as it remained profitable.

The ghetto even had its own microeconomy, complete with postage stamps and banknotes. The one-mark note was emblazoned with a seven-branch candelabra, while the five-mark note had a Star of David. Torn between keeping the Jews alive to make money and their desire to slaughter them for the Nazi ideal, the Germans also set up a skeleton infrastructure in the ghetto to keep it and its inhabitants functioning enough to turn a profit. There was a Jewish fire department—the only Jewish institution to be allowed a motor vehicle—a horse-drawn ambu-lance, hospitals, schools, orphanages, and soup kitchens.

And there was profit for the Nazis. There survives a photograph of Biebow in his office, gloating over his loot. He is surrounded by piles of foreign currency and jewelry seized from Jews, and a confiscated tablet of the Ten Commandments stands on his bookcase, which is filled with orderly files. Just as in Budapest in 1944, where the strug-gle for control of the Manfred Weiss industrial combine triggered an intra-Reich battle between SS Reichsführer Heinrich Himmler and Herman Goering, the Lódz ghetto was battled over between com-peting Nazi factions. For while the Nazis were racial fanatics, dedi-cated to purging Europe of Jewish blood, money often triumphed over ideology, and the army vied with the SS for control of this eco-nomically profitable giant concentration camp until its elimination in the summer of 1944. The Lódz ghetto even had its own special police unit, charged with discovering and looting Jewish possessions, to be shipped to Germany.

But however much money its inhabitants made for the Third Reich, their living conditions were deteriorating rapidly. Fuel became as valu-able as food. By January 1941 the Lódz Judenrat (Jewish Council) had begun a ghetto-wide dismantling of uninhabited sites to obtain wood, and swarms of ghetto residents attacked the buildings with hand tools. Isaiah Trunk in his book *Lódzher geto* quotes one contemporary observer on the hordes of freezing Jews as they advanced "like crows on a cadaver, like jackals on a carcass. They demolished, they axed, they sawed, walls collapsed, beams flew, plaster buried people alive, but no one yielded his position." Social relations and any notions of Jewish sol-idarity collapsed under these conditions.

In Lódz the thousands of better-off Jews who arrived from Austria and Czechoslovakia took over the black-market supply of bread. Hunger and cold even spawned their own grim poetry:

> When we had nothing to eat,
> They gave us a turnip, they gave us a beet,
> Here, have some grub, have some fleas,
> Have some typhus, die of disease.

In this hell, Velvel Singer had an important job. As long as the Germans needed the Lódz ghetto, whose sewing factories were making millions of Reichsmarks for the Third Reich, they needed Velvel Singer. His wealth was gone, together with the grand family home in the city, which was just a few miles away but had long been appropriated by the Nazis. However, his expertise and manufacturing skills would grant him a few more years of existence ("life" is too grandiose a term for daily conditions in Lódz). Ghetto survivors, such as Jack Weisblack, still remember him as a *mensch,* that Yiddish term which roughly translates as a cross between a person of integrity and a plain human being.

Weisblack, who was born in Lódz and now lives in New York State, was held in the ghetto from the winter of 1939 to August 1944. He was one of 200 workers in a factory run by Velvel Singer. "I worked with Velvel Singer for four years in the Lódz ghetto. I was eighteen and he was an older man. I was fixing machines and he was the boss. He looked like a boss; he carried himself like a boss; he was a wealthy man; he was in business. He was a generous, kind man, a quiet man. He didn't bother nobody—he was a good man. I know that Velvel Singer was a rich man. For a man in our town, in his line, he was the richest, although there were other Jews with more. I cannot tell you how many millions he had, but he was a wealthy man.

"The Germans took everything from us and concentrated us in a ghetto, and he was running the show in the factory. He was the man with the knowledge. We were mechanics and we had to work. We had tailors, machinists, making German uniforms and shoes. Life in the ghetto was murder. There was no food. We were freezing in the winter, stifling in the summer. We didn't have any contact with the Germans, and none of them showed us any humanity."

News of the Nazi extermination percolated in, but the inhabitants were insulated from the full horror of Auschwitz. "We knew there were death camps, but we didn't know it was that bad until we found out in 1944. We were closed in the ghetto, no mail and no newspapers," said Weisblack.

The Lódz ghetto seemed "almost an island of serenity in a sea of blood," writes Lucy S. Dawidowicz in her book *The War Against the Jews, 1933–45.* "Its residents, working in the industrial enterprises that appeared to justify their existence, hoped they would live to see the defeat of the Germans." Unlike in Warsaw or Vilna, there was no armed resistance movement in Lódz. The Jewish political parties such as the Communists and the Socialists had no arms-smuggling channels to their Polish comrades outside. Lódz was so sealed off that even food could not be smuggled in, let alone enough weapons for an uprising. The strategy was to organize communal welfare, wait, and hope.

On 6 June 1944 the news of the Allied invasion of Normandy reached the ghetto, and its inmates went wild with joy. The Lódz ghetto dwellers celebrated in vain, for the Nazis had already decided to liquidate the ghetto months earlier, in the spring. In June mass deportations to the Chelmno extermination camp began. In Lódz, as in every city under German control, the Judenrat was forced to help organize the deportations, by bringing those about to be deported to special assembly points. Deportations to Chelmno were halted in mid-July, but the cattle trucks began running again on 7 August, destination Auschwitz, whose gas chambers had been busy exterminating the remnants of Hungarian Jewry, such as Katalin Csillag's family.

Some, such as Mindla Zarzewska, chose suicide, as recorded in *The Chronicle of the Lódz Ghetto,* a remarkable account of day-to-day life—and death—in the Holocaust, written by ghetto dwellers all through the Nazi occupation. Many suicides chose "death by wire," by simply walking up to the barbed wire that surrounded the ghetto and letting the policemen shoot them dead, as they were ordered to. Mindla Zarzewska had to struggle to be killed, though, as the chronicle relates:

> [She] showed that she intended to climb over the barbed-wire fence. The Schupo [policeman] hurried over and tried to reprimand her. A mature, sensible reserve policeman, and by no means trigger-happy, he tried to reason with her, make her understand the danger she was in. But she refused to be turned back. . . . The

regulation is strict: "Anyone who crosses the barbed wire will be shot to death!" And so the shot rang out. A woman weary of life had been granted her wish.

In August Jack Weisblack too was taken to Auschwitz. "There was no food, and they put us in cattle cars. It took a day and a half. I was there for a month, but the Germans wanted mechanics, so I was taken to Chemnitz, to make vehicle parts."

By November the ghetto was virtually empty, but a skeleton Jewish underground still remained, including a Dr. Daniel Weisskopf, who ran a secret radio-listening network. He was betrayed by an informer, and the Nazis discovered his bunker on 6 November. Hans Biebow was called to carry out the arrest. Weisskopf went out fighting, attacking both Biebow and the informer. A German policeman shot him dead as he tried to strangle Biebow.

About 800 Lódz ghetto inmates survived in the city, to be liberated by the Red Army on 19 January 1945. In that same month, the Soviets captured the last German-occupied blocks of Budapest, including Wesselenyi Street. Velvel Singer was not among the Lódz survivors. He perished in Auschwitz sometime in November 1944 when he was taken out to a pit and machine-gunned.

NOT FAR from the Toronto offices of Sergio Karas lives Ron Singer, nephew of Velvel Singer. Singer, a professor of theater at Toronto University, has for years been attempting to recover funds deposited by his uncle Velvel before he perished in Auschwitz.

"Velvel Singer was my uncle," Ron Singer says. "His real name was Wolf. . . . He was known as one of the wealthiest Jews in Poland. He had an estate home that was supposed to be the most beautiful home in Lódz. This was told to me by a number of people who were in Auschwitz with him and were in the Lódz ghetto with him, and people who worked for him and who are still alive.

"He was the supervisor of all the machine shops for sewing garments in the ghetto. The Lódz ghetto survived longer than any other because they were working for the Nazi war machine more than any other ghetto. They were turning out uniforms for the soldiers. He was known by most of the people in the ghetto. I asked a survivor if it was conceivable that my uncle could have had millions in the bank. He said, 'Absolutely. Your uncle was one of the wealthiest Jews in Lódz.'

"There is an incredible irony in the fact that the Swiss bankers created secret accounts almost exclusively for wealthy Jews who were trying to save their funds and their savings and send the money to Western Europe, a neutral country, [and they] suddenly find that the very thing which was designed to protect them is now being used against them. I find the Swiss behavior to be reprehensible. There is no excuse. It borders in some cases on the techniques that we have accused the Nazis of using. They created secret accounts and then denied that there were any accounts there. Or there were people trying to escape the Nazis and then finding that the Swiss were saying, 'We'll take your money, but sorry, we can't accept you.' There are many stories like that."

The story of Velvel's deposits in a Swiss bank has been part of the Singer family lore for decades, according to Ron. "In 1945, as the war ended, a man came to our house in Montreal. I vividly recall him coming to our house, talking to our father. He told my father that Velvel told him, 'If you survive this and you manage to get to my brother in Montreal, please tell him that there is four million dollars in U.S. funds in a [Swiss] bank."

But which bank? Like most Holocaust victims who had deposited funds in Switzerland, Velvel Singer was reluctant to reveal the details before he died, for fear that an impostor could claim the money.

Ron goes on to say, "I met another Auschwitz survivor, who had worked with my uncle in the Lódz ghetto, and he asked me if it had bothered me that my uncle said 'in a bank' but didn't say which bank. I said, 'Of course.' He told me that was one of the most common things that people who were about to die, and who knew that they were going to die, did. They were terrified that their savings, their money, would not be found, so they told someone near them who might survive, but they would not give the specifics, for fear that person would go and get the money. They hedged their bets and hoped like hell that the relatives who were in line for the money would somehow find it. He said it's very common to hear this 'in a bank.' "

Singer has been searching in earnest for his family funds since January 1987, even hiring a private investigator, Terry Howes, to track Velvel Singer's assets. Like Holocaust survivors before him, Howes got the brush-off from the Swiss authorities. A letter to Howes from a Mr.

D. Blatter, then consul general of Switzerland, dated 12 February 1987, encloses a leaflet outlining the procedure for searching for assets in Swiss banks.

Paragraph three of point one says, "In order to be in a position to reply to inquiries of an heir, it is necessary for the latter to furnish legal proof of the death of the customer and the capacity of the inquirer as heir." Meaning, provide us with a death certificate and we might aid you.

"When they told me that, I was incensed," Ron Singer says. "I was furious, naturally. To hear someone say, 'You produce the appropriate documentation like a death certificate for your uncle that died in Auschwitz, and we may consider looking for the money.' What kind of nonsense is this? It's people who are playing the ultimate bureaucratic role and saying rules are rules, end of game. This is an image I have got of the Swiss, of people who are idiotic bureaucrats to an extreme that is so ludicrous that they have to stand up and answer for it. We come from efficiency to bureaucracy to outright thievery, and we have hit that point now.

"Terry Howes did some research for me and found that the wealthy Jews in Eastern Europe, particularly in Lódz, would do their banking in Zürich. They would go on Thursday and make it back in time for the Sabbath on Friday. I am saying that, whether the money is there or not, the Swiss have an obligation to look and to let me know, which finally they are doing. It's conceivable it's not there, but my uncle was a wise man who traveled a great deal, and, given the research that was done, I would say the odds are that it was there. The Swiss banks have stonewalled for decades: they were arrogant, they were rude, they have lied in a number of ways. It has been awful. They closed ranks and functioned as though they had the God-given right not to have to answer. If they can finally respond in a true and honest way to the many people associated with the Holocaust, I will feel that I have accomplished something.

"My uncle would be furious if he knew about this. Who would like to think that they put away money and people other than their family got the money? That you put away money, and some banker lived off that for sixty years, and then contended that they had no idea there was money there?"

There is quite a simple solution to the problem of dormant accounts held by Holocaust victims, says a former U.S. State Department official,

Seymour Rubin: publish a list of dormant accounts, and invite those with a claim on them to forward as much information as possible to make their claim. The procedure is not perfect and needs plenty of safeguards, but it works and provides some just reparations, however late. The Austrian authorities' return of Zoltan Csillag's family silver box is testimony to that.

Rubin says, "The Swiss banks should make a real effort to take a census. [In] the state of New York, every once in a while, on the back pages in the business section, there will be a list of bank accounts, with names. These are bank accounts which have been sitting there, unused, untouched for a period of three, five, twenty years. The state is saying to everyone that can read: these are the accounts that have had no activity in them for a long period of time, and we would like to know if anyone has any claim on them. If not, we will take them into the treasury of the state of New York."

Now eighty-two and living in Washington, D.C., Rubin during the Second World War was a senior official working on Operation Safehaven, a joint U.S. State and Treasury operation with responsibility for tracking the flow of looted assets to neutral countries and monitoring Swiss banks as they accepted stolen gold.

Rubin asserts, "There is no reason why the Swiss could not take a census of all of their banks—they must have very clear records: that's one thing everybody believes that the Swiss are very good at—and find all the accounts that were established between nineteen thirty-three, thirty-five, something like that, just after Hitler, and nineteen forty-something, when it became impossible to openly move large amounts of money. You can take all those accounts that were established and say, 'These are accounts in which there has been no activity since they were established. We will publish the names and numbers, as much information as we have.'

"There are very few of those accounts which nobody knows about. My understanding is that those numbered accounts were established by some trusted person within the bank, or outside if you had a friend, knowing what was there. That could be a start: by publishing whatever information you have, you could find out from the records if the people are no longer alive. Or you publish the numbers and say, 'These accounts and these amounts were established in these years.' If they are from Germany, or Hungary, they are probably from people who were trying to keep their money away from the authorities, perhaps just for tax purposes, or were trying to hide it. I don't know why they haven't done this—I really don't see the difficulty in that."

None of the banks' supposed difficulties in locating funds prevented Switzerland from using unclaimed assets of Holocaust victims to persuade Communist governments in Eastern Europe to pay compensation for nationalizing and confiscating Swiss-owned property. In 1949 Switzerland signed a bilateral compensation treaty with Poland that called for Warsaw to pay SF52.5 million ($11.5 million) to Switzerland for property the Communists had appropriated. Similar agreements were reached with Communist regimes across Eastern Europe. The Polish deal had a secret protocol attached that ceded Poles' bank accounts and life insurance policies held in Switzerland to Poland, to be turned over to the country's central bank, if they were unclaimed by 1954, the Swiss foreign ministry has admitted. As 3 million Polish Jews were exterminated in the Holocaust, these assets were not very likely to be recovered by their original owners.

Much of this research was carried out by Swiss historian Peter Hug, who was quoted as saying: "For me what is morally very, very questionable is that for fifty years Switzerland did nothing to try and find the people this money actually belonged to." Once they had plowed through the dead Jews' bank accounts and insurance policies, the Swiss officials promised Poland $1.6 million of unclaimed funds, although less than $400,000 was actually handed over.

Just as reprehensible as the Polish agreement, says Swiss journalist Gisela Blau, was the fact that the Swiss government had refused to give up some German assets to the Allies, thus contravening the terms of the 1946 Washington Agreement between the Allies and Switzerland that governed the terms of Swiss repayments of German gold and assets to the Allies. "The Swiss banks said they could not liquidate private assets because it would be unethical from a banking point of view and these were private firms, with private clients," says Blau. "But at the same time they were absolutely prepared, without any discussion, to liquidate the assets of private clients who happened to be Jewish and who perished in the Holocaust. They had a dual ethical conception of banking. This is a scandal. That word is used very often, but this was a scandal, to do one thing with the German assets and another with the Polish Jewish ones. The government took this decision. The foreign minister said they were not forced to adopt the Polish law of 1946, but they thought it was normal at the time. The people who had dormant accounts had been Polish, so why not give them back to Poland, where they had come from? It was a fantastic example of double standards."

German assets were saved, but Polish Jewish ones disposed of. Why was there enough information to locate the Polish accounts, but not enough to return money to relatives of Holocaust survivors? It's a question to which surviving members of the Lessner, Haraszti, and Singer families are still demanding answers, but so far without success.

Velvel Singer's wealth, and that of almost every other Holocaust victim who entrusted his assets to Swiss banks, cannot be located, according to the Swiss banking ombudsman, Hanspeter Haeni. Claims are sent to Haeni's office; if he judges them to be sufficiently credible with adequate information, they are then forwarded on to the relevant banks. Ron Singer submitted his in late spring 1996. The reply came a couple of months later: there was no trace of any of Velvel Singer's money. But by mid-November Haeni announced he had found valid claims for SF1.6 million ($352,000) of dormant assets.

Of these, he said, SF11,000 ($2,200) belonged to Holocaust victims.

2

Looting a Continent

*You know, my child, they treated me with an electrical apparatus . . .
they have maltreated me in vain. I have told them I was not informed
of fortune matters.*

> The seventy-seven-year-old mother of Alexander Leitner, civil
> leader of the Jewish ghetto in Oradea, Romania, to her son after
> being tortured for details of nonexistent wealth

The acquisition of gold by any means, including deceit and brutality.

> Extract from an Allied secret interrogation report on the purpose
> of the Devisenschutz Kommando, a special SS looting unit

Safe in Bern and Zürich, the Swiss bankers gave little, if any, thought
to the Holocaust as it unfolded just a couple of hours' drive away. At
Auschwitz, the Csillags and the Harasztis were clambering out of the
stinking cattle trains, dazed and terrified, stepping over corpses as they
stumbled into the selection lines, while German SS guards screamed
out orders to them as they lined up. One path led to the gas chambers,
the other to a usually brief spell of labor, before being killed.

The gas chambers didn't look menacing: a sign announced BATHS
over the lawns, with their borders of flowers. An orchestra played as the
victims lined up, usually selections from *The Merry Widow* and *The
Tales of Hoffman,* something light and reassuring to keep the shuffling
Jews moving. The Jews were herded into the chambers while, outside,
orderlies waited to drop the crystals of Zyklon-B down the vents. A
Sergeant Moll gave the go-ahead, usually shouting, "All right, give them
something to chew on," before laughing as the gas poured out from

the vents. There was nothing to chew on, even less to breathe, and it took several minutes to die. Panic erupted as the Jews clawed desperately at the sealed door, climbing over each other in a futile bid for freedom as their bowels and bladders voided in their terror.

Swiss government officials, at least, well knew of both the effects and the initial methodology of the Nazi genocide, from its outset. Swiss army doctors had served on the eastern front, at the invitation of the German military, treating Nazi soldiers wounded in Operation Barbarossa, the invasion of the Soviet Union, says Professor Yehuda Bauer, professor of Holocaust Studies at Hebrew University, Jerusalem. At that stage of the genocide, the Nazi killing machine operated mostly by mass shootings, carried out by the Einsatzgruppen, special extermination squads, with assistance from regular Wehrmacht (army) soldiers.

According to Bauer, "Already in the autumn of 1941, there were Swiss doctors who were invited by the German military to help with medical work, with wounded German soldiers on the eastern front. They didn't see the Einsatzgruppen, but they saw the effects of the German policies and the murder of the Jews. They reported back to the Red Cross and the Swiss government, which had access to those reports because they came in the name of the Swiss army."

How much did the Swiss government and the bankers know about the mass extermination camps and the gas chambers? Certainly the Swiss elite, both financial and political, knew that dreadful things were happening to the Jews in areas under German control. The Swiss National Bank's legal office report, dated 1943–50, mentions the deportations and persecutions of the Jews. The Nazis and their local accomplices had been carrying out mass murder by gassing, first with gas vans and then in gas chambers, since September 1941. It is hard to believe that the Federal Council and the bankers, with their ties of language and culture to, and extensive business and diplomatic contacts with, the Third Reich had not heard of the gassings in Poland. Either way, it was Swiss telegraph machines that clattered out the first truths about the extermination of the Jews, transmitting information relayed through contacts in Switzerland.

One of the earliest reports of the true extent of the Holocaust reached the West on 8 August 1942 from Switzerland, in a telegram sent by Gerhart Riegner, the WJC's representative in Geneva, to Sidney

Silverman, M.P., in London and Rabbi Stephen Wise, president of the American Jewish Congress, in New York.

> Received alarming report that in Führer's headquarters plan discussed and under consideration according to which all Jews in countries occupied or controlled Germany numbering three and a half to four million should after deportation and concentration in east be exterminated at one blow to resolve once and for all the Jewish question in Europe. Action reported planned for autumn; methods under discussion including prussic acid. We transmit information with all necessary reservation as exactitude cannot be confirmed. Informant stated to have close connections with highest German authorities and his reports generally reliable.

That informant was Eduard Scholte, a Leipzig businessman who was in Switzerland on business and wanted to get news to the Allies about the Holocaust. Scholte's sources are not known, but the chain of events that led to the Riegner Cable, as the WJC's representative's telegram became known, are a matter of record. Scholte gave his information to a Swiss intermediary, who in turn informed a Jewish journalist, Dr. Benjamin Sagalowitz, who ran the Swiss Jewish Press Agency. On 1 August Sagalowitz informed Riegner, and a week later the cable was sent. In fact, the information in the Riegner Cable was almost a year old, but it was still a watershed, because it confirmed other reports about mass extermination that had trickled through to the West. After several months of debate and discussion about the cable's contents and likely veracity, backed up by a similar report from another Jewish leader based in Switzerland, Isaac Sternbuch, that was sent in September, Rabbi Wise finally broke the story to the press on 24 November 1942. After that, even the bankers of Zürich could not say they didn't know about the Holocaust.

But, genocide or not, all through the war in Switzerland it was business with Berlin as usual, especially at the Swiss National Bank. And even less did the bankers worry about the origin of the gold bars, franked with the insignia of the Reichsbank, as they neatly slid into the vaults under the quiet and orderly Swiss streets. The Swiss National Bank's own report on its gold deal with the Third Reich, written in 1984, points out that SNB officials were not adequately suspicious of where the German gold was coming from. Chapter 3 explains in detail why SNB officials should have questioned the provenance of the Nazi gold shipments, but the SNB report puts it most succinctly: "It is hard to understand that [in 1944] the SNB's Governing Board still trusted the criminal Nazi regime."

It was the international scandal that erupted in the spring of 1996 over Holocaust victims' dormant accounts that first kicked Swiss banks' murky wartime record of economic collaboration with the Nazis into the headlines. But however many million Swiss francs still sit in the accounts opened by Jews who perished in the Nazi genocide—although only "peanuts" remain, according to Robert Studer, chairman of the Union Bank of Switzerland—the documents in British and American archives reveal a much deeper and more sinister pattern of economic collaboration. Holocaust victims' accounts are just the opening payoff. These formerly secret reports show how, for all Switzerland's claims of neutrality, the Swiss National Bank accepted gold that its officials must have known was looted, while private Swiss banks were key financial foreign-currency providers of the Nazi war machine. The escudos and dollars the Swiss banks provided paid for everything from steel to build Panzer tanks to tungsten to strengthen Messerschmidt fighter planes— for a war, especially a world war, is fought on the economic battlefield as much as the military one. Swiss banks were the international economic pivot of the Nazi war machine that stretched from Berlin to Lisbon, and Buenos Aires to Bern.

HOW DID the looted gold make its way to Switzerland? Behind the sparse prose of the Allied intelligence documents lies a bloody trail of stolen wealth. The actual process by which the Nazis lined their pockets was rather less civilized than the Swiss bankers' deliberations as they sent telegrams back and forth to the Reichsbank and forwarded stolen gold and the Nazis' occupation profits on to Fascist Spain and Portugal, which, like Switzerland, were also neutral but whose leaders shared some limited ideological sympathies with Hitler. Being occupied by the Nazis was an expensive business, and countries such as France and Poland had to pay staggering amounts for the privilege of being ruled by the master race. There were SS and Gestapo salaries to be paid, Wehrmacht soldiers to be fed, Gauleiters (district leaders) to be provided with comfortable accommodation. Seizing national gold reserves was just the start. In February 1944, Count Schwerin von

Krosick, Nazi finance minister, judged the total of occupation payments received by Berlin as RM48 billion ($19 billion). The Third Reich extracted a total of RM104 billion from its new lands, according to a study by the U.S. Strategic Bombing Survey. Holland, for example, paid RM10 million ($4 million) to the Third Reich as a "war contribution," the Reichsbank vice-president Emil Puhl told his Allied interrogators after his capture at the war's end. And Poland was to be put through the Nazi economic mill until it was wrung dry. "I shall endeavor to squeeze out of this province everything that is still possible to squeeze out," said Dr. Frank, its Nazi governor-general. Reichsmarshal Goering liberally plundered the art treasures of the Third Reich's new territories. As soon as Poland was conquered he ordered the seizure of its art, and within six months the country was almost entirely stripped of its artistic wealth.

France's artistic heritage, of course, offered much greater bounty than Poland's. Goering, who fancied himself as a connoisseur of art, wanted the lot. Alfred Rosenberg, the supposed "Philosopher King" of the Third Reich, later hanged as a war criminal at Nuremberg, set up a special unit to plunder France's museums and châteaux, including the Louvre. This was the Einsatzstab Rosenberg. On 5 November 1940 Goering issued a secret order detailing how objects plundered from the Louvre would be disposed of, putting them into categories:

- Those art objects about which the Führer has reserved for himself the decision as to their use
- Those . . . which serve the completion of the Reichsmarshal's [i.e., Goering's] collection . . .
- Those . . . that are suited to be sent to German museums

Removing a painting from a museum or stealing a statue from a country was a relatively straightforward task. In extermination camps such as Auschwitz, special Kommandos were set up to search for victims' valuables. Their members were relatively privileged camp inmates, whose job it was to sort through the mountains of baggage that arrived every day with each fresh intake of Jews: the deported Jews, who believed they were on their way to a new life, were encouraged to bring their valuables with them.

They sat in a large room, surrounded by suitcases containing the few possessions that the Jews had managed to bring from their homes, and sorted through the detritus of the victims' former lives. Jewelry, foreign currency, antiques, all these were immediately put to one side. Gold items were especially prized, for they could be sent to Berlin to be smelted down before being turned into ingots. Occasionally a Kommando member would cry out as he recognized the possessions of a relative or loved one. Even so, the work was preferable to climbing over piles of the dead Jews, examining their mouths and yanking out gold fillings or silver dental work. That was the task of the Sonderkommandos, camp inmates with the worst job of all. About half an hour after the Zyklon-B had done its work, the Sonderkommando teams, dressed in rubber boots and wearing gas masks, would wade into the pile of twisted humanity and the pools of blood and excrement that slopped around the gas chamber floor. After washing away the bodily fluids, the Sonderkommandos used nooses and hooks to drag the corpses apart, before starting to look for gold dental work that could be melted down for the Reichsbank's precious-metals department, although dental gold is of lesser quality than normal gold reserves.

But there were profits in more than teeth. Nazi businessmen even worked out how to make soap from dead Jews. A document offered by Russian prosecutors at the Nuremberg trials detailed how a firm in Danzig constructed an electrically heated tank for making soap from human fat. The recipe was "twelve pounds of human fat, ten quarts of water, and eight ounces to a pound of caustic soda . . . all boiled for two or three hours then cooled." German firms rushed to submit bids for the crematoria at the extermination camps, for genocide was good business.

After Auschwitz had been liberated by the Red Army, the Allies discovered a lengthy correspondence between the firm of I. A. Topf and Sons, of Erfurt, heating equipment manufacturers, who won the contract to build the crematoria there. There was no question that the directors of this family firm knew precisely what was being burned in their furnaces. Here is an extract of a letter from the firm, dated 12 February 1943:

> To the Central Construction Office of the SS and Police, Auschwitz: Subject: Crematoria 2 and 3 for the camp

> We acknowledge receipt of your order for five triple furnaces, including two electric elevators for raising the corpses and one emergency elevator . . .

A practical installation for stoking coal was also ordered, and one for transporting ashes. Nor were the ashes wasted, for there were Reichsmarks to be made with them as well. Testimony was offered at Nuremberg that the ashes of Holocaust victims were sometimes sold as fertilizer.

But it was the Third Reich's mania for gold that most exercised the Nazis. So greedy were they that sometimes they couldn't even wait to kill their victims before pulling out their teeth. In Minsk, Belarus (formerly the Belorussian Soviet Socialist Republic), the German warden of the prison forced a Jewish dentist to extract gold dental work from prisoners' mouths while they were still alive. All the Jews "had their gold bridgework, crowns, and fillings pulled or broken out. This always happens one or two hours before the special action," he recorded in a secret report. "Special action" was, of course, the Nazi euphemism for killing the prisoners. As a good German bureaucrat he dutifully recorded the numbers killed under his command and the amount of dental work pulled from their teeth. In one six-week period, in the spring of 1943, 516 Russian and German Jews were executed, of whom 336 spent their last hours having their gold dental work extracted. Their fillings were sent on to the Reichsbank to be smelted down at the mint.

ECONOMIC efficiency was always a prime factor in the Holocaust. Even the special preparations the Nazis made at Auschwitz in the spring of 1944 for the elimination of Hungarian Jewry proved inadequate as the extermination machine went into overdrive. There were too many people to kill. The gas chambers could not keep up with the stream of condemned Jews, and so the Nazis reverted to the favored method of extermination, honed on the eastern front in 1941 and 1942: mass shootings of naked Jews, standing or kneeling in front of open graves. As the Holocaust entered its final stages, the commanders at Auschwitz complained that even the refurbished crematoria were not only inadequate but "uneconomical." The Nazi obsession with value for Reichsmarks had marked the Holocaust from its early days. As early as 1938, when the Third Reich annexed Austria, to the cheers of onlookers, contemporary observers, such as the foreign correspondent William Shirer, who witnessed the Nazi occupation of Vienna, noted the Germans' greed as they jailed Jews and stole their goods. "I myself, from our apartment in Plosslgasse, watched squads of SS men carting off silver, tapestries, paintings, and other loot from the Rothschild palace next door," Shirer writes in his book *The Rise and Fall of the Third Reich.*

Money, in sufficient quantity, would often buy a wealthy family a ticket to freedom. Baron Louis de Rothschild bought his way out of Vienna by handing over his steel mills to the Hermann Goering works, just as the wealthy Hungarian Weiss family would hand over their Budapest steel mills to the Germans in 1944 in exchange for safe passage out. The Nazis even set up a special looting unit of hand-picked SS troops, the Devisenschutzkommando (DSK), charged with locating and acquiring gold for the German war effort and for officials' personal enrichment. DSK officers were ready and willing to use violence and torture to get information.

The *stated* purpose of the DSK—to control the currency traffic between Germany and the occupied territories in Western Europe and within the territories themselves—was pure camouflage, according to a secret Allied intelligence report on the interrogation of one Dr. Rudolf Noltmann. Born near Osnabruck in 1904, Noltmann, an expert on animal diseases, served in the German air force but never received any military training. Nor was he qualified as a medical doctor, but he still spent a comfortable war quartered at the Hotel de Calais in Paris. There his medical knowledge was put to use treating high-ranking officers of the various Nazi intelligence and counterintelligence services for venereal disease. Several of his patients served in the DSK.

Dr. Noltmann surrendered to Allied forces on 22 September 1944 and was interrogated on 29 May 1945. He claimed to have witnessed DSK interrogations and, like many Nazi officials in Allied custody, was, in the words of the report, "anxious to cooperate," hoping that by incriminating his former colleagues he would be treated more lightly by the Allied authorities. Based at Rue Pillet-Will 5/7 in Paris, the DSK was headed by one Staffeldt, charged with running operations in France, Belgium, and Holland, the report details. Like any multinational corporation, the DSK had offices abroad as well, and Staffeldt had headquarters in Bordeaux, Marseilles, Brussels, and Amsterdam.

Staffeldt flew out of Paris before the arrival of the Allies, but his deputy, named Hartmann, was ordered to stay behind in the case of Allied occupation. Staffeldt and Hartmann had ten assistants, all members of the SS, equipped with fake British passports and French identity cards and other false papers. Hartmann and other officers who were ordered to stay behind after the arrival of the Allies were instructed to guard the looted gold, and even obtain more when possible, probably to help finance the Nazi Werewolf operation of resistance behind Allied lines and fund the clandestine escape routes from Germany to South America for escaping Nazis. DSK officers were thugs, according to the report. It lists such luminaries as these:

- ObInsp. Blumenstein. From Silesia. Opened Marseilles branch of the DSK in the summer of 1944. Blumenstein was particularly brutal. . . . His private secretary was Frl. Erna Bertinchamp, reportedly from the Saar. PW saw her physically mistreating DSK victims during interrogations.
- Obltn. Hugo Doose. In charge of Channel Islands. Lived in Granville. His favorite method of interrogation was to break a beer glass over a victim's head.
- Obltn. Ludwig Jaretski. Austrian. Employed burning matches on stripped victims, to obtain information. Lived at 3 or 5 Blvd. Emil Augier, Paris with Knoblauch, and their girlfriends.

Anyone dragged in for interrogation by the DSK could only hope to be interrogated by Knoblauch, a former customs officer, according to the report:

- Obltn. Karl Knoblauch. Also a member of the SS. Civilian occupation ObzollInspec. Residence in Germany Hannover—Cossina Str. Had seven passports. Less brutally inclined. Paris address same as Jaretzki's.

The DSK could not function without the active help of dozens of French citizens, ready to inform on their compatriots in return for favors from the Nazis. The French DSK auxiliaries, about eighty in number, were known as V-men (Vertrauensmann—confidential agent), and were drawn from "the lowest levels of society to the highest circles, including prominent lawyers, as well as some White Russian residents in France," according to the intelligence report. To be a V-man in Nazi-occupied France could be quite lucrative, as they worked on a commission basis, receiving 10 percent of any loot that the DSK acquired.

V-men were armed and were equipped with false identity cards and counterfeit American dollars and British pounds. Many of these fake banknotes and passports had been crafted by concentration camp victims, for the Nazis set up a network of forgers' workshops in the camps to produce counterfeit currency and documents. The DSK operated by using property sales to attract potential buyers with liquid assets, preferably gold. Once the victims had expressed interest in the house or land for sale, DSK officers would arrest and interrogate them. The report says that "torture was a common practice in these interrogations." After their interrogations, the DSK's victims were usually relieved to be transferred to the jails of Sante, Cherche Midi, or De La Repremiere.

What did the Nazis do with the gold acquired by the DSK? It was used to finance agents in German-occupied countries and for "other purposes," according to the report. Some would have found its way back to Berlin and the Reichsbank, to be sent on to Switzerland, but as the Allies advanced it became easier to send the loot south, to Spain. One of the last gold transports to leave Paris was intended for Spain, while the very last to leave, on 17 August 1944, was bound for Rheims, the new headquarters of the DSK. As the Allies advanced and the DSK's supply of victims began to run low, its members expanded their area of operations to include intelligence work and used their skills in extracting information on political interrogations.

In Paris the DSK SS officers used lit matches to torture their victims. In Oradea (now in Romania), a city near the Hungarian border which had been returned to Budapest's rule after Hungary joined the Axis in 1941, the Nazis and their local collaborators preferred to beat their victims senseless or wire them up to an electric-shock machine to force them to surrender their valuables.

Like most of their coreligionists, the Jews of Oradea were first forced into a ghetto, before being sent on to Auschwitz. A few survived, including Alexander Leitner, chairman of the Orthodox Jewish community and civil leader of the ghetto. Leitner even made it to the safety of Switzerland, where, after the Allied victory, he wrote his memoirs, entitled *The Tragedy of the Jews in Nagyvarad,* as the city was known in Hungarian. He escaped on a secret train from Budapest in June 1944. It departed for Switzerland, via Bergen-Belsen; there, its passengers were held in a special annex, where conditions were easier than in the main concentration camp complex. The train was known as the "Kasztner Train," after the city's wartime Zionist leader, Rezso Kasztner, who concluded a secret deal with Adolf Eichmann, brokered by an SS officer called Kurt Becher, a key figure in the Nazi acquisition of looted wealth. The negotiations among Kasztner, Eichmann, and Becher were a central point in the triangle connecting Germany, Hungary, and Switzerland, and much more follows about them in subsequent chapters.

The Leitner report is a heartrending document, written in the stilted English of the nonnative speaker, whose anguished and clumsy style makes its pages even more poignant. Leitner's detailed daily entries catalogue the terror that engulfed the city's Jews, a terror organized by the SS and the Gestapo, with the ready aid of local members of the Arrow Cross (the Hungarian Nazi Party), civil police, and the gendarmerie, the last in particular being prime engineers of the Hungarian Holocaust, as they robbed and looted to fill the treasuries of Berlin and Budapest.

The yellow star for Jews was introduced on 5 April 1944, soon after the German occupation, Leitner writes. "First day of the Jew badge, the yellow star. The days of the darkest Middle Ages have come back. . . . The leper Jews should be recognized by their yellow star (10cm diameter) from afar. A very important ingredient of the Hitlerite conception. First stair that leads to the deportation."

When the Nazis introduced similar rules in Denmark, virtually the whole population donned the badge. The Danes then organized a mass exodus of the country's Jews to the safety of neutral Sweden. In Bulgaria the government refused to cooperate in the Holocaust, and the pressure of public opinion prevented the deportations of that country's Jews. However, many Hungarians, conditioned by decades of institutionalized anti-Semitism under the rule of Admiral Horthy, couldn't wait to get their hands on the assets of the country's Jews, before putting them on the cattle trains to Auschwitz.

By 11 May the Nazi and Arrow Cross hunt for gold in Oradea was in full swing. Jews were brought in for interrogation, to make them reveal where they had hidden their wealth. Most had none, or at the most a few items of jewelry, such as wedding rings. But with their perceptions shaped by decades of propaganda, neither the Germans nor their local auxiliaries would take no for an answer. Even when there was nothing to surrender.

There was a set pattern for beating information out of Jews under interrogation. Leitner reports:

One of the hangmen asks the delicvent [sic] "Confess, what have you hidden or entrusted to the Christians." If he is confessing he would beat him still, that he might be thoroughly mollified, should he be obdurate, then he would be exposed to still harder scourging. 4–5 are rushing at him, shoes, clothing, underwear would soon be torn from him, two of them would beat the heels, two others, the hands, arms and other parts of the body . . . the gendarme detective are [sic] really not of the sort that he would shrink back from belaboring the more sensible parts of man.

If systematic beating did not work, the electric-shock machine was brought in. "One of the 'treated' during the afternoon, has someone told, that he was tantalized by electrical apparatus too. And this, what appearance has it, we asked him," records Leitner.

The victim explained: interrogators would wind a length of wire, fifty to sixty centimeters long, around the victim's left wrist, and insert the other end into the machine, while an electrode would be applied to various parts of the victim's body, including the penis or vagina. "The iron 'tormentor' would be pressed, as you please, at the head, heart, sexual organs, thigh, shank, heel. This produces terrible shocks and unbearable pains."

Not surprisingly, this particular victim, who had given a few valuables to a Christian neighbor for safekeeping, soon succumbed to the machine's electric shocks. He described his ordeal to Leitner:

My brain turns out, my heart leaps into my throat. "I will confess all," I have screamed, but it was in vain. They continued it. We torment you stinking Jew until you will be mollified as butter and would not retain the least. In conclusion as they saw, that I was at the end of my knowledge and hardly able to inhale, they have stopped. Naturally they obtained everything from me. I have confessed all. It vexes me now, that my honorable Christian friend will have uneasiness, he was so trustful and I betrayed him.

The next day, 12 May, brought further horrors for Leitner. At eleven in the morning he looked out into the courtyard of the building where he was held. An old man shuffled forward, "his face swollen on both sides, traces of scourging, look on the surface of both hands, red and strongly swollen. His feet were to be sure also treated, as he went limping." It was Leitner's father, who had just been beaten for information about valuables. Father and son embraced, and the elderly man lay down on Leitner's cot.

A few minutes later the gendarme accompanying the prisoners returned to ask the elder Leitner if his wife lived with him. The younger Leitner argued in vain for his mother to be spared the torture chamber. A few minutes later she took her turn at the electric-shock machine before returning.

> In half an hour was my dear mother also with us. To my surprise no traces of violence outwardly. "What have they done with you?" I asked her. "You know my child they treated me with an electrical apparatus." Have you had great pains? "Yes, but it will pass away. You know my child they have maltreated me in vain. I have told them, that I was not informed of fortune matters. Even if they will kill me, they will not be more informed. Then it was too dull for them and [they] stopped with the torments."

Still the gendarme wasn't satisfied, and soon after he returned, to take Leitner's mother away again. This time she was gone for almost an hour. Returning to her husband and son, she explained how the enraged gendarme had driven her back to the family home to search for nonexistent valuables. "He worried me during our drive to tell him, where have we hidden our gold, silver, jewels, and cash. I always repeated I don't know, gold and jewels we had not at all, silver and cash have been declared and deposited in the bank, as I am informed by my husband." Transfixed by greedy visions of hidden wealth, the gendarme refused to accept her denials and, drawing his revolver, threatened to shoot the elderly woman in the street unless she revealed where the hidden gold was. She put on a brave display of defiance.

"Well, I told him, drive me only into our court and I will show it to you. We have arrived there. Our court is fully asphalted. He saw it, and incites me, 'Then show me, where have you digged your gold?' Hither, showing to him a corner in the court. 'Don't make a punch of me, you old woman,' and he became furious, there is old asphalt everywhere."

If the Leitners had hidden their valuables under the asphalt, the gendarme was welcome to dig it up, for surely there would be marks on the ground to indicate its hiding place, she asserted. "At last it became too imbecile to him and white of rage he began to cry, 'That is impossible. Here is nothing digged.'"

Meanwhile, in Budapest, government ministers were closely monitoring their underlings as they tortured Hungarian Jews for details of their supposed hordes of gold, and financial clerks totted up the latest total of loot. On 18 May two important visitors from the capital arrived in Oradea, reports Leitner. "One of them, unimportant, antipathetic figure wears Hungarian national costume, the other a civilian dress. After two minutes they have withdrawn."

The man in national costume was Secretary of State Laszlo Endre, the friend of Eichmann, and a major architect of the Hungarian Holocaust. His companion was Desiderius Nagy, a senior figure in the department of state finance. The two officials were well satisfied with their visit. The loot was piling up, all for the glory of Hungary and its ally, Nazi Germany. Leitner writes:

> Mr. Director of Finances had also no ground to be ashamed before the almighty Secretary of State. The booty gained out of Jewish assets grows successfully, having estimated reached about 30 millions already merely the values brought in and who might know to what level it might rise still.

In Hungary—as in every Nazi-occupied country—not only did looted Jewish assets line the pockets of everyone from the gendarme switching on the electric-shock machine to senior government officials, but by stealing the wealth of hundreds of its own citizens, the wartime Hungarian government could fund its war effort, quickly, cheaply, and efficiently. Who needs special war bonds when you can just kill your own citizens and steal their wealth? Or, as Dr. Leitner put it:

> Has this not proved to be the best invention? There needs not to subscribe war bonds loans (by the experience of the last war it would fail without that) neither taxes on war profits, nor supplementary taxes, nor assessment, nor collecting of them. Nay, nor are a bulk of civil servants are wanted. It goes with some county police, gendarmes, a number of hangman's assistants, three chauffeurs and as many motor cars. And they produce miracles. The state revenue gained by torturing of Jews amounts to much more in a few days, than tax collection in some years by ordinary methods imposed on every race of the town population.

The Nazis were so efficient at plundering occupied Europe that, by the end of the war, the Third Reich had more loot than it knew what do with. In the spring of 1945 Allied troops had discovered a mountain of hidden booty at an abandoned mine in Merkers that Nazi officials had not been able either to smelt down or to send on to Switzerland.

As well as the main gold hoard found at Merkers, Allied troops found a separate group of 189 containers, carefully piled up in a corner of the cave away from the main haul. These containers, identified by Albert Thoms, chief of the Reichsbank precious metals department, to his Allied interrogators as SS loot, included sacks of gold and silver dental work, not all of which had been melted down. Each container had been carefully labeled, showing its contents, the name of the sender—the Reichsbank in Berlin—its weight, a package number, and the name "Melmer." In April and May 1945 the containers were opened. They held "every conceivable kind of personal article of value and considerable currency," according to a report, stamped "secret," from the Special Finance Division of the Supreme Headquarters Allied Expeditionary Force (SHAEF), dated 8 May 1945. This was not the wealth of national treasuries; it was not piles of neat gold bars, relocated to Berlin and dispatched by clerks in the Reichsbank to their colleagues in Bern; not merely a cog in the machine of international finance that kept running all through the war, between the neutral countries and both the Nazis and the Allies. Rather, the booty listed in the SHAEF report was the bloody crop of the Nazi killing fields.

The SHAEF report gives details of what qualified as SS loot: "ornamental silver—trays, candlesticks, etc.; flat silver—knives, forks, spoons; Passover cups and candlestick holders, silver; gold and silver dental work, some melted down (full bags); watch chains and cases, gold and silver; cigarette cases, gold and silver, some with engraved names, some with names scratched out."

Here is the archeology of genocide: a list of personal effects, whose owners needed them no longer, the last vestiges of Jewish communities eradicated by the Nazis. And so the list on the SHAEF report goes on—a morbid catalogue of the piles of once-treasured valuables, presents for birthdays, anniversaries, school graduations, final mementos of happy family celebrations for their now-dead members. Nothing should be left behind, if it could bring in a pile of, or even a few, Reichsmarks. These personal belongings too were found at Merkers: "powder puff cases; opera glasses; spectacle frames; rings, gold and silver and with precious stones—wedding, engagement, anniversary, etc.; necklaces and strings of beads—apparently diamond, pearl, silver, gold; earrings; bracelets; stickpins; cufflinks; tiaras; coins and currency of many nations and denominations. . . ." And the list concludes: "silk stockings."

That discovery led to further investigations by British and American intelligence officers and a fresh round of interrogations of German bank officials, together with searches of Reichsbank local branch vaults. The results were staggering as U.S. officers discovered a haul of looted gold, currency, precious metals, and centuries-old antiques that Reichsbank officials had stashed away all over Germany.

A top-secret cipher telegram, signed by Dwight D. Eisenhower, commander of Allied Forces in Europe, and sent to the Joint Chiefs of Staff on 6 May 1945, details the reports of loot discovered by U.S. troops, worth hundreds of millions of dollars, some of it looted by those same DSK SS officers in Paris, the rest looted from all over Nazi-occupied Europe, from Holland to Hungary, including, probably, the Jews of Oradea. Here are some extracts from Eisenhower's telegram:

> Halle branch of Reichsbank. 16 boxes containing 64 gold bars 7 bags and 2 boxes containing individual deposits of gold and foreign exchange assets appearing to have been taken from safe deposit boxes. Reichsbank records indicate that gold was delivered by Devisenschutzkommando France and had been moved to Halle from Eisenach where it had been taken in Sept. 1944 when the Germans fled France.
>
> Nurnberg branch of Reichsbank. 34 bags and 2 chests containing gold bars which according to records at Reichsbank branches in Nurnberg came from Niederlanschen Bank Amsterdam.
>
> Magdeburg branch of Reichsbank. 6,000 silver bars 500 cases of silver bars which according to Reichsbank records at Magdeburg belonged to Magyar National Bank of Hungary and said by local Reichsbank officials to represent Hungary's silver reserve. Also found 12 bags records of precious metals department of Reichsbank [Author's note: this department oversaw the gold smelted from looted jewelry and teeth of Holocaust victims]. . . . Found two envelopes said to contain foreign securities from Holland, Spain, and Switzerland deposited with the bank by Magdeburg customs officer.

The Plauen branch of the Reichsbank yielded a particularly rich haul, according to Eisenhower's telegram. But then branch records showed the deposits were credited to the bank account of SS Reichs-führer Heinrich Himmler, the man who would be Hitler's successor. No one could accuse Himmler of failing to take advantage of the spoils of war. In Plauen's vaults sat the following: "35 bags of gold containing 250,000 U.S. gold dollars, 1,000,000 Swiss gold francs, 98,450 Dutch gold guilders, and 151,560 Norwegian gold kroner all of which gold according to the records of the Reichsbank at Plauen was deposited by the Sicherheitsdienst (SD) [SS Security Service] of the Wehrmacht for the account of the SS Reichsführer (Himmler). Also found 18,000 RM value [Yugoslav] dinar and [Hungarian] pengö currency."

High-ranking Nazis, such as Richard Wendler, head of the Lublin concentration camp, had also used the SS to deposit their own private booty. Like Himmler, Wendler was a greedy man, according to the telegram. In Hof, U.S. officers discovered a church's gold chalice, dated 1722, reportedly deposited for him. They also found in a nearby spinning mill twenty-three crates of boxes jammed with gold and silverware, as well as "valuable cloths and rugs," deposited by Wendler.

As well as the loot they discovered at Merkers, Allied soldiers also found Albert Thoms, Chief of the Reichsbank Precious Metals Department, whom they captured and interrogated. Like many of his Nazi colleagues, the senior Nazi economic official was ready to cooperate with his interrogators and explained in further detail the history of the relationship between the SS and the Reichsbank.

In Berlin, Reichsbank officials struggled to cope with the mountain of Nazi booty, as vaults and corridors were filled to overflowing with war plunder. It was simple to send looted gold from concentration camp victims to the Reichsbank in Berlin to be melted down, but works of art and jewelry sometimes needed to be sold in their original condition to swell the coffers of the SS. The Reichsbank's answer was to set up the Melmer system.

The Melmer system worked like this: Loot arrived at the Reichsbank, where its value would be estimated. If, for example, Reichsbank officials estimated that a consignment of valuables was worth RM100,000, then that amount would be credited to the Max Heiliger account. The account was opened in the name of Max Heiliger, but Max Heiliger was just a cover name for the SS. Allied intelligence believed that much of the money deposited in the Max Heiliger account went straight into the pockets of Heinrich Himmler.

But what to do with all this loot and how to convert it into Reichsmarks? The Reichsbank's directors decided to sell it through the Berlin municipal pawnshop, so converting a silver candlestick from a Jewish family in Smolensk, or a gold watch stolen in Warsaw, into cash. The Melmer system used the municipal pawnshop as a channel both to sell stolen valuables and to enrich the SS.

The Max Heiliger account was opened in 1942 with a telephone call from an SS officer called Frank to Reichsbank vice president Emil Puhl; and, soon afterward, Albert Thoms was instructed to receive the deliveries of SS loot. These were marked "Melmer," with their value, after assessment by Reichsbank officials, to be credited to the Max Heiliger account. Thoms's interrogation report, dated 8 May 1945, details how the Reichsbank accepted the loot: "Melmer payments arrived in truckloads of suitcases, boxes, packages, and bags. Either Thoms or a clerk would issue an itemized receipt for the contents of each container. 'Once or twice Thoms noted a container stamped "Konzentrationlager" [concentration camp],' " the report details.

This was the Melmer system. The pawnshop also sold silver and gold extracted from camp victims' teeth, but mainly abroad, according to Thoms's interrogation report. Like most Nazis, Thoms claimed to know very little about this, the report says: "[He] claims to have regarded the stuff as ordinary 'booty' or spoils of war from Jews and other peoples in the occupied east. Of concentration camps he claimed to have known only of Dachau and Oranienburg until his recent trip . . . to Buchenwald."

Thoms's claims, were of course, nonsense. By his own admission he knew that the Berlin municipal pawnshop was selling considerable smelted-down gold and silver dental work, which demanded some sort of permanent site and systematic extraction process, not a job that could be carried out by front-line fighting troops. The Reichsbank enjoyed a close relationship with the SS, closer than with the Wehrmacht proper, whose soldiers generally—but not always—spent more time fighting their armed opponents than lining up Jews and shooting them, before pulling off their wedding rings. "Ordinary" Wehrmacht booty went to the Treasury, Thoms's interrogation report says; "in the case of SS loot, however, the bank handled everything, coins and currency and personal booty. Gold and silver bars were bought by the bank at full value."

Small items such as rings were sent to the mint and were smelted. Larger items were sent to the Degussa firm, Germany's biggest firm dealing in precious metals. All the SS's revenue from these, whether through the Reichsbank, the mint, the Melmer-system municipal pawnshop, or Degussa, was then credited to the SS account in the name of Max Heiliger.

Every war is marked by looting and profiteering, and even now the streets of Zagreb and Belgrade are filled with swaggering Mafiosi, bedecked with Rolex watches, driving top-of-the-range Mercedeses and BMWs, who stole their wealth on the killing fields of Bosnia. But no other regime has devoted as much planning and manpower to plundering its conquests as did the Third Reich.

The Nazis have no rivals in the organized-booty stakes. In fact, there was a major contradiction between the Nazis' ideological campaign to eliminate European Jewry and the concomitant economic effort needed for the design and engineering of the Holocaust and the Third Reich's aim of turning a fast Reichsmark. For as far as the progress of the German war effort was concerned, the Holocaust was an economic nonsense that used up vital war resources: manpower, transport facilities, construction work. Millions of Reichsmarks were diverted from the army and the front lines, and spent instead on building a network of extermination camps, transporting the Jews of Eastern Europe there, killing them, and disposing of the bodies—a complicated and expensive undertaking. It would have made far more financial sense—moral questions aside—to have used Eastern Europe's Jews en masse as forced labor. But while slave labor was occasionally exploited, as in the Lódz ghetto, where Velvel Singer toiled before being killed in Auschwitz, the SS—as distinct from the Third Reich in a broader sense—needed dead Jews rather than live laborers, to properly exploit their wealth. Far easier to shoot and gas Jews and harvest rings, bracelets, and gold dental work from a pile of corpses than deal with live human beings, who needed to be housed and fed, even at below-subsistence levels. But even that giant haul of booty had to be bureaucratically processed, much of it through the Melmer system.

An extract from a Reichsbank memo, sent from Berlin and dated 31 March 1944, explains in more detail how Melmer worked in practice, after an agreement reached by the Reichsbank vice-president Emil Puhl and Berlin government officials:

The Reichsbank has undertaken to convert the domestic and foreign money, gold and silver coins, precious metals, securities, jewelry, watches, precious stones, and other valuables accumulated by this bureau. These articles will be handled under the codeword "Melmer."

Jewelry and similar items not already smelted will be turned over to the City Pawnshop, Dept III Central Office, Berlin N 4, Elshasserstra. 74, for redemption at the best possible price.

Much of the loot stolen on the eastern front would be converted into Reichsmarks through the Melmer system, the memo explains, under the order of Walther Funk, minister for economics (who was also head of the Reichsbank), and Lutz Schwerin von Krosick, minister for finance.

The Reichsbank has been informed by the Reichsmarshal and director of the Four-Year Plan (Goering) that the considerable gold and silver wares, jewelry, etc., of the Head Trustee Office for the East will be turned over to the banks by orders of Ministers Funk (Economics) and Von Krosick (Finance). These articles will be redeemed in the same manner as the Melmer deliveries. Goods from the occupied West will also be similarly redeemed.

A letter from the Reichsbank to the Berlin municipal pawnshop, dated 15 September, lists the latest booty, including 154 gold watches, 1,601 gold earrings, 132 diamond rings, 784 silver pocket watches, and "160 diverse dentures, partly of gold."

As well as supplying Berliners with a supply of cheap looted jewelry and gold and silver valuables, the Melmer system was also designed to sell war booty abroad, and so acquire the vital foreign currency the Third Reich needed to keep the Nazi war machine going. The Reichsbank memo concludes:

Regarding the large accumulation of foreign exchange expected through sales of such articles abroad, and the not inconsiderable accumulation of gold and silver from smelting of unexported items, prompt establishment of a uniform arrangement for handling these items is required.

That vital foreign exchange would, of course, be purchased through Swiss banks. True to form, once brought to trial at Nuremberg, Nazi officials were falling over themselves to implicate each other and shift the blame for this gruesome traffic. Oswald Pohl, head of the SS economic office, testified that Reichsbank president Funk knew full well where the funds earned from looted goods deposited in the SS's Max Heiliger account had come from. He clearly recalled talking with Reichsbank vice-president Puhl about the origin of the piles of valuables, reports the foreign correspondent William Shirer: "In this conversation no doubt remained that the objects to be delivered (came from) Jews who had been killed in concentration camps. The objects in question were rings, watches, eyeglasses, gold bars, wedding rings, brooches, pins, gold [teeth] fillings, and other valuables."

Dr. Funk even took guests on a tour of the Reichsbank vaults, to inspect the piles of valuables looted from Holocaust victims. Just as at the Wannsee conference and the Siofok meeting, where Nazi officials planned the Holocaust and its Hungarian chapters, the tour was followed by a multicourse dinner. The various Nazi luminaries chatted merrily over their haute cuisine, washed down with a selection of fine wines, as they discussed the unique nature and special provenance of the newly acquired valuables.

Reichsbank officials knew full well the origin of the mountains of gold that were suddenly appearing in its vaults. As trained professional bankers, they realized that the gold suddenly appearing for them to deposit was of a different quality from that used in normal banking procedures. One Reichsbank official testified at Nuremberg that he noticed much of this new gold came from the Polish city of Lublin and, of course, Auschwitz. "We knew that these places were the sites of concentration camps. It was in the tenth delivery, in November 1943, that dental gold appeared. The quantity of dental gold became unusually great," he said.

Gold extracted from the teeth of dead Jews is a ghastly motif throughout the Holocaust Bonanza. Even after the war, some officials of countries occupied by the Nazis wanted their former citizens' teeth back. A letter dated 23 September 1945 from two Czechoslovak finance ministry officials to U.S. military officials requests the return of valuables confiscated by the Nazis, including silver bullion and gold jewelry, found by U.S. forces in the Regensburg branch of the Reichsbank. The gold jewelry includes such macabre items as one tooth bridge, twelve gold teeth, five gold teeth crowns, one false-teeth plate, and two false teeth.

"In this inventory they list gold teeth, teeth crowns, silverware; we know exactly what they are talking about, whom those assets belong to: to murdered Jews," says an official of the World Jewish Congress.

The Melmer system, one of several methods of channeling funds from SS loot into the Max Heiliger account, was secret, known only to a few Nazis at the top of the Third Reich's economic hierarchy, according to the Thoms interrogation report. The Reichsbank "appears to have acted as the personal agent of Himmler in converting SS loot into orthodox financial assets," the report says, before adding that only a handful of people knew the code words "Max Heiliger" and "Melmer," and what they meant.

But however secret was the true purpose of Heiliger and Melmer, such a complicated operation needed considerable assistance from other Nazi financial organizations. The Nazi web of looted gold was spread across the Third Reich, and the 8 May report names the Reich finance minister, Von Krosick, the mint, the Reich pawnshop, and the precious-metals firm Deutsche Gold und Silber Scheideanstalt (Degussa) as helping in the two operations.

After the war, the Allies too were much exercised by the quality of Nazi gold they discovered stashed all over the Third Reich. Assessing the reparations payments demanded from Germany necessitated a proper assaying of the quality of looted Nazi gold. Dental gold is worth less than gold used in international finance, and it was proving tricky for the Allies to value gold bars made out of smelted teeth fillings. A letter from Livingston T. Merchant, minister-counselor for economic affairs at the U.S. embassy in Paris, dated 19 July 1946, addresses the problem of Shipment No. 1: "A question mark has been placed against the item of 4,173 bags said to contain 8,307 gold bars inasmuch as these gold bars may, after proper assay and expert consideration, be determined to represent melted down teeth fillings and therefore classifiable as nonmonetary gold." But, whether the gold was of monetary quality or merely of dental grade, it would always find a ready home in Swiss banks.

3

The Financiers of Genocide

[The Swiss National Bank in 1944 showed] . . . a degree of credulity which is impossible to comprehend. It is hard to understand that the SNB's governing board still trusted the criminal Nazi regime.

Extract from an internal SNB report on its relations with the Reichsbank, written in 1984

The Nazis . . . needed that one thing: hard cash. And there was only one place they knew they could find it, in Switzerland, and they knew they could only get it if they left the Swiss alone. The Germans made the Swiss so dependent on them that the Swiss could not slam the door in their face. But whose fault was that? The Swiss.

Marc Masurovsky, consultant historian to the U.S. Senate Banking Committee on Switzerland and looted Nazi assets

The musty paper trail that so damns Switzerland for its decade-long record of economic collaboration with the Third Reich stretches from London to Washington and Bern to Berlin. Included in the archives' piles of files are many thousands of declassified former intelligence reports, diplomatic notes, records of interrogations at the Nuremberg war-crime trials, and, most poignant of all, the telegrams sent by Jewish leaders abroad, many based in Switzerland, as they helplessly watched the elimination of their coreligionists. As the only neutral country bordering Nazi-occupied Europe, as well as its allies Vichy France and Fascist Italy, Switzerland was a natural base for Jewish relief organizations.

News poured from all over the Third Reich, via refugees, diplomats, and journalists, to the Jewish leaders based there. The Riegner Cable from the Geneva representative of the World Jewish Congress, sent in August 1942, caused a great sound and fury among international Jewish organizations and the Allied press. But with the Allies refusing to bomb even the railway lines to Auschwitz, there was little that Swiss Jews could do to slow down the Holocaust.

The attempts by Swiss Jews to help their coreligionists in Eastern Europe were of little concern to the members of the governing board of the Swiss National Bank in Bern. Their aim was to maximize their profits on the gold arriving from the Reichsbank. But just how much? Nazi gold, whether extracted at gunpoint from the treasuries of the Third Reich's newest territories, or pillaged from Holocaust victims, before being sent on to be resmelted at the Prussian State Mint to be franked and stamped, has become a modern myth. Even now, over fifty years since the defeat of the Third Reich, the phrase still resonates with a morbid appeal, its continuing fascination in part echoing ancient anti-Semitic stereotypes about hordes of Jewish wealth. Nazis and Jews; Jews and gold; piles of teeth and spectacle frames; mountains of looted art; the lost secrets of the Third Reich—this is the macabre recipe of which adventure films and airport thrillers are made. Nobody knows the precise total value of the gold, currency, and works of art stolen by the Nazis, from both countries and individuals, although it certainly runs into billions of dollars. Few records were kept when the SS Ein-satzgruppen arrived in a Polish shtetl (Jewish village) to round up its Jews and shoot them, before burning down the synagogue and keeping a silver candlestick or ripping gold wedding rings from their victims' fingers.

As the war progressed, even the fabled German bureaucracy could not cope with the amount of loot pouring into Berlin. The Melmer system and the Max Heiliger account were overrun with booty, and the loot that could not be sold or processed was piled up at the Merkers mine. But, if precise figures of how much loot the Nazis acquired were unavailable, the Allies had a fairly clear idea at least of the approximate amounts of gold stolen by the Nazis from the national treasuries of countries annexed by the Third Reich. An Allied economic intelligence document, dated 5 February 1946, entitled "Allied Claims Against Swiss for Return of Looted Gold," reveals how Nazi booty found a ready welcome in Switzerland and how the Swiss National Bank (SNB) washed looted gold, reexporting it to neutral Spain and Portugal. The document says that its detailed figures are based on "a complete inventory of the gold found in Germany at the end of the war and a thorough examination of the records of the Reichsbank, including a detailed tracing of the processing and disposition of more than half of the gold originally looted."

Here, then, is the mathematics of how the Nazis stole the gold assets of their new territories. The document asserts:

> It has been determined from available ledgers of the German Reichsbank that a total of at least 398 million dollars worth of gold was shipped to Switzerland by the German Reichsbank during the war. This figure does not include the following, which when verified and amounts definitely determined should be definitely taken up with the Swiss: a) one additional shipment known to have taken place after these books were closed and evacuated from Berlin[;] b) other shipments believed to have taken place early in the war and to have been recorded in earlier ledgers of the German Reichsbank which are not now available[;] c) an amount of approximately 12 million dollars worth of gold which the Germans seized when they looted the Italian gold but delivered directly to the Swiss.

But Germany didn't have $398 million worth of gold at the beginning of the war. A table attached to the document lists an estimate of German gold movements from April 1938 to May 1945. The Third Reich started the war with estimated gold reserves worth $100 million, according to the column headed "Income." To that was added gold looted from Austria, Czechoslovakia, Danzig, Poland, Holland, Belgium, Yugoslavia, Luxembourg, France, Italy, and Hungary, making $648 million in total.

The column marked "Outgo" details where the looted gold went. Between $275 million and $282 million was sold to the SNB, with another $20 million worth of gold possibly sold to Swiss commercial banks before 1942. A hundred million dollars' worth was "washed through the SNB depot account and eventually reexported to Portugal and Spain (larger part by far to Portugal)," the report says.

Why did the Reichsbank sell so much gold to the SNB? In small part because the gold helped to satisfy the Third Reich's financial obligations to Switzerland outside the terms of the 1934 clearing agreement that governed the terms of nearly all payments between Switzerland and Nazi Germany. But, far more important, the Swiss francs the Nazis received for the gold were universally accepted as hard currency, whereas some other countries were uneasy about accepting bars of Nazi gold. As the 1984 SNB report says, "These gold sales swelled the Reichsbank's holdings of Swiss francs, which were used to pay countries highly unwilling to accept German gold, notably the Portuguese, Spanish, and Romanian central banks. Inasmuch as these banks converted their Swiss francs into gold at the [Swiss] National Bank, the SNB functioned as a gold transit point."

Not only did Swiss bankers accept looted gold, but they must have known that it was stolen. As the managers of Europe's key financial center, with up-to-date information about the treasuries of countries under Nazi occupation, simple arithmetic indicated to the Swiss bankers that most of the gold they were accepting was looted. As the 1946 intelligence document says: "Monetary experts all over the world (Switzerland has monetary experts at her disposal) knew, or ought to have known, roughly the figures and movements as contained in the above estimate [of 5 February 1946]—certainly they knew the gold holdings and gold reserves of the German Reichsbank." In fact, Swiss bankers had been warned that all Germany's prewar gold stocks had been used up by mid-1943 at the latest, and therefore all the gold coming from Germany must be presumed to be looted gold, the report concludes.

A realistic assessment of the amount that had been looted was about $289 million, the document asserts, adding that "there is a possibility that all gold received by the Swiss from Germany was looted." The bankers at the SNB knew all this. But, by the SNB's own admission, its wartime officials still accepted gold consignments from the Third Reich, totaling SF1,638 million (approximately $384 million), between September 1939 and May 1945, according to an internal SNB report, published in autumn 1984, written by the archivist at the time, Robert Vogler. Swiss officials are now very keen to discount the mountain of declassified Allied intelligence documents detailing Swiss banks' economic collaboration with the Nazis as a melange of uncorroborated gossip and speculation, but the SNB's figure of SF1,638 million is extremely close to the sum of almost $400 million worth of gold that was shipped to the SNB according to the 1946 intelligence document.

In June 1943 Paul Einzig, a journalist with the *Financial Times*, wrote an article that sent nervous tremors through the offices of the

Swiss banks. Referring to a declaration by the Allies in January 1943 that all transfers of property from conquered countries to owners of different nationality are invalid, even if the property was bought, and bought by a neutral buyer, he wrote: "This means that neutral central banks will be called upon to restore to their rightful owners the gold they acquired from Germany during the war. As the Reichsbank's own gold reserve was very small at the outbreak of the war, and is now about the same, the assumption is that any gold acquired by neutral central banks since September 1939 is looted gold."

The reaction to Einzig's article, which coincided with other similar warnings in the Allied press and on the BBC, was rapid. In the next month, July 1943, the SNB Bank Committee (an inner circle of key decision-makers) met to discuss whether it should continue accepting the Nazi gold. Chairman Ernst Weber took the view that having a gold standard meant Switzerland was compelled to accept gold from foreign states, but other board members disagreed. The SNB decided to ask the Federal Council, and on 9 October it briefed the Federal Council on its consignments of gold from the Reichsbank. The 1984 SNB report details how the SNB's October 1943 briefing also referred to the fact that the SNB's wartime representative in Washington had been advised by U.S. officials that some of the gold might be looted. The SNB could not argue that it was acting in good faith, U.S. officials warned. The SNB letter to the Federal Council stated that the SNB had not been alerted that the Germans had been looting gold, although any suspicions that the gold had come from Nazi-occupied countries could not be entirely dismissed.

Such suspicions, though, did not trouble the Federal Council. In its reply to the SNB, dated 19 November 1943, it said that it was unanimously in agreement with the line the SNB had taken to date, although it would welcome efforts by the SNB to ensure that these gold dealings took on more modest proportions in the future. The light was still green for the SNB to accept Nazi gold, looted or not. Or as the 1984 SNB report says: "The SNB had thus received a stamp of approval from the highest authority."

Just as the Nazi war criminals who looted the gold turned on each other at the war's end, so did SNB officials. Directors Rossy and Hirs accused each other of having known that looted gold was being transferred to Switzerland. In 1946 Rossy told SNB officials that Hirs "purchased stolen Belgian gold from the Reichsbank in 1943 and 1944 while being fully aware of the nature and the provenance of this gold."

The Allies' extensive intelligence networks in Switzerland and other neutral countries such as Spain and Portugal kept London and Washington well informed about the Nazis' looting and gold movements. Most of the gold sent to Switzerland was shipped via the Reichsbank's Bern depository, which was opened in May 1940, the SNB report says. Of this SF1.6 billion ($3.5 million) worth of gold, SF1.2 billion was sold to the SNB, while the remaining SF400 million was transferred to the Bank for International Settlements (BIS) in Basel—whose directors included Reichsbank president Walter Funk and his assistant Emil Puhl—other central banks with gold custody accounts at the SNB, and various other Swiss banks, the report goes on. Most of the Reichsbank's gold sales to the SNB were transacted between the fourth quarter of 1941 and the start of 1944, soon after Nazi Germany had exhausted its prewar gold reserves.

"This is the period when Switzerland was almost completely encircled by German forces," notes Robert Vogler author of the report, an elliptical reference to the oft-repeated Swiss argument that, surrounded by the Nazis and their allies, Switzerland had no choice but to collaborate economically with the Third Reich. By early 1944, as it became clear that they were winning the war, the Allies began to plan for a postwar Europe, and U.S. Treasury Department officials began to pressure the SNB over its acceptance of looted gold. In February of that year the U.S. Treasury informed the Swiss that the Allies would not recognize any ownership claims to looted gold, other than from its original owner. "The United States formally declared that it does not and will not recognize the transference of title to the looted gold which the Axis at any time holds or disposed of in world markets," Treasury Department officials announced. In response to this outspoken warning, the SNB's legal office prepared a report detailing the bank's gold operations.

Written in April 1944, by which time even the most ardent Nazi could see that the war was more or less lost, the SNB's legal office's report is a feeble document. Its proposals included significantly reducing the volume of future gold purchase and, in addition, as quoted in the 1984 SNB report, "demanding a binding, general written declaration from the Reichsbank establishing—possibly even proving—that it was the rightful owner of the gold to be delivered to the SNB, and restricting purchases to ingots bearing the Reichsbank stamp and accompanied by a consignment note, and not accepting gold coins minted in occupied countries." All of which was a tacit admission that, until then, the SNB had not required the Reichsbank to properly prove that it was the rightful owner of the gold it was sending to Switzerland. This response by the SNB to the Treasury warning was both weak and tardy. The idea that the words of men such as the Reichsbank officials Walther Funk and Emil Puhl—who would both be convicted of war crimes—would be sufficient to guarantee the Nazi gold's provenance was so bizarre it was surreal. Or, as the 1984 SNB report says, "From today's vantage point, the last requirements testify to a degree of credulity which is impossible to comprehend. It is hard to understand that the SNB's governing board still trusted the criminal Nazi regime. It appears not to have considered the possibility of the then German government recasting foreign ingots, marking them with Reichsbank stamps, and providing new papers."

In his report, Vogler outlines how the SNB accepted gold looted by the Nazis from Belgium. When the Nazis attacked Belgium, its government arranged for its gold reserves to be sent to France, where they would hopefully be safer. With the Nazis at the gate, France arranged for the Belgian gold deposits, then worth about $223 million, to be transferred to Dakar, capital of its colony French West Africa (now Senegal). But once the pro-Nazi Vichy regime took power the Belgian gold was sent on to Berlin, on riverboats, on camel trains through the Sahara desert, and by plane to Marseilles. From Marseilles it went to Berlin, where it was smelted down, stamped with prewar markings in an attempt to disguise its provenance, and most was then sent to Bern, and the SNB's vaults. Vogler's report explains: "Large amounts of this [Belgian gold] were subsequently recast by the Prussian mint and marked with prewar stamps. Exact records kept of this recast gold show that a specific quantity was sold to the SNB." The extent of the SNB's relationship with the Reichsbank was no surprise to Vogler. "Germany has always been and still is, before the First World War and after, the most important trade partner of Switzerland, at that time even more than now, to a large extent bigger than the other countries. So it is not astonishing that the SNB was dealing with the Reichsbank, it has traditional roots which go far behind the Nazi regime," he says.

Like many business relationships, the SNB's connection to the Reichsbank began on a small scale, before it grew to such an extent that it was, Vogler says, in effect, unstoppable. "The SNB slid into this affair, it started with small amounts, then bigger and bigger. You must imagine that Switzerland after the summer of 1940 was completely encircled by the Germans and Italians. The Germans controlled everything, and before it was not like that. It didn't start from nil, there was already gold traffic before, they ran into bigger amounts, and then I can imagine there was a point when they thought it was dangerous to say no. They thought: 'We are encircled so what can we do?' "

One option would have been to check the source of the bars of gold arriving in Bern and refuse to accept them without adequate guarantees, in accordance with international law. There was, after all, only so much gold in the world, and it didn't need a financial genius to work out that, each time the Nazis annexed another country to the Third Reich, Berlin's gold reserves suddenly rocketed and then found their way to Switzerland.

How much of the SF1.6 billion worth of gold that the SNB bought from the Nazis was looted is unknown, says Vogler. "We only know what was looted in Belgium, and in Africa, [Dakar], through the French, for the Germans. It didn't all come directly to Switzerland. We don't know how much of the looted gold came to Switzerland. Today we can only calculate what has been looted and how much came to Switzerland, but what happened in between we don't know."

Why didn't the SNB refuse these deposits? The supposed threat of Nazi invasion has been discounted by some Swiss historians, as well as by Marc Masurovsky, an independent historian working for the Senate Banking Committee. The Nazis' lust for looted wealth—and the need to deposit it somewhere, preferably Switzerland—demolishes the Swiss argument that, surrounded by Nazi Germany, Vichy France, and Fascist Italy, they had no choice but to cooperate economically with the Nazis, Masurovsky says, and continues: "Switzerland was essential for the Nazis. It was a warehouse of currency. The Nazis were dealing with the Swiss banks from the very beginning. The main economic collaborators of the German Reich, the bankers, the brokers, the insurance people, were working hand in hand with Swiss entities. The bottom line was that they needed that one thing: hard cash. And there was only one place they could find it, in Switzerland, and they knew they could only get it if they left the Swiss alone. The Germans made the Swiss so dependent on them that the Swiss could not slam the door in their face. But whose fault was that? The Swiss."

There was never any serious attempt by the Nazis to annex the country. Invading Switzerland would have been a costly exercise, both militarily and economically. The Swiss citizens' army would have put up stiff resistance to the Germans. Its plan was to abandon the plains and fight a partisan-style guerrilla war from the Alps, and the Wehrmacht would not have marched into Bern as easily as it did into Paris and Prague. There was little pro-Nazi feeling among the population at large, especially among the army, although much of the political and financial elite, and some senior army officers, supported Germany. Perhaps more important, a Nazi takeover would have immediately triggered the collapse of the Swiss franc, ruined the Swiss banks' international credibility, and so closed the Nazis' main haven for looted gold and their chief source of vital foreign currency. In fact, Hitler didn't much like the Swiss or Switzerland, even describing the country at one dinner as "a pimple on the face of Europe that cannot be allowed to continue"; but he knew that Berlin needed Bern to keep the Nazi war machine rolling across Europe.

"We know that anyone in the Reich at that time who even suggested the possibility of invading Switzerland would have been sent to the Russian front," says Marc Masurovsky. "The Nazis were crazy, they were ideologically bent on destroying half of Europe and purifying it racially, but the other side of the Reich was just like any other government, interested in making money, in hoarding money and expanding. They understood that they can't do that without the banks."

Even if the Nazi threat was taken seriously, Swiss history could have taken a different, more honorable course, had there been the desire to stand up to the Nazis. Vogler says: "The Swiss National Bank could have behaved differently in its relationship with the Reichsbank, if there had been a political will behind it. The SNB could have gone to the government, and said, 'Look, we have a problem, they [the Nazis] want to sell us more and more of their gold, is that okay for us, for the country, if it is then we will do it. Please give us the power to do it.' But they didn't do that, the SNB informed the government very late about the affair. The first information to the SNB was given in 1943, before that it was business as usual, and by then a substantial amount had come through. They didn't ask, they just informed the government what they were doing.

But the size of the gold dealings between the SNB and the Reichs-bank was never modest, at least after 1940, as the SNB report details. Gold poured into Bern from the treasuries of Nazi-occupied Europe and other, more gruesome sources. It paid for the foreign currency that kept the Nazi war machine rolling. Spanish tungsten, Brazilian diamonds, Argentinian beef—none of these could be bought with Reichs-marks. Neutral traders, and neutral countries' central banks, wanted Swiss francs. The conclusion is simple: without the active economic aid of the gnomes of Zürich, the Germans could never have maintained their genocidal grip over half a continent for so long.

Probably the most disturbing intelligence report in the paper trail that details the importance to the Nazis of Swiss economic collaboration is known as the "Red House" document. Stamped "Secret" and dated London, 27 November 1944, it was compiled by Lt. Col. John W. Easton of Economic Section of G-2 (U.S. military intelligence) based at SHAEF, the Supreme Headquarters, Allied Expeditionary Force. Its subject is "Plans of German industrialists to engage in underground activity after Germany's defeat; flow of capital to neutral countries." Its source is an unnamed agent of the French Deuxième Bureau. That the Red House document has only a single source has led some historians to be skeptical of its contents, but the plans outlined on its pages for a reborn economic Fourth Reich are in accord with what we know of the Nazis' plans to use commercial and economic channels after the war's end. It says: "This agent is regarded as reliable and has worked for the French on German problems since 1916. He was in close contact with the Germans, particularly industrialists, during the occupation of France, and he visited Germany as late as August 1944."

The Red House document is named after a hotel in Strasbourg, where on 10 August 1944, six months after Rabbi Taubes's telegram, after the Holocaust had reached its climax—the elimination of three-quarters of Hungarian Jewry—Nazi industrialists and military officials reportedly met to organize how the Third Reich would live on, after its inevitable defeat by the Allies. Launching the Fourth Reich would be an expensive affair, and these forward-thinkers realized they would need a financial base. Its site, of course, was obvious: Switzerland. Swiss banks would be used to export capital for the Fourth Reich, while Swiss agencies would buy property for the Nazis under false names, helping the Nazis of Berlin establish a new base in Bern, the report says. The ready welcome Swiss bankers had given looted Nazi gold made the country a natural choice for those at the Red House meeting.

Among those alleged to have attended were representatives of key German firms such as Krupp, Messerschmidt, Volkswagen, and Rhein-metall, as well as engineers from factories in Poland and the German naval ministry in Paris. The meeting was presided over by one Dr. Scheid, who held the rank of SS Obergruppenführer. There was a brief discussion of the worsening Nazi military situation. The battle for France was lost for Germany, and the defense of the Siegfried line (guarding Germany) was the main problem, said Dr. Scheid. Allied tanks might be advancing on Berlin, but the Third Reich would be reborn as a new Nazi economic empire, based in Switzerland but stretching across the globe to the United States, he explained.

"From now on German industry must realize that the war cannot be won," Dr. Scheid is quoted as saying in point two of the report, "and that it must take steps in preparation for a postwar commercial campaign. Each industrialist must make contacts and alliances with foreign firms, but this must be done individually and without attracting any suspicion. Moreover, the ground would have to be laid on the financial level for borrowing considerable sums from foreign countries after the war."

However realistic his assessment, Dr. Scheid was living dangerously—this was high treason. Berlin's policy was to fight on, until ultimate victory. So the Nazi industrialists must make contacts and alliances with foreign firms, but subtly, without attracting too much attention, he argued.

This would be achieved partly through the links between American companies and their German trading partners. Dr. Scheid cited Zeiss (lenses), Leica (cameras), and the Hamburg–America shipping line as firms with American offices that had allegedly been "particularly effective in protecting Germans interests abroad." He handed out the addresses of their New York branches to the industrialists at the Red House.

Dr. Scheid was not the only Nazi official looking out for his own future. Even though such a dangerous discussion as took place at the Red House hotel was treasonous, farsighted Nazis across the Third Reich were already planning for eventual defeat. By this stage in the war much of the command structure of the Third Reich had collapsed.

The Red Army was thundering across Poland, and the Allied forces were scything through the Nazi lines in France. With military defeat inevitable, high-ranking German army officers had even tried to assassinate Hitler in July 1944, although they had been happy enough to follow his orders as their soldiers had laid waste half of Europe and the Soviet Union. But, while they could capture a string of countries for Berlin, they were incapable of organizing a simple bombing, and Hitler survived to string up the conspirators on piano wire, film their slow deaths, and then endlessly watch reruns of their grisly ends.

By late 1944 Himmler, Hitler's would-be heir apparent, was starting to put out separate peace feelers to the Allies, trying to split London and Washington away from Moscow, even using Saly Mayer, leader of the wartime Swiss Jewish community, as an intermediary in a series of extraordinary negotiations between the SS and President Franklin D. Roosevelt's representative on the War Refugee Board, Roswell McClelland. On 5 November 1944, two days before the Red House report was compiled by Allied intelligence, one of the most bizarre meetings of the Second World War took place at the Hotel Baur in Zürich. Sitting around a table were McClelland, an SS officer called Kurt Becher—who as Himmler's representative worked with the Budapest Zionist leader Rezso Kasztner in ransoming Jews—and Saly Mayer. There is no other publicly recorded instance of a high-ranking U.S. government official meeting with an envoy of the Nazi leadership to try to stop the Holocaust, in exchange for a separate peace. The discussion was in total contravention of official Allied policy to demand unconditional German surrender. But then Switzerland was always a good place to bend the rules, whether of finance or diplomacy. Dr. Scheid too knew this, which is why Switzerland was the base of choice to finance the Nazi Party when it went underground after the coming military defeat.

By point three, the Red House document appears to turn into the plot of a thriller, so extraordinary are its contents. These are extracts from the proceedings of a second, smaller meeting, attended by an official from the Nazi armaments ministry and representatives from German industry:

> German industrialists must, it was said, through their exports increase the strength of Germany. They must also prepare themselves to finance the Nazi Party which would be forced to go

underground as Maquis [resistance]. From now on the government would allocate large sums to industrialists so that each could establish a secure postwar foundation in foreign countries. Existing financial reserves in foreign countries must be placed at the disposal of the party so that a strong German empire can be created after the defeat.

It was important that the new German economic entities, to be based in Switzerland and other foreign countries, should be fully cloaked, the report said. "It is also immediately required that the large factories in Germany create technical offices or research bureaus which would be absolutely independent and have no known connection with the factory." Only Nazi Party chiefs and senior industrialists would know of these bureaus, the report said. "As soon as the party becomes strong enough to reestablish its control over Germany the industrialists will be paid for their effort and cooperation by concessions and orders."

So where will this money be sent, and who will move it around the world, according to Berlin's instructions? The answer, of course, is Switzerland, and Swiss banks, as point five makes clear: "The German industrialists are not only buying agricultural property in Germany, but are placing their funds abroad, particularly in neutral countries. Two main banks through which this export of capital operates are the Basler Handelsbank and the Schweizerische Kreditanstalt of Zürich [Credit Suisse]. Also there are a large number of agencies in Switzerland which for a 5 percent commission buy property in Switzerland, using a Swiss cloak." No wonder, then, that in his 1946 book, *Germany Is Our Problem,* the U.S. wartime treasury secretary, Henry Morgenthau, advocated a deindustrialized Germany. Just as the German industrial conglomerates such as Krupp and Volkswagen had helped Hitler run the Nazi war economy, German big business would play a pivotal role in any future Fourth Reich. Morgenthau knew of the Nazis' plans, outlined at the Red House meeting.

"These funds will be at the disposal of the Nazis in their underground campaign (but the industrialists will be repaid by concessions and orders when the party candidates come to power)," he wrote. "Two Swiss banks through which operations may be conducted were named, and the possibility of acquiring a Swiss dummy at a cost of 5 percent was noted."

While Swiss banks would be the instrument for the export of capital abroad, the Nazi underground avoided opening accounts at the banks, in favor of stashing loot with private individuals, according to a British intelligence document dated February 1945. "The German underground movement disposes of considerable funds in Switzerland. The assets consist chiefly of Devisen [foreign currency], mostly in Swiss banknotes and of diamonds, probably also of other precious stones," according to the report. "From the beginning of its activity in Switzerland the underground movement had avoided opening bank accounts with Swiss banks, and not even bank safes were used. The assets at the disposal of the movement are deposited in the safes of private individuals."

It is a curious feeling to hold a copy of a document such as the Red House report in your hands. Like almost all of the declassified documents it is typewritten, and the edges of the letters are fading slowly. The language is dry, factual, without adjectives, but its contents are part of the secret war, fought on the front lines of intelligence gathering, a battle as vital as that between opposing armies. The writer of the Red House document knew its importance. The Red House report is stamped "Secret" in two places, on the top and the side. The document is a valuable piece of the Allied intelligence jigsaw that highlights the importance of Switzerland as a Nazi banking center. For organizations such as the World Jewish Congress who are fighting the Swiss banks for the return of assets still held in Holocaust victims' dormant accounts, reports such as the Red House document are vital ammunition in this, probably the last stage of the Second World War, an ongoing war fought with documents and publicity, instead of tanks and artillery.

"These are documents of immense historical importance," said a senior WJC official who has been heavily involved in the dormant-accounts issue. "I almost feel proprietary about them. The Red House report is scary, like something out of Robert Ludlum or Graham Greene. You look at these things and if you have any sense for them, as grotesque as they are, you have to show some humility for them. You have the lifeblood of history in your hands, look at it: an SS Gruppen-führer, Krupp, Messerschmidt, [all allegedly meeting] in late August 1944, a month after the Hitler plot, a year before the end of the war. It would never have turned up in [Operation] Safehaven, except for the fact that part of the plan was to funnel this capital through two particular Swiss banks. As part of the larger context this document makes you understand why these assets were being moved through Switzerland."

Historians have long argued over the Red House report and the importance of its contents. There is no longer any debate over its existence, although whether or not the Nazis launched a secret economic plan for a Fourth Reich still bears investigation. Either way, that the Nazis considered Switzerland their major base for international economic operations and conduit for the supply of vital foreign currency is clear from the Red House meeting. The Nazi economics minister and Reichsbank president Walther Funk had admitted as much in 1943, when he told a secret Nazi trade policy committee that he couldn't do without Swiss banking facilities for purchasing foreign exchange for even two months. Unnamed in the Red House report, two of Berlin's main economic allies—according to a confidential U.S. government memo (no. 2694, dated 30 January 1945, prepared by the Foreign Economic Administration) to the American mission in Bern—were Credit Suisse of Zürich and the Union Bank of Switzerland. Most of the gold looted by the Nazis was sent on to the Swiss National Bank, rather than private banks such as Credit Suisse and the Union Bank. Their job in financing the Nazi war effort was to supply foreign currency and forward it on to Nazi economic agents based outside the theater of war, in cities such as Lisbon, Madrid, and even Shanghai, as the memo makes clear.

It was in the neutral capitals that the Third Reich could finance the purchase of vital war materials. Credit Suisse was happy to help, according to the memo. "It appears from the memorandum that Credit Suisse of Zürich and the Union Bank of Switzerland have been guilty of violations not only of the standard of conduct which this and the British government indicated in June 1944 was expected of them but also of the less rigid regulations which the Swiss Bankers' Association put into effect on September 19, 1944."

Memo 2694 outlines how Credit Suisse performed financial services to the Nazis, making available SF1,930,731 ($429,051) between 26 September and 24 November 1944, for purposes "other than those for recognized trade purposes; at least this appears to be true from the intercepts." Credit Suisse, during this period, also took part in two other transactions, which benefited the Reichsbank in Berlin and Deutsche Bank in Hamburg, the report says. Of the two Credit Suisse transactions mentioned above, the first supplied the Reichsbank with escudos, paid for by the sale of SF500,000 ($110,000) supplied to Credit Suisse, while in the second Credit Suisse acted as an intermediary for the payment of SF30,000 ($6,700) to one Kurt Meisner, probably based in

Tokyo, by a company in Hamburg. In just under a month, from 2 to 29 August 1944, Credit Suisse supplied the Germans with SF1,620,800 ($360,180), the memo says, while together with its branch in Basel the bank helped the Germans obtain 500,000 escudos and 200,000 kroner.

There are twenty-eight dated intercepts of Credit Suisse's and Union Bank's communications attached to memo 2694. Allied intelligence services based in Switzerland, as well as in other neutral capitals such as Lisbon, Madrid, and Ankara, devoted much time and energy to economic warfare and monitoring the movement of Nazi money. Telephones were tapped, telegrams surreptitiously copied, and employees bribed to find out where the Third Reich's money was going, what it was buying, and who was moving it. Agents of the Office of Strategic Services (OSS), forerunner of today's CIA, were very active in intercepting interbank communications. Nine of the twenty-eight intercepts on memo 2694 concern transactions in the financial triangle connecting Germany, Switzerland, and the Iberian peninsula. Like other neutral capitals, Lisbon and Madrid were jammed with spies of every shade, double agents, triple agents, and some who had so many paymasters they were no longer sure for whom they were working.

Madrid had been a spies' capital for a decade. The battlefields of the Spanish Civil War were a testing ground for the Nazi Luftwaffe, as its pilots honed their techniques of dive-bombing hospitals and strafing columns of refugees with machine-gun fire. The NKVD, forerunner of the KGB, and the GRU, Soviet military intelligence, also maintained extensive networks in Madrid, although they expended much of their energy in the Civil War eliminating supposed Trotskyists and executing anarchists.

General Francisco Franco kept Spain neutral during the Second World War, for, although he was a fascist with a natural sympathy for some aspects of Nazi totalitarianism, he refused to join the Axis and, like Mussolini, did not share Hitler's maniacal anti-Semitism, counting Moroccan Jewish businessmen among his friends, from his time as a government official in Spanish Morocco.

In neighboring Portugal, also neutral, the wartime leader Antonio Salazar made no secret of his admiration for Hitler, even ordering that flags be flown at half-mast on Hitler's death.

At about the time telegrams were buzzing back and forth between Credit Suisse and the Reichsbank in Berlin, Spanish diplomats based in

Budapest, along with their Swiss and Swedish colleagues, were issuing protective papers to Hungarian Jews, to try to save them from Eichmann's plans for deportation to Auschwitz. That said, Admiral Wilhelm Canaris, the chief of the Abwehr (Nazi military intelligence) usually found a ready welcome from General Franco when he traveled to Spain to meet with the fascist leader and the Spanish chief of staff, as Hitler's emissary.

As well as serving as intelligence listening posts, Lisbon and Madrid were the site of years of an economic warfare campaign waged by the Allies to prevent the Third Reich's purchase of tungsten, alternatively called wolfram, from Spain, which was a major producer of the vital element. Tungsten, a super-strong metallic element, is vital for waging modern warfare, as it has the highest melting point of any metal, the highest tensile strength above 3,000 degrees Fahrenheit, and the least expansion when heated. It is used in everything from making dies for the manufacture of shells to hardening iron and steel. Extraction of tungsten from wolframite and scheelite (another tungsten-related mineral that is a source of tungsten and its compounds) is a lengthy process, and a ton of rock yields just 1.5 grams of the element. The Nazis set up a network of front companies in Spain and Portugal to try to disguise their attempts to acquire the metal, which is twice as rare as uranium. These were real firms, in that they operated to make money, but whether or not they turned a profit was incidental, for their real purpose was to provide a cover for Nazi acquisition of war material as well as espionage operatives.

Front companies were an old Nazi intelligence-gathering device. In prewar France, the Abwehr had set up a company that published brochures describing the views train passengers might enjoy from their window as their train ran along a main line. It was a perfect cover for Nazi agents to take frequent train rides and regular photographs of stations, bridges, and crossings, and so gather the sort of information needed to plan an invasion. Import-export firms were another favored setup, as their staff would need to travel frequently—a precursor of Universal Export, for which James Bond supposedly worked in Ian Fleming's novels. Madrid, with its connections of history, language, and culture, was also an excellent forward base for Nazi espionage and economic operations in South America.

Argentina, which, like Spain, was neutral but pro-Nazi, was host to three Nazi spy rings. Information gathered in Buenos Aires was sent on

to a Nazi front company in Rio de Janeiro, from where operatives transmitted it on to Berlin via a clandestine radio. One such Abwehr import-
export company in Argentina was so well run that it even turned a
profit and was able to pay for the costs of running the resident Nazi
agent.

The Reichsbank and private German banks transferred millions of
Swiss francs to banks in Madrid and Lisbon via Switzerland, the intercepts on memo 2694 show. On 13 October 1944 Credit Suisse made
SF700,000 available to the Reichsbank to purchase escudos, according
to intercept ref. H (FE) 1009, based on an OSS report; while on 6 April
1944 "Reichsbank, Berlin, offered to sell to Banco Lisboa e Acores,
Lisbon, the SF500,000 Reichsbank supplied Credit Suisse, at Monday's
value," the memo records.

Credit Suisse in Zürich found the Reichsbank a valued customer,
according to the intercept of 24 May 1944: "Reichsbank, Berlin, sent
the following message to Acores, Lisbon: 'Sell SF800,000 we furnished
Kredit (Credit Suisse) Zürich value Saturday, wire execution.' "

As well as the above transactions, Credit Suisse had engaged in
numerous smaller transactions, not just in Europe, but also in the Far
East, including acting for Japan and Germany in occupied China, the
memo reports.

It is the details of the intercepts of the banks' transactions, complete
with dates, times, and amounts of cash sent around the world for the
Third Reich, that help detail Swiss banks' economic collaboration with
the Nazis, says the WJC official: "This is one of the most important
documents, because it is based on intercepts, where they intercept
actual transactions. This is not simply estimations, or the word of
German officials; it mentions the two leading banks of Switzerland, so
it's not as if you can say these are rogue operations. It's very clear, that's
why we have a precise date. What this document does is demonstrate
that the U.S. had them caught cold in 1944, and labels it 'Objectionable
activities' and delineates it."

As for Credit Suisse now, its officials don't want to talk about the
bank's wartime activities. "We are not ready for a meeting, because we
are still going through the archives," the bank's press officer, Seraina
Conrad, told me, after I requested a meeting with an official of the
bank to discuss these intelligence documents. As for UBS, the bank's
spokesman said: "We do not comment on single documents."

In Madrid British intelligence and other Allied operatives were shadowing the Third Reich's economic agent, Sofindus, as the firm procured war material for the Nazis, using funds transmitted via Swiss banks. "Sofindus" was an abbreviation of Sociedad Financiera Industrial, run by the German businessman Johannes Bernhardt, who in 1936 had passed Hitler a letter from Franco that had led to German support for the Falange armies as they battled and eventually helped bring down the republican government. In Berlin Walter Schellenberg, head of the Nazi Party foreign intelligence service, sent Sofindus RM50,000 ($20,000) a month, to fund the firm and help purchase pesetas for the German war effort. British intelligence records show that virtually every telegram Sofindus employees sent to Berlin, and the instructions they received, were intercepted, decoded, and forwarded on to London, where economic intelligence officers sifted and evaluated the torrent of information about how the Nazis were spending their looted gold in neutral countries.

Sofindus used Swiss francs and gold, both supplied by Swiss banks, to purchase the Nazis' war material, the intercepted telegrams show. Allied intelligence quickly cracked the code words Sofindus used to try to disguise the financial details of his work:

Stab = Swiss francs
Pilz = pesetas
Ring Wurm = Reichsmarks

As ever, the Swiss National Bank was a prime mover in shifting Nazi assets. On 23 March 1944 Berlin telegrammed Sofindus outlining the progress of its latest funds: ". . . gold deposit is to be made available to Reichshauptbank Baer [=Berlin] at the Swiss National Bank Bern with telegraphic advice to Reichshauptbank give instructions for this and wire execution." This triggered some confusion at the Sofindus office. Should the gold be made available in Bern, or merely its value in Swiss francs? That Bern would organize the transaction was not in doubt, as the telegram in reply, sent on 30 March, shows: ". . . wants to know whether your original bars are to be sent back or whether you agree to provision of equivalent quantity of fine gold in Bern or countervalue in STAB. If so wire back countervalue in STAB or new place for handing over."

Sofindus was also used to purchase the chemicals needed for war material, such as ammonium sulfate. Allied intelligence closely monitored movements of such goods, so purchases had to be clandestine, Berlin made clear. "We inform you in strict confidence that there is a possibility of delivering ZOO [=10,000 tons] of ammonium sulfate. Matter is not to be dealt with through official channels if this has already been done Spitz [=Bethke, a German official based in Berlin] requests you to inform him by wire urgently."

This was important intelligence information, for intelligence analysts could deduce part of an enemy's military strategy by monitoring its economic activities. A massive purchase of chemicals needed to make explosives could herald a new offensive or defensive buildup, for example, while a sudden purchase of bales of silk could mean new parachutes and a coming attack.

So busy were the Swiss sending Nazi gold all over the continent that sometimes bank officials became muddled over exactly what was to be sent where, as the telegram of 3 March 1994 makes clear: "Gold deposit was allegedly sent to this end in error by the Swiss with the other Spanish consignment so that the bars are at Zunft. Zunft will however make them available again in Zürich free of charge," Sofindus instructed Berlin.

At the same time, Sofindus's brief also included black marketing and currency speculation. On 21 February 1944 he telegrammed to Berlin that he had received an offer of SF800,000 ($18,000) to be sold on the black market, asking whether this was of interest. Berlin was not sure. After waiting in vain for ten days, Sofindus, worried the Swiss francs would come off the market, sent another telegram asking for instructions: "Concerning STAB, Buche [=Becker, who was working with Sofindus in Madrid] has still not been given instructions please hurry up decision from your end as offer cannot be maintained indefinitely."

By June 1944 Reichsbank officials, overwhelmed with the amount of looted gold the SS were bringing into the Max Heiliger account, were looking for the best return on converting the metal into neutral currency. The Melmer system of selling looted valuables through Berlin pawnshops was proving too slow to move the mountains of booty. A mass export of looted gold to Madrid, where the Nazis already ran an economic operation, could be the answer, depending on exchange rates. On 9 June Berlin sent a telegram to Sofindus asking about the technicalities of converting gold into Swiss francs:

"BLATT has inquired by order of REICHSBANK:

I. How many STAB will be paid for one kilo pure gold.

II. What is desired: A coins and which [coins]; B ingots.

III. Where the countervalue will be made available in STAB and in what form.

At present question of transport is being gone into here."

Beneath the dry language of the telegram, Berlin is asking Sofindus how many Swiss francs a kilo of gold will fetch and what is the preferred type of gold (coins or ingots). Finally, Berlin wants to know where the Swiss francs can be collected and whether they will be notes, coins, or a payment by bank transfer.

Like Switzerland, Portugal also turned a tidy profit during the Second World War, so much so that the Bank of Portugal's gold reserves nearly quintupled between 1939 and December 1944, according to its own records. A State Department memorandum, dated 6 December 1946, reports Portuguese officials as admitting to accepting looted gold, either directly from Germany or via middlemen based in Switzerland. U.S. officials believed that Lisbon held substantial amounts of looted Nazi gold, probably from the treasuries of Belgium and Holland. Portugal felt "under no obligation to return any German gold," noted one State Department official. In 1946 a furious diplomatic row erupted between Portugal on one side and the United States, Britain, and France on the other after Lisbon attempted to use looted Nazi gold to pay for Polish coal. When, in the autumn of 1996, the spotlight briefly shifted away from Bern to Lisbon, the Bank of Portugal confirmed that it had received gold from Nazi Germany, but a spokesman denied charges of money laundering: "During the Second World War our [gold] reserves did grow, but this was because we were selling goods and services, such as wolfram, which is used in explosives, to Germany. They had no proper currency with which to pay, so we took gold."

When a Reuters reporter asked the Bank of Portugal spokesman if the gold might have been stolen from Jews he replied, "How could you tell? Gold has no race."

4

Capital *über Alles:* The Bank for International Settlements

Throughout the war we [the BIS] continued working with the Reichs-bank, our contacts with it, and our relationship with it. We received, throughout the war, up until the end of the war, gold shipments from the Reichsbank.

> Piet Clement, official historian of the Bank for International Settlements

A symbol of Nazi instrumentality . . .

> Henry Morgenthau, U.S. wartime treasury secretary, on the BIS

Gold has no race. That might have been the motto of the Bank for International Settlements (BIS), the Third Reich's second main conduit for channeling looted gold, after the Swiss National Bank. Based in Basel and still operating now, the BIS is relatively unknown outside the business pages of the world's newspapers. But the wartime history of this global financial institution is part of one of the Second World War's most bizarre episodes, which highlights how, throughout the war, financial channels were kept open between the Allies and the Axis, through Switzerland. For as well as accepting looted Nazi gold—the bank was forced to return $4 million worth after the Allied victory—the BIS forwarded some of the profits of that Nazi plunder on to its own founders. These included the central banks of the Allied nations, such as the Bank of England, which accepted into its coffers the proceeds of Nazi looting.

Each year, both before and during the Second World War, the BIS paid out a dividend of several million Swiss francs (the amount varied) to be divided up among its owners. Part of the BIS's annual dividend was funded by German interest payments to the BIS on the bank's investments in Germany. Germany partially financed these interest payments by looting the national gold reserves of Holland and Belgium. So a proportion of the BIS's income, which paid for its annual dividend, and was funded in part by stolen Nazi gold, ended up boosting the Allied war effort. The ultimate provenance of the BIS's dividend was irrelevant, even to the Allies, for the rules of international capitalism meant that some economic channels had to remain open across the continent, even in the middle of a world war. But the complexities of this extraordinary financial web that linked Berlin, London, Paris, and Brussels all through the war were no surprise to the BIS's wartime directors and staff. They included officials representing all the major warring countries' national banks, including the Reichsbank, the Bank of France, and the Bank of England, who continued to hold their positions for the benefit of the BIS, while just over the Swiss border, in France, Germany, and Italy, soldiers from their home countries were slaughtering each other on Europe's battlefields.

The BIS's president was an American, Thomas McKittrick; the general manager a Frenchman, Roger Auboin; and the assistant general manager was Paul Hechler, a German and Nazi Party member. The BIS's wartime directors included two war-criminals-to-be, Reichsbank vice-president Emil Puhl and his boss, Walther Funk, as well as bankers from London, Brussels, Rome, and Japan. While Funk did not visit Basel, Puhl was a regular caller, discussing the BIS's affairs with McKittrick. And, conveniently for Berlin, the BIS even shared a wartime chairman with the Swiss National Bank—the main channel for looted gold—in the person of Ernst Weber.

British staff members too worked alongside their Nazi colleagues, such as Hechler, at the BIS during the war, according to the Swiss historian Gian Trepp. "Four Britons worked with Hechler during the war, who was a Nazi Party member. Churchill knew the British employees were there. The chancellor of the exchequer defended their presence in the BIS, by saying the Germans were not taking advantage of the BIS, but that was not true."

What, then, was this extraordinary bank, where Nazis worked in harmonious cooperation with Allied citizens between 1939 and 1945? The BIS was founded in May 1930 by the world's central banks, under the Young Plan, to channel German reparations owed to the Allies for the First World War. The BIS's owners were a conglomeration of key international financial institutions: the Bank of England, the Reichsbank, the Bank of Italy, the Bank of France, and the First National Bank of New York, whose host countries, as well as Japan, supplied the directors. The BIS founders planned for a possible repeat performance of the 1914–18 conflict, and its charter detailed how the bank could never be closed, seized, or sanctioned, even if another global conflict erupted between the directors' home nations. When the Young Plan was accepted at the Hague conference in January 1930 it included a general description of the future BIS's functions and role. The Swiss government even signed a special convention that gave the BIS a constituent charter having the force of law, together with the governments of Belgium, France, Britain, Italy, and Japan. In his booklet, "The Bank for International Settlements, 1930–1955," Roger Auboin outlined the perks that the BIS enjoyed in the world of international finance, which he described as "certain special advantages." These were considerable. The most important of these, he wrote, was that, "the bank, its property and assets, and all deposits and other funds entrusted to it are immune in time of peace and in time of war from any measure such as expropriation, requisition, seizure, confiscation, prohibition, or restriction of gold or currency export or import, and other similar measures."

The BIS, in its relations with the U.S. Federal Reserve and the Treasury, had the same status as central banks such as the Bank of England, and so could buy and sell gold from and to the U.S. Treasury. At the same time the BIS could also carry out the following financial operations, wrote Auboin: "buy, sell, exchange or hold gold for its own account or for the account of central banks, make advances to or borrow from central banks, discount, rediscount, purchase or sell, with or without its endorsement, bills of exchange and other short-term obligations of prime liquidity." Perhaps most significant, the BIS could also accept deposits from central banks on current or deposit account, and other government deposits.

For bankers such as McKittrick and Puhl, the interests of international capital always triumphed over mere nationalist squabbles, even if their respective governments were at war. "The world needs in time of war a place where moneymen can gather, because money is stronger than nationalism," says Trepp. "Even during the war the moneymen of different nations needed to keep in touch, because when the war stops, you have to rebuild and you need free trade."

At its inception the BIS's capital was fixed at SF500 million ($110 million), to be guaranteed by five central banks: the Belgian National Bank, the Bank of England, the Bank of France, the Bank of Italy, and the Reichsbank. A banking group acting for the Bank of Japan also took part, together with another triumvirate of three American banks: J. P. Morgan and Company, the First National Bank of New York, and the First National Bank of Chicago. The BIS's main purpose was to act as a trustee for the governments of its directors. But, more than that, it had a large measure of control over those reparations payments. Or, as Auboin wrote, "Its function was much wider, for it was also to play an essential part in the execution of the Young Plan by 'setting up machinery which will provide an elastic element between the payments to be made by Germany and their realization.'"

How was this to be done? By granting direct aid to the Reichsbank in foreign currency credits or by investing part of the annuity payments in Reichsmarks back in Germany, with the agreement of the Reichsbank. The BIS's investments in Germany were considerable. By June 1931, eighteen months after the bank's founding, they reached 444 million gold Swiss francs ($98 million), although by the end of 1932, thanks in part to the international financial crises of the early 1930s, the BIS investments there had been reduced to about 300 million gold Swiss francs ($66 million). As the economic situation in Germany worsened, representatives from the national central banks met in Basel to discuss what to do. In September 1931 the first "standstill agreement" was concluded, covering six months' worth of short-term banking credits to Germany. Under the agreement, foreign bank creditors maintained existing short-term credit lines, allowing capital owed by Germans to stay in the German debtors' hands for the duration of the agreement. Commissions and interest, however, were collected as before. This was part of about $1 billion worth of credit granted to Germany, much of it organized by the BIS.

The background to the early years of the BIS is important, because beneath the dry legalese of the BIS's charter lay an international financial institution with fabulous potential for the Nazi war machine. Here was a bank that everyone, from Hitler to Churchill, agreed could never be closed down or have its assets appropriated. It could buy and sell gold either for itself or for other national central banks and even had the same status as, say, the Bank of France or Bank of England in its dealings with the U.S. Treasury. Its focus of attention was on Germany, and while it was ostensibly set up to collect reparations payments, its officials expended at least as much energy in overseeing its investments of 300 million Swiss gold francs (three-fifths of its start-up capital) in that country to help rebuild its economy. In addition the BIS could even introduce "an elastic element" in Germany's reparations payment schedule. In effect the victors of the First World War were financing a part of their own reparations by providing capital to the BIS, which then invested its assets—Allied money—in Germany. In Berlin, the Nazi minister of economics, Hjalmar Schacht, took a close interest in the affairs of the BIS, seeing the institution as a useful channel for business as usual with Germany's international trading partners, in the event of another war.

Many German industrial concerns maintained networks across the globe, such as Zeiss lenses and the Hamburg–America shipping line, allegedly singled out at the Red House meeting as key centers for the soon-to-be-reborn economic Fourth Reich. It was a vital Nazi financial interest to have a sympathetic base in Switzerland with connections to Allied countries where German companies had branches. The BIS, whose own finances were closely interlocked with the Nazi economy, fitted the bill perfectly. Hitler himself chose two of the German directors: Walther Funk and Emil Puhl. Their colleagues included Hermann Schmitz, of the Nazi industrial giant IG Farben, and the banker Baron Kurt von Schroeder.

BIS directors were unwilling to oppose Nazi racial policies after Hitler came to power, as the case of one BIS director, Karl Melchior, shows. Melchior, a prominent German Jewish banker, of the Warburg Bank in Hamburg, was one of the first directors of the BIS. But, once Hitler took power in 1933, Melchior was forced to resign his position. He was not supported by his fellow directors, says Gian Trepp. "He was forced out because he was a Jew, by Hitler and Schacht. The BIS said it couldn't do anything if the Germans were 'retiring' their personnel." Germany's reparation payments through the BIS stopped in 1931, and the Lausanne conference in 1932 failed to solve the question of future payments, but the Nazis continued to pay interest on their obligations all through the war; such was the importance that Berlin gave to maintaining correct relations with its helpers in Basel.

At the same time, the BIS's investments in what was then the Third Reich stayed in place all through the war. "The BIS investments remained in Germany, and when the war started it was decided to continue business as usual by the board of directors, to continue to receive the interest payments," says the Swiss historian Piet Clement, who has been commissioned by the BIS to discover the truth of the BIS's relationship with the Third Reich, by examining its archives. "It was argued that Germany had shown the willingness to at least pay these interests, and it was a drain on the German economy, that every year they had to pay ten to twelve million Swiss francs [$2.2 to $2.6 million]. As long as the Germans were willing to continue to pay the interest it was thought wise that the BIS went on receiving these payments."

All of which leads to the question: why did the Nazis, who spent most of their energy laying waste to Europe, bother keeping their international obligations to pay interest related to their reparations from the First World War, while they were busily pursuing the Second World War? Why not just sever relations with the BIS? The Third Reich, after all, was not noted for its adherence to other aspects of international law.

The Reichsbank payments were vital to keep the BIS functioning through the war, says Clement. "That is the most interesting part of the story. The Germans thought they had an interest in maintaining good relations with the BIS. The Germans knew that if they stopped the interest payments that would have meant probably the end of the BIS, because during the war there was not a lot of opportunity for the BIS to do business anyway," says Clement. "Those interest payments constituted the bulk of the money that came in. The BIS would probably have failed without those interest payments. First of all, the Germans counted on the BIS, that once the war was over it would be a good instrument to rebuild some sort of international financial system, because that didn't exist during the war. There were more practical reasons as well, in that the Germans paid their interest through the BIS and received in return payments from the BIS, about a third as much as they paid in."

And here the story of the BIS, recipient of looted Nazi gold, takes perhaps its most bizarre twist: as well as receiving money from the

Reichsbank, the BIS paid some of it back to the Nazis each year as well, as part of its dividend obligations. Step back from this web of complicated finance—and, in many people's eyes, treasonous meetings between the BIS staff with their Nazi colleagues—and consider the bank's genesis and history so far. Set up by the victors of the First World War to channel Germany's reparations payments to the Allies, the BIS invests massively in Germany to help rebuild its economy, so that Germany can meet its international obligations to pay the Allies. Most of the money for those investments came from the Allies in the first place. The bank then pays a dividend each year on its work channeling German reparations. But as the Reichsbank is one of the founders of the bank set up to accept Germany's reparations payments, Nazi bankers too get their share of the BIS's dividend, which was initially funded by the Allies' capital to help rebuild the German economy, so that Germany can meet its obligations under the Young Plan, and so and so on—an endless circle of money sloshing across a war-ravaged continent.

Money talks in wartime, and nowhere louder than at the BIS between 1939 and 1945. In its official history, the BIS says that it suspended meetings of directors when war broke out in September 1939, but bank officials of warring nations still came together to discuss the BIS's work. Its officials were "a sort of club," McKittrick told a visiting U.S. Treasury official in 1943.

For many in London and Washington it was a club of high treason, serving the economic interests of the Third Reich, over and above those of the Allies. There were civilized discussions in the BIS's boardroom, a lot more pleasant than the conditions at Auschwitz or on the eastern front, where the looted gold that was channeled to the BIS, via Berlin, was first gathered by the Nazis and the gas chamber Sonderkommandos. While the BIS's president, McKittrick, denied that its gold was looted, one man who knew its true provenance was his colleague Emil Puhl, vice-president of the Reichsbank and a frequent visitor to Switzerland. Walther Funk was the president of the Reichsbank, but when it came to dealing with international financiers, Berlin preferred to send the relatively sophisticated Puhl, instead of Funk. As a homosexual with a drinking problem, in the Third Reich, where gay men were incarcerated in concentration camps, Funk was easy to blackmail and pressure and lacked Puhl's savoir faire in the world of international high finance.

Like his boss Funk, Puhl too was captured by the Allies after the war and tried as a war criminal in 1949. He was sentenced to five years but served only a fraction of that before being freed. Puhl paid for his crimes in other, more personal, ways. An intelligent man, he was later troubled by his role at the Reichsbank and suffered a nervous breakdown. His wife committed suicide. Like many of his colleagues Puhl, once in custody, was ready to explain how the Nazis financed their war machine, as his interrogation report of 6 June 1945 outlines. The Reichsbank did not want to seize the Belgian gold as war booty, and it was deposited there in the account of the National Bank of Belgium, as opposed to being added to the Third Reich's general gold stocks. Whatever the technicalities of accounting used to keep track of the Belgian gold, the Reichsbank was happy to dispose of it. The Belgian gold arrived in 1942; a substantial part was sent on to Romania in 1943.

"All the Belgian ingots had been previously remelted in Berlin by the mint," explained Puhl to his interrogators. "It is a tradition of the Reichsbank to remelt all the ingots that it received, in order to avoid deceptions," he said, although a more pressing reason to remelt loot and place false stamps on it was to satisfy the cursory inquiries of the Swiss National Bank as to whether the bars had been looted. Puhl also outlined where the looted Belgian gold went: Romania, between RM80 million and RM100 million ($40 million); Hungary RM20 million ($8 million); Bulgaria RM20 million; Slovakia RM20 million; Albania RM20 million; Greece RM30 million; while about RM300 million ($120 million) worth remained in Germany. The Hungarian gold, he explained, was partly deposited in Budapest, while some was sent to Switzerland.

But Funk and Puhl had—almost literally—blood on their hands. Testifying at the Nuremberg trials in May 1946, Funk said Puhl had been in charge of gold deposited by the Gestapo into the Reichsbank before being sent on to Switzerland. Teeth fillings from Holocaust victims, coins, watches, and cigarette cases were all melted down into gold bars that weighed twenty kilograms each. Looted gold was not sent directly to the BIS but to an associated account at the Swiss National Bank. In 1945 SNB officials told the U.S. Treasury representative Orvis Schmidt that, to ensure they were not receiving looted gold, they had requested that a Reichsbank official certify that each delivery of gold was not looted. Schmidt asked who this was—perhaps not surprisingly, it was the BIS director Emil Puhl. As Funk said at Nuremberg, "It was very difficult to pay [for foreign exchange] in gold. . . . Only in Switzerland could we still do business through changing gold into foreign currency." The Nazis also used looted gold to fund their interest payments to the BIS, says Piet Clement. Like their colleagues at the Swiss National Bank, the directors of the BIS were easily satisfied with the Reichsbank's cursory attempts at disguise. But then the men in charge of channeling loot, Walter Funk and Emil Puhl, were directors of the BIS.

"Now we know that throughout the war the Germans paid their interest with gold, gold they had stolen from the other central banks," says Clement. "But the BIS directors at the time didn't know, they couldn't know, the gold was looted, in the sense that the amount involved was so small in comparison to the SNB there was no way for them to tell. Some of the gold bars they received were falsified by the Germans with prewar German markings, so they were considered to be prewar Reichsbank property, or in 'good delivery' as they called it. The BIS received gold from the Nazis for the interest payments in two periods during the war: in early 1941, and from the beginning of 1943 until the end of the war. During the periods in between, the payments were made in Swiss francs. The BIS received around twelve tons of gold from the Reichsbank.

"After the war there was the Tripartite Commission for the Restitution of Monetary Gold, which was established by the Paris Reparations Conference in 1946. The Allies investigated the BIS. They had their hands on files and records from the Reichsbank and the Prussian mint," Clement continues. "They were able to compare those records with our records of the numbers of gold bars we received from the Reichsbank, and through that it was established that of the twelve tons, 3.7 tons were looted gold, mainly from the Belgian National Bank and the Dutch National Bank. The Belgian looted gold had been melted down, and . . . the bars as we received them were all with German marks from 1935 to 1937, and through Reichsbank records and the Prussian mint it was established that these were melted bars from the Belgian national bank reserve."

As for the grislier origin of looted Nazi gold, the movements of those sacks' contents after their arrival at the German mint has never been comprehensively traced. Did the BIS accept looted gold that had been extracted from dead Jews' teeth? "That is a very difficult question. It is known that the Reichsbank received directly from the SS gold that was taken from the camp victims. It is very hard to establish what happened to this gold, where it ended up and how it was remelted, whether it was mixed with gold from other origin. It is a different quality, but it can be remelted and refined. The gold that was received by the BIS and identified as looted—that, as far as we can tell, was established then as only originating from the Belgian National Bank and the Dutch National Bank. The weight and fineness of the bars corresponded in detail to every bar; it was just the markings that had been changed."

The man who did know was, of course, the BIS director Emil Puhl. "Puhl was in charge of gold dealings for the Reichsbank, and he was perfectly aware of all the gold that came in from the SS. He was in charge of the operation of remelting the gold that had been looted from different occupied territories. He declared that the BIS management, or at least the president, were aware that the gold they received was looted gold, from central banks. Puhl stated that he had made this clear from the beginning, and especially in the later war years, according to Puhl, McKittrick knew. Of course, according to McKittrick, he never knew. "They said after the war that they asked the Reichsbank to only deliver gold in 'good delivery,' but the Reichsbank never put this in writing. Puhl was on good terms with the management of the SNB and the BIS. He visited the SNB; he visited the BIS throughout the war."

It is impossible to believe that the senior managers of the BIS did not suspect that some of the gold was stolen. The BIS was the central banks' bank. Its directors were drawn from the national banks of the very countries that had been invaded by the Nazis, or, in Britain's case, were at war with Germany. BIS board members were probably better informed than any other bankers about national gold reserves and the movement of international capital.

"The people who should have known, if anyone should have known, were McKittrick, Hechler, and the general manager, Auboin," says Clement. "Of course, after the war they denied that they had any knowledge of it. There is no written proof anywhere that they knew, although McKittrick must have been very naive to believe that the Germans were doing business as usual in a clean way. Maybe he fooled himself into believing it."

The keen attention Hitler had paid to the affairs of the BIS had paid off as early as 1938, when the bank sent on the Czech national gold reserves to Berlin, where they were used to finance the early stages of the war. What, then, was the BIS's role in this? In March 1938, when the Nazis marched into Prague, the directors of the Czech National Bank were immediately arrested and held at gunpoint. The Nazis demanded that they hand over the $48 million national gold reserve. The Czechs announced that the gold reserves had already been sent to the BIS, from where they were to be forwarded to the Bank of England. The Nazis' reply was to order the Czechs to ask the BIS to get the gold returned to Basel. Montagu Norman, governor of the Bank of England, who, like many British financiers and members of the establishment, was pro-Hitler, quickly obliged. The gold was returned to the BIS and then sent on to Berlin.

Such a scandal, though, could not be kept secret for long, and soon afterward it broke in the press. The journalist who got the scoop, Paul Enzeig, met with the Labor MP George Strauss, who began asking questions in Parliament. On 15 May 1938 Strauss asked Neville Chamberlain—the prime minister forever damned by history for his appeasement of Hitler, and who coined the phrase "a faraway country of which we know little" about Czechoslovakia—the following question: "Is it true, sir, that the national treasure of Czechoslovakia is being given to Germany?" Chamberlain's reply: "It is not."

But it was a lie. About the gold reserves of this faraway country both Chamberlain and the chancellor of the exchequer, the man charged with running the British economy, knew a lot. Eleven days later Strauss asked a further question about the Czech gold, this time of the chancellor of the exchequer, Sir John Simon. Winston Churchill, outraged at this craven compliance with Nazi demands and at collusion in them by leading British financial officials, led a verbal attack on the chancellor in the House of Commons.

In Washington, Treasury Secretary Henry Morgenthau too had been putting the pressure on Sir John Simon, even telephoning him in the countryside on a Sunday night to find out what was happening. Unfortunately for Morgenthau, Merle Cochrane, his representative at the BIS in Basel, was far more in sympathy with the aims of the bank than was Morgenthau, who was concerned about its role in building up an economic base for the Nazis. Cochrane's letter of 9 May was a typically emollient piece of diplo-speak, couched in the kind of language preferred by the U.S. State Department, home to the princes of isolationism, and engaged in a perpetual struggle for control of foreign policy with the Treasury Department: "There is an entirely cordial atmosphere at Basel; most of the central bankers have known each other for years, and these reunions are enjoyable as well as profitable to them. I have had talks with all of them," wrote Cochrane. "The wish was expressed by many of them that their respective statesmen might quit hurling invectives at each other, get together on a fishing trip with President Roosevelt or to the World's Fair, overcome their various prides and complexes, and enter into a mood that would make comparatively simple the solution of many of the present political problems."

Smack in the middle of the dispute about the Czech gold reserves, a new president was appointed to the BIS, Thomas Harrington McKittrick. A Harvard graduate, born in St. Louis, who was chairman of the British-American Chamber of Commerce, McKittrick was the archetypal banker: politically conservative and concerned only with the continuing movement of capital across the world, whether or not its nations were at war. But then this was the man who, all during the Holocaust, worked closely with the Reichsbank vice-president Emil Puhl, as they discussed how to keep the BIS operating. After the war McKittrick slid into a comfortable new post as a senior official of the Chase National Bank in New York. He died as he lived, as a scion of the American financial establishment, his extensive record of economic collaboration with the Nazis diplomatically glossed over. After he died in 1970 the *New York Times* published a respectful obituary of him, entitled "T. H. McKittrick, World Financier."

In 1940, as it became clear that the United States and Nazi Germany would eventually go to war, McKittrick traveled to Berlin to meet Kurt von Schroeder at the Reichsbank, to discuss how business could continue as usual in the coming difficult trading circumstances. McKittrick was also a channel from the BIS official and Nazi Party member Paul Hechler to the U.S. ambassador in Bern, according to Gian Trepp. "The Reichsbank had Hechler living in Basel, as an outpost of the Reichsbank, working together with McKittrick, the American and the British. The BIS was the international arm of the Reichsbank. Hechler's loyalty was one hundred percent to Berlin, and he could function in Basel."

McKittrick was back on Axis territory in the spring of 1943, after being issued an Italian diplomatic visa to travel to Rome by train and car, although he was not a diplomat and he was a U.S. citizen, writes Charles Higham in *Trading With the Enemy*. He was given safe conduct by Himmler's police at the border, before proceeding to Lisbon and back to the United States on a Swedish ship. From there he went to Berlin to meet up with his old friend Emil Puhl.

"McKittrick must have been aware what the Axis was up to in terms of looted gold, but he was a typical banker, and he wasn't worried about moral considerations," says U.S. historian Marc Masurovsky. "He was the quintessential financial bureaucrat. The State Department loved having him there at the BIS. The opposition to what he was doing came from the Treasury and Morgenthau." Meanwhile, in London, the Labor MP George Strauss was still posing awkward questions and demanding awkward answers. In May 1942 he asked Sir Kingsley Wood, then chancellor of the exchequer of a country at war with Nazi Germany, about the BIS's activities. Not just in Basel, but in London too, some financial officials wanted to keep channels open via the BIS. "This country has various rights and agreements in the BIS under our international trust agreements between the various governments. It would not be in our best interests to sever connections with the bank," said Sir Kingsley. Given McKittrick's pro-Axis activities, it was not surprising that, in February 1942, the Nazi and Italian governments, as well as the Reichsbank, employer of McKittrick's friend and colleague Emil Puhl, approved McKittrick's reappointment as BIS president. There was an argument of sorts that the Allies should have kept their wartime financial connection to the Axis through the BIS. Meetings between BIS officials—citizens of countries at war with each other—were an excellent opportunity for economic intelligence gathering and the passing back and forth of both information and disinformation. Chitchat over drinks and dinner, gossip about events at home, it was all grist to the Allied intelligence mill.

At the same time, the BIS's role as a clearing center for international payments, mail, and telecommunications provided a valuable opportunity for Allied agents to sift and evaluate the volume, direction, and type of Nazi communications traffic, all of which would be eagerly devoured by the various Allied intelligence services as they monitored Europe's lines of communication. There was no real attempt by the Allies to strategically disrupt the internal postal services of the Third Reich, so payment records—for letters between Germany and Sweden, for example—and the addresses of the correspondents could provide valuable information about potential German-Swedish business relationships.

Stung by criticism in the British press in the winter of 1942 about the role of the BIS, McKittrick went on a PR offensive with Allied diplomats in Switzerland. A letter from the British embassy in Washington to the U.S. State Department, dated 2 November 1942, includes an account of McKittrick's arguments about why the BIS should continue trading. If Britain withdrew from the BIS's board of directors, it would make his position impossible and open the way for a Nazi takeover. "Germany would represent the bank as now being the financial organ of the New Order in the hope of restoration in countries like Hungary, Romania, and Bulgaria, which were beginning to demand something better than credits in exchange for their goods," argued McKittrick in the letter. He also claimed that a British withdrawal would open the way for the Nazis to seize the SF100 million held by the BIS in Switzerland and convert it into a credit for the Reichsbank.

Both the Swiss National Bank and Credit Suisse refused to allow me to interview any of their officials, but the BIS was more cooperative. Piet Clement, the official historian of the BIS, willingly answered all my questions, and so did the bank's general manager, Andrew Crockett. BIS managers admit they are not exactly overjoyed about the sudden glare of media attention on this murky episode in its past.

"We, as the management and the directors, have felt that this is a historical episode that people are entitled to know about," says Crockett. "We will open our archives to Senator D'Amato's commission. It's not something that we feel comfortable about, but this is a unique historical episode, which is *sui generis;* because of its sensitivity. We will make everything that we have, on appropriate terms, available."

Those terms did not include letting me into the archives, but I still had many questions to ask Andrew Crockett about the bizarre wartime history of this institution. I reproduce our conversation here, as his answers are complicated and deserve adequate space.

Q: "Why was it so important that the BIS continued trading through the war?"

A: "I think it is probably fair to say that it was at a relatively low level of operation during the war. As an organization which had been started during the 1930s, those who had been in charge of it during the war undoubtedly felt that it was desirable to preserve its existence, not so much for what it could do during the war, but in order, as they saw it, to be a base for cooperation after the war. Probably those who were in charge of the BIS during the war devoted more effort than maybe subsequently appeared appropriate to trying to promote reconciliation. Certainly the economic adviser, Per Jacobssen, who subsequently became manager of the International Monetary Fund, being from a neutral country—he was a Swede—I know, saw one of his missions to try to promote reconciliation, to try to encourage armistice, or peace. He saw that as a real hope, longer than it was truly realistic. He shuttled between Berlin, Stockholm, London, and Washington.

"It wasn't only operating in the interests of reconciliation and the interests of the Germans. The transactions that the BIS had with the Germans during the war involved primarily receiving gold from Germany—approximately half of the gold we received during the war was in payment of transactions that were, in effect, reparations payments for the First World War. Maybe it was seen as being in the interest of the creditor countries, who were primarily the Allied countries, that the BIS should continue to receive payments from the debtor country, in this case, Germany.

"The BIS did receive some gold that was subsequently determined to be looted, about four tons; as far as we can see there was another three tons, which it is very difficult to determine the provenance of. The total that we received to the best of our knowledge was thirteen tons; roughly six tons was clearly in the possession of the Reichsbank before the war—we know the history of the bars. The other seven tons is much more difficult to trace. Four tons seems fairly clearly to have been Belgian and Dutch gold . . . the other three tons, it is very difficult, now that we look back, to determine that it was legitimate, and it is also difficult to say where it came from. It will never be solved, but we should let people know that is the situation."

Q: "What happened to these tons of gold?"
A: "They went to the Swiss National Bank, and they were held in the SNB. They were used in the way that gold is used and transferred on. It is recorded where it went."

Q: "So the BIS's role was to sort out the German reparations payments, and some of this gold that you held in your position as trustee of the reparations payments [during the Second World War] went to the

Allies. So does that mean that the Allies accepted looted gold as reparations payments?"

A: "In an indirect way. . . . In the 1930s there was a moratorium, and subsequently it was canceled, so a lot of payments weren't made. In the early 1930s, in an effort to reestablish payments, the BIS made a loan to Germany in order to enable it to pay reparations, so what the BIS received was interest on that loan made to Germany. It wasn't, strictly speaking, a reparations loan: it was a loan made in order to facilitate reparations payments. They [the Germans] then paid, and in that sense, in that the Allies were creditors of the BIS, it was to the benefit of the creditors of the BIS, but the gold didn't necessarily go directly to the Allies."

Q: "Did some of the staff of the BIS know that some of the gold was looted?"

A: "You will have to determine that. It will be part of what you write. There is no open-and-shut evidence that would enable me to say categorically: they have to have known. You cannot trace that—it would have to be by inference. I think you will have to draw your conclusions from what you find. I wouldn't like to be on the record as saying they knew, or I thought they knew. There are suspicions that, as a banker, one ought to have about the provenance of funds that come."

Q: "Did they have those suspicions, or act on them?"

A: "You will have to judge. I think I have said enough to point you in the right direction."

Q: "Did officials from the countries at war still meet with each other during the war?"

A: "People came here, but we don't have great records of it. It is probably not true to say that there were meetings of belligerent countries here, under the aegis of the BIS. We know the Germans came here. Puhl certainly came, and it's likely that others came. But I don't think the British came, or the representatives of the two Belgian banks, one under Axis control, the other Allied."

Q: "What was the BIS's role in the return of the Czech gold?"

A: "After the invasion of Bohemia and Moravia, the BIS received instructions to transfer ownership of gold that was held in London to the ownership of the Reichsbank. The BIS sought authentication of these records and received it, naturally, and then sought clarification from the British authorities, concerning what they should do. Not receiving information to the contrary, they authorized a transfer. In terms of strict legality, they probably followed what banking records said you should follow, in terms of authentication and so on.

"Again, it is a matter of interpretation. Knowing the circumstances under which this request had been received from the Czech authorities, were you entitled to think it was not done under duress? You can form your own answer to that. I think it is generally recognized that it was a wrong thing to have done. I don't think anybody tries to pretend that it was appropriate. The people at the time would have said that this gold is held in the Bank of England and they have said to go ahead, so we have done everything we could. But it was obviously a transaction undertaken under duress, so both the BIS authorities, and the French and the British, should have taken a more imaginative view, and stopped it."

Q: "How close was the relationship between the BIS and the Reichsbank?"

A: "I would guess it was fairly close. The head of the banking department was a man called Hechler, from the Reichsbank, who had worked under Puhl, and who was a member of the Nazi Party. There was a quite close relationship. That was entirely in the nature of the institution up until the war, when the parties were not formally at war with each other and they had ordinary commercial relations. There are pictures of Schacht [the Nazi economics minister] and Norman [the Bank of England governor] together, which you could say was normal until 1939. The question is: what happened after that?

"What happened during the war is not something the BIS is particularly proud about, as an institution, but it happened. We haven't found anything beyond the facts that were there. There are questions of interpretation, like you asked: did people know [if the gold was looted]? And I think that is a legitimate question to ask for the historical record. I'm not sure that the answer is going to be all that flattering to those people, but that has to be an interpretation."

In July 1944 a Norwegian economist, Wilhelm Keilhau, tabled a resolution at the International Monetary Conference at Bretton Woods, New Hampshire, that the BIS be dissolved as soon as possible. State Department officials in the American delegation, such as Dean Acheson, secretary of state, went into overdrive to save the BIS. The pro-BIS faction had a powerful ally in the figure of Maynard Keynes, who argued that the BIS should be kept going until a new world bank was set up, while Henry Morgenthau wanted the BIS shut down. Eventually the U.S. delegation approved the death of the BIS. But it would live on.

McKittrick launched a furious campaign to save his bank. He fired off letters to both Morgenthau and the British chancellor of the exchequer, arguing that after the war's end the Allies would have to pay for the rebuilding of Germany and that the BIS would be needed to channel these. His support for the Reichsbank, implying his willingness to let the Nazis use the BIS as a channel for looted gold, was justified as a macabre kind of bookkeeping operation.

"When the war is over you'll find it all carefully segregated and documented. Anything that's been looted can be identified. When the gold was offered to us, I thought it would be better to take it and hold it rather than refuse it and let the Germans keep it for other uses," he told a U.S. Treasury official, Orvis Schmidt. After the war's end McKittrick continued his attempt to whitewash the role of the BIS. On 2 May 1945 he wrote to Clifford Norton, minister at the British legation in Bern. He justified the BIS's record in accepting Nazi gold as part of its obligations under the Young Plan to arrange German reparations, under which the BIS was originally set up.

"During the early years of its activity the BIS, as part of the duties devolving upon it under the Young Plan and acting upon special recommendations put forward by the creditor governments, was called upon to effect substantial investments on the German money and capital markets," McKittrick wrote. Translated from bankerese, this meant that the BIS's ostensible purpose of overseeing reparations payments gave the bank the perfect excuse to lock its own fortunes into those of the Nazi economy, under the supervision of the Nazi economics minister, Schacht.

McKittrick continued: "Interest on these investments has been regularly transferred by the Reichsbank to Switzerland, up to the end of

1942 in Swiss francs and thereafter in gold. The transfer of this interest also forms part of the obligations assumed by Germany under the
Young Plan." Translated, this meant that the BIS had a perfect legal
cover for accepting shipments of looted Nazi gold, whether stolen from
the national treasuries of Nazi-occupied Europe or from the corpses
littering the gas chambers' floor.

And more: "In order to ensure further transfers of interest, even
in the event of an interruption of communications, the Reichsbank in
November 1944 agreed to place at the disposal of the BIS a considerable amount of gold from which monthly transfers of accrued interest were to be effected." This meant that the Reichsbank was so keen
to ensure continued relations with the BIS and to further its economic
relationship with the bank that, even as the Nazi war effort crumbled
under the Allies' onslaught and the situation across the Third Reich
became more precarious, the Reichsbank would still guarantee
enough gold for the BIS to keep their mutually beneficial relationship
functioning.

And then the details, as outlined by McKittrick: "As a result of negotiations which began in March this year, the Reichsbank placed at the
disposal of the BIS at its Constance branch approximately 1,526.6 kilograms of fine gold consisting of German gold coin and gold bars, which
were purchased by the BIS, being understood that this gold should be
transferred to Switzerland as soon as possible." The relevant gold was
marked for the account of the BIS at the Constance branch of the
Reichsbank, McKittrick's letter says. But the BIS gold, instructs McKittrick in his letter, should on no account be confused with the general
booty of looted Nazi gold (so much of which would be discovered by
U.S. troops in local branches of the Reichsbank in spring 1945).

The BIS gold had been exactly assayed for its correct value in relation to the assets of the BIS. The BIS gold was "held apart from the
gold holdings of the Reichsbank and packed in forty cases clearly
marked as the property of the BIS. The quantity of gold so earmarked
corresponds exactly to the interest accruing on the investments of the
BIS in Germany up to the end of this year," McKittrick wrote. McKittrick never got his gold. The Constance gold was eventually sent to the
French National Bank.

But consider anyway for a moment the importance of this bald
phrase of banker's language. Here is Thomas Harrington McKittrick,

president of the BIS, a citizen of the United States, a country engaged in all-out war with Nazi Germany, who holds his post with the full knowledge of his government, arguing to a British diplomat that not only has his bank been investing in Nazi Germany, but that the BIS is entitled to the interest accrued on those same investments. The interest was to be paid in gold, and McKittrick must have known that by 1944 the Third Reich had long ago spent its own gold reserves and was funding the Nazi war effort through looting. In his letter, McKittrick does point out that the BIS received the express assurance of the Reichsbank that German ownership of the gold in question dated back before the outbreak of war.

But the Reichsbank's assurances to McKittrick were meaningless on two counts. First, even if the gold had been owned by the Nazis before the outbreak of the war, it could still have included the looted Czechoslovak gold, which the BIS had sent on to Berlin in 1938, over a year before the war started. Second, however favorably McKittrick wished to portray his friends Emil Puhl and Walther Funk—the BIS directors who were Reichsbank president and vice-president respectively—the organization for which they worked was not a model of financial rectitude and integrity. The Reichsbank was the economic motor that drove the Nazi extermination machine, funding Hitler's genocide on the proceeds of genocide and looting. Which is why Walther Funk, who took his dinner guests on tours of the Reichsbank's vaults to gawp at the piles of Nazi loot stolen from dead Jews, was put on trial at Nuremberg and sentenced to life imprisonment.

But Funk's gruesome record as the paymaster of the Holocaust mattered not to McKittrick as he fought for the BIS's share of Nazi gold. "In order to safeguard the rights of the bank, we have considered it indispensable to draw attention to the existence of this gold deposit of the BIS at the branch of the Reichsbank in Constance," he wrote. "The BIS would refer in this connection to the privileges concerning the free disposal of its deposits, granted by terms of Art. X of the Hague agreement dated January 20th, 1930."

And those privileges were considerable. But who benefited most from them? Not the Allies. A U.S. government study in 1945 of the BIS's activities during the war reported that investigators "repeatedly encountered evidence of the Reichsbank's remarkably close and solicitous relationship with the Bank for International Settlements throughout the war, which raised strong suspicion of still unrevealed wartime advantages accruing to the Reichsbank."

Over five decades after the end of the Second World War, the BIS is still functioning. It no longer oversees trafficking in looted Nazi gold or payments for international mail and telecommunications. The BIS has many more members, such as the national banks of Turkey, Spain, and Iceland. Its role now, says Andrew Crockett, is to "promote financial cooperation among the central banks, to do with banking stability and payment."

In 1977 the BIS moved into a new building, a circular tower block that dominates the Basel skyline. Its directors still meet in the city to discuss the BIS's affairs, not far from where Thomas McKittrick dined with Emil Puhl.

5

Whose Safehaven?

Because of Jewish involvement and ties with England, Lombard Bank can not be recommended!

> Handwritten note on a telegram asking whether the Swiss Banking Society could recommend Lombard Bank as "suitable for very confidential special transactions of the Reichsbank"

A "fund" in which were placed the assets and titles of property taken by the Nazis from Jewish businessmen in Germany and the occupied countries.

> Description of Trustee Account Gustloff Stiftung, payments to which were channeled through Bank Johann Wehrli & Co., Zürich, according to Safehaven report no. 11902

The existence of the BIS might have been perfectly legal in international law, but the fact that an American ran, as president, a Nazi-dominated bank that had accepted looted gold enraged many in Washington—probably none more so than Treasury Secretary Henry Morgenthau. Morgenthau, himself Jewish, loathed the BIS and its policy of trading with the Nazis. As the head of the Treasury Department he was the general of a financial fighting force, one dedicated to combating the Third Reich through international economic and financial channels, rather than on military front lines. Backed up by his battalion of highly motivated staff, Morgenthau decided that if he couldn't close down the BIS he could at least help direct Operation Safehaven.

Operation Safehaven was run jointly by the U.S. Treasury Department, the State Department, and the U.S. Foreign Economic Administration, the American equivalent of the British Ministry of Economic

Warfare. Safehaven's aims were summed up by Resolution VI passed at the international monetary conference at Bretton Woods in July 1944. They were: to call on neutral governments to immobilize looted assets; to uncover and control enemy property; and to hold German assets, which would then be disposed of by the Allies once they took control of a defeated Germany. Safehaven's aims were to secure Allied control of Nazi loot and German assets and to prevent their use in any further aggressive activities.

Safehaven officials initially focused on using economic warfare and intelligence to help defeat the Third Reich, but as 1944 stretched into 1945 the emphasis moved on to preventing the Nazis from using their looted assets after the war. There was in the closing years of the war considerable apprehension in Allied capitals that the Nazis were preparing to go underground at war's end in preparation for a reborn Fourth Reich, with the sort of plans outlined in the Red House document, the Allied intelligence report that details the plans of German industrialists for a postwar resurrection of Germany.

Safehaven focused on Switzerland, but its officials were also monitoring Nazi economic activity and financial deals in other neutral countries, including Sweden, Turkey, Spain, Portugal, and Spanish North Africa. Safehaven agents worked with Allied intelligence reports, particularly from the Office of Strategic Services, forerunner of the CIA. It was these agents on the ground who used their contacts to tap telephones, intercept telegrams, and utilize other clandestine means to obtain the bank records that detailed Swiss economic collaboration with the Nazis. Like every government operation run by three different departments, Safehaven was riven by interdepartmental rivalry and infighting, particularly between the more militantly anti-German Foreign Economic Administration and the more emollient State Department. After the war, Safehaven reports gave the Allies much of the vital economic intelligence they needed to take control of German assets and use them for reparations payments.

Over fifty years later, those same reports detailing Swiss economic collaboration with the Nazis that passed across Morgenthau's desk are now rattling the bankers of Zürich. But however important Swiss banks were to the Nazi war effort, Treasury officials, as part of Operation Safehaven, were also monitoring how Berlin also spent much time and resources on maintaining clandestine financial and economic links with the United States.

According to the Red House document it was no accident that when, in November 1944, the Nazi industrialists and SS officers met at the Red House Hotel to plan the Fourth Reich, the meeting's chairman, Dr. Scheid, allegedly singled out the New York branches of German companies, such as the Hamburg–America shipping line, as future economic bases for the rebirth of Nazism. The Nazis had for years run an extensive network of German immigrants charged with gathering information and influencing domestic opinion across the United States, and the German immigrants, organized in groups such as Friends of the New Germany, or the German-American Bund, provided a base of recruits ready to carry out Berlin's orders. American intelligence knew this too, which is why the FBI ran agents in these pro-German groups, and why the Treasury monitored the business activities of German companies.

The Nazi propaganda machine also exploited the natural inclinations of many Americans toward isolationism and the belief that the war was essentially a European affair and of no real consequence to small-town America. Hitler might decry the United States as a mongrel nation, degenerated by intermarriage and "Judaization," but the Nazis worked hard to use banks based in the United States to aid the German economy. The United States' links of trade and geography with Central and South America, home to large German expatriate business communities—which would later provide sanctuary to fleeing Nazi war criminals—only increased its importance for Berlin.

But if the Reichsbank realized the potential aid that financial institutions based in the United States could give the Third Reich, so did Henry Morgenthau, whose agents were spying on companies with German links. No American firm could trade directly with the Nazis, but Berlin had a more subtle plan. German companies would exploit their connections with supposedly neutral middlemen for the Nazis' economic advantage, to keep financial channels clear from Berlin to New York. The German firms would use Swiss middlemen, under the cloak of Switzerland's neutrality. New York's importance as an international financial center, and the United States' massive resources of industry and agriculture, spurred Berlin on to pour money and resources into maintaining networks across the United States.

German-owned foreign funds in U.S. banks also provided valuable revenue. In 1940 the Abwehr obtained permission for a Berlin firm working with it to pay out $10,000, held in a German company's account at the Bankers' Trust company, New York, writes David Kahn in *Hitler's Spies*. The money, which was paid to one of the firm's board members, then in New York, was supposedly to buy patent interests in film and photographic appliances. It went straight into the coffers of the Abwehr. That was a direct payout, but when middlemen were needed they could be found at the several Swiss banks with headquarters in New York.

These banks were used to transfer ownership of German and Italian companies to Swiss or American names, thus allowing them to continue trading, and to use Switzerland as a channel for supplying both goods and currency to the Third Reich, Treasury officials believed. Which is why Treasury officials spied on Swiss financial institutions in New York as well as their deals with the Nazis, sealed at their head offices in Switzerland. An interoffice Treasury Department communication, from a Mr. Foley to Secretary Henry Morgenthau, dated 2 June 1942, asked for permission to install Treasury agents in the New York branches of the Swiss Bank Corporation, the Swiss American Corporation, and Credit Suisse, to examine all of their files and records. All three banks had, since June 1941, been operating in New York under Foreign Funds Control licenses, and the Treasury had kept enough representatives on their premises to monitor their operations.

Much useful information had been gathered in the economic intelligence war, the memo says, as Treasury employees occasionally checked their records. Now it was time to step up the operation and launch a comprehensive examination of all their files, in order to "obtain the information contained therein concerning the background of companies in this country with European connections and other significant information concerning transactions effected through these banks during the past decade." It would be difficult to avoid the conclusion that these Swiss banks were fronts for Nazi economic interests in the United States, the memo says, actively aiding the Third Reich under the pretense of neutrality.

"Representatives of these banks participated actively in the affairs of Swiss-German industrial concerns in this country and in the management of Swiss firms which we have reason to believe are still camouflaging for German interests," it continues. The Holocaust profiteers included one Felix Iselin, who represented IG Farben in Switzerland and also had a place on the board of the Swiss Bank Corporation, as chairman of IG Chemie. Together with his colleague

Gottfried Keller, who sat on the board of Credit Suisse, Iselin had been added to the Proclaimed list in May 1942, the memo said. The list, compiled by the U.S. government, contained the names of individuals and businesses abroad that American citizens and businesses were forbidden to trade with.

Not every Swiss banker or financial official was seduced by the siren call of the profits to be made from the Nazi conquest of Europe. At least one official of the Swiss Bank Corporation had resigned in disgust over its officials' pro-Nazi leanings, the memo said. "A former top executive of the Swiss Bank Corporation in Switzerland, who now resides in New York, recently stated in a letter written to a colleague that he had resigned because of the fact that certain high officials of the Swiss Bank were allowing themselves to be unduly influenced by Germany's apparent success in establishing a new European order." It was that enthusiasm for the Nazis' new order that led many Swiss bankers into the bloody embrace of the Reichsbank, and their ready acceptance of the looted gold with which it funded the Nazi extermination machine.

After the war, as the Allies used the information gleaned in Operation Safehaven to try to work out the full extent of the Third Reich's plundering of Europe—and so utilize those assets for German reparations—Washington and London sent their senior officers running Safehaven to Switzerland to negotiate with Swiss officials and try to determine the provenance of the gold sitting in the vaults of the Swiss National Bank and its private partners in the Holocaust Bonanza, such as Bank Johann Wehrli. Among those officials dealing with the Swiss was Seymour Rubin, a senior State Department official. Rubin remembers that the Swiss were not particularly contrite about channeling loot for the Third Reich: "I don't think they thought they had done anything wrong. . . . They said they knew we had some legitimate worries about Swiss firms having done business with the Germans [and that] they tried to keep that to a minimum, probably the minimum was more than we thought, but that's the way it was."

As a senior official in the State Department, Rubin helped set up the international monitoring operation. "I was one of the people who thought up Safehaven. Its aims were to mobilize whatever assets the Germans had hidden primarily in the neutral countries and mobilize them as semi-reparations payments. Operation Safehaven showed that a large number of German people were putting money into Swiss

banks. We were interested basically in Germans and their money. Theoretically we were interested in Japanese money too. We were looking
for money that could be used to make reparations to the Allies or to the
persecuted."

Safehaven took its name from the frantic attempts by German Jews
to try to shift their assets to Switzerland, efforts that greatly intensified
once the Nazis took power in 1933. It was a place that they thought—
wrongly—would provide a safe haven for their wealth. Rubin says, "If
you were living in a country like Germany, where the fiscal controls
were becoming stricter and stricter, from the 1930s on after Mr. Hitler
unfortunately came to power, and if you had a large Jewish population
with special reason—it turned out quite rightly—to fear what was
coming, you took every cent you could and got it to some kind of safe
haven, which is where the phrase Safehaven came from. I am sure that
a large amount of [Jewish] money left Germany and the occupied countries as well and went to Switzerland, the thesis being that Swiss banks
were a safe depository."

Although Safehaven had input from both the Treasury and State
departments, the interdepartmental rivalry between the two affected
its operations. The Treasury, under Morgenthau, was in charge of the
financial controls in the United States, while the State Department had
a division dedicated to tracking the progress of Nazi money across
Europe. Rubin recalls: "I was more or less directing Safehaven in the
State Department. There was a certain amount of rivalry between the
two. I worked very closely with a variety of people. There was a division
in the State Department that had a lot to do with the very heart of
Safehaven, the question of where money was going. The Treasury had
some feature in that: they were operating the controls in the United
States; but we were running the blacklists, so that you couldn't do any
business with the people in the neutral countries who were dealing with
the Germans in a way in which we considered to be excessive."

American intelligence was closely monitoring the Nazi spy rings
and front companies based in nearby Central and South America, and
in September 1943 Rubin traveled to Colombia, to encourage the government to clamp down on the Third Reich's networks there. "I went
to talk to the Colombians about sequestering German assets in
Colombia, who might be using them either for espionage or propaganda," he says.

Safehaven officials drew up a list of companies across the globe with whom American companies were forbidden to trade, as part of their battle to disrupt, and preferably break, the Swiss–Nazi economic relationship. "We made every effort that we could to prevent Swiss companies from dealing with the Germans. The blacklist was the principal weapon. There must have been two hundred, three hundred companies on it. They were all over the world, machinery companies, companies in any kind of trade," says Rubin. "If these companies were on the blacklist, no American company could do business with them. We tried to blockade them. If we discovered that any of their products were on ships coming through Argentina, shall we say, we would try to do whatever we could to prevent that shipment. We did whatever we could to prevent those companies propping up the German economy."

The Allied intelligence agents based in Switzerland were one of the main conduits for the torrent of information that poured into London and Washington about the progress of Operation Safehaven. Known Nazis based in Switzerland were followed, their telephones tapped, their telegrams intercepted, and the same subterfuge was applied to breaking into the confidential communications of their Swiss partners. In Bern, Allen Dulles, head of the city's OSS station, was funneling information on to Washington, although there are questions as to whether his motive was in supplying genuine economic intelligence or merely building a complicated empire of information and disinformation that reached from Bern to Berlin and back again.

"We had all sorts of information coming out of Switzerland," says Rubin, "and out of other places as well. During World War Two we had censorship of communications, and we pretty much had control of communications. Intercepts came across my desk in the State Department. I didn't see the most sensitive ones, but I did see the ones having to do with funds. There were a lot of intercepts: somebody sent a letter through Switzerland, or a telegram, the letter got picked up."

But whatever the motives of their chief, OSS operatives passed on their intelligence gleanings to Safehaven officials.

"I'm sure that we got stuff from Dulles' operation," Rubin says. "I'm sure that the OSS in Switzerland was picking up information from time to time. The telegraph lines were not sacrosanct. Back in those days when you had to communicate you weren't able to use the machines you can now that garble everything. Even then, we were able to break the latest codes. There were a lot of people snooping. There were means of getting hold of communications. There were spies for us as well as the other side," says Rubin.

Over fifty years later, Rubin looks back on Safehaven's achievements with mixed feelings. A lot was achieved, but not as much as could have been done, he says. "I certainly think it was a good cause. Do I think the results were good? On a scale of one to ten I would give it a four. If we had been able to get a census for the Swiss accounts, for example, we would have done a better job. If we had been able to recover all the looted gold, some of which went through Portugal—and I am not at all convinced we got all of that—we would have done a better job, [or] if we had been able to find all of the Germans who, I am sure, got hold of a lot of the Jewish assets when they located them in Germany or in Switzerland and got away with them. We did as good a job as we could under the circumstances."

BUT HOWEVER extensive the reach of Operation Safehaven, and however diligent the work of the Allied spies and diplomats based in Switzerland who were tracking the flow of looted Nazi assets, they could hope merely to *monitor* the movement of the Third Reich's booty into Switzerland, for the only way to finally *stop* the flow was an Allied military victory. Nazi officials in the financial and economic ministries, as well as the Reichsbank, were running an international operation of military precision as they shifted loot across Europe, one that was no match for tapped telephones and intercepted telegrams.

Two Allied intelligence documents that are part of the Safehaven paper trail—one an interview by a U.S. intelligence officer with a senior Reichsbank official, the other detailing the deposition of loot in the Johann Wehrli & Co. bank in Zürich—illustrate how the Third Reich's extermination machine was funded, on both the long-term strategic level and the short-term tactical one, by looting and the transferring of that loot to Switzerland and Swiss banks.

The Nazi economy was designed by Hjalmar Schacht, the Third Reich's economics minister and the financial genius who had stabilized the German economy after the madness of Weimar, when it took a wheelbarrow full of notes to buy a loaf of bread. Schacht, who was also a driving force behind the establishment of the Bank for International Settlements, and who had connections on Wall Street, designed the Nazi economy around preparations for total war, a machine of pillage, to be oiled in large part by a steady flow of loot. In Berlin at least, capital of Prussia, this was not a new concept, for in the seventeenth and eighteenth centuries over half of the state revenue was spent on the army and its virtually ceaseless wars with its neighbors.

The Nazis coined the term "Wehrwirtschaft," or war economy, to describe the Third Reich's economic setup, a term which included both the buildup to war and the necessary preparations as well as the actual military struggle. Major General Georg Thomas, chief of the Military Economic Staff, best summed up this economic philosophy: "History will know only a few examples of cases where a country has directed, even in peacetime, all its economic forces deliberately and systematically toward the requirements of war, as Germany was compelled to do in the period between the two world wars."

In May 1935 Hitler appointed Schacht plenipotentiary-general for war economy, authorizing him to begin the necessary preparations for war. These had already begun. Earlier that month Schacht submitted a memorandum to Hitler outlining how "the accomplishment of the armament program with speed and in quantity is *the* [his italics] problem of German politics; everything else therefore should be subordinate to this purpose."

Nine months earlier, in September 1934, Schacht had submitted a report to the Führer entitled "Report on the State of Work for War-Economic Mobilization as of September 30, 1934." In this report he proudly stressed that his ministry has been "charged with the economic preparation for war," notes William Shirer. In his memo Schacht related how the Nazi war machine had been funded with assets taken from "enemies of the state" and blocked foreign accounts. "Thus our armaments are partially financed with the credits of our political enemies."

Schacht's reward for building the economic base of the Third Reich had a certain poetic justice. In the last few months of the war, after the army plot against Hitler, he was imprisoned in a concentration camp and was later tried as a war criminal at Nuremberg. Although he had played no part in the plot to bring down the leader of the Third Reich, the army officers wanted him to run the economy after their takeover.

In wars, as in secret plots and coup attempts, everyone needs to keep capital flowing. Just as both the Axis and the Allies kept the BIS functioning all through the war for their own purposes, the anti-Hitler plotters saw a key role for the man who, perhaps more than any other, had built up the economic base of the Nazi war machine. In the dock at

Nuremberg, Schacht—to the amazement of onlookers—argued that he had played no part in the plan to mobilize Germany for war. The Nazi records told a different story. Schacht, according to the Wehrmacht newspaper published in January 1937 to mark his sixtieth birthday, was "the man who made the reconstruction of the Wehrmacht economically possible."

But, once the German armed forces had been made economically viable, the coming battles had to be paid for. Much of that would be paid for by the acquisition of looted gold from the national treasuries of countries invaded by the Nazis, and by the purchase of foreign currency, preferably through neutral countries, organized by the foreign exchange department of Schacht's economics ministry, operating through Swiss banks.

That Nazi–Swiss connection was always carefully maintained: Schacht's successor as economics minister was Walther Funk, who in 1939 also took over the Reichsbank. Like the Reichsbank vice-president Emil Puhl, Funk was a director of the Basel-based Bank for International Settlements. A key intelligence document detailing the extent of Swiss financial collaboration with the Nazis is dated 1 February 1946. Formerly classified as secret, it is the record of an interview by a U.S. military official with one Dr. Landwehr, former head of the foreign exchange department of the Nazi economic ministry, then working for the Berlin city administration.

Dr. Landwehr was happy to explain the details of his expertise and cooperate with his interrogators—so keen in fact to help that he even gave his interrogator, unnamed in the report, a booklet containing an accounting report as well as a record of his own work for the Reichsbank and the Nazi economic cause until the Allied victory. The good doctor showed signs of exhaustion and undernourishment from the period of his imprisonment, the report notes.

After the Allied victory furious arguments raged between the Allies and the Swiss over the amount of looted Nazi gold that either remained in or had passed through Swiss banks, and, as Seymour Rubin states above, the Swiss were not particularly contrite or willing to reveal the full extent of their collaboration with the Nazis. Dr. Landwehr was more forthcoming, and so, being keen to help and to reduce the length of any possible prison sentence, he stated that "the estimates on the total of the transactions which took place through Switzerland were really far from the Swiss estimates and closer to the Allied point of view," the report says. "Dr. Landwehr estimated that all in all the sum of German assets which passed into Switzerland amounted to at least fifteen billion Reichsmarks. I could not conceal my astonishment and asked him to explain this." The estimate by the Swiss that the sum total of Nazi assets passing into their coffers was RM1 billion was dismissed by Dr. Landwehr with "an ironic smile." Much of the money passed as a straight sale of gold by the Reichsbank to the Swiss National Bank, to acquire foreign currency, he said.

Even more damning was Dr. Landwehr's assertion that the Swiss authorities granted a stream of permits to allow the Nazis to disguise their economic holdings under a Swiss cloak. The Reichsbank created special war chests in Switzerland by underinvoicing goods exported there from Germany, such as coal from the Ruhr, which operated through a special Ruhr fund, the details of which were recorded in a file in the Swiss account. If, for example, Switzerland bought SF1 million worth of coal, Berlin sent an invoice for, say, SF700,000. The remaining SF300,000 was allowed to stay in Switzerland, to be used by Berlin to purchase war material or just sit and earn interest. As the document says, "Special permits were granted which permitted the related companies in Switzerland to hoard considerable funds over the years and camouflage them in Swiss holdings."

The Ruhr coal fund was the first of these cloaks for German economic interests in Switzerland, said Dr. Landwehr. Each of the competing sections of the Third Reich—for the Nazi regime was perpetually riven by factional infighting, over politics, strategy, and the acquisition of loot—wanted a slice of the Swiss funds pie. Dr. Landwehr explained: "In the same way steel and the chemical industry were also used upon the instigation of the different Dienstellen [departments] in the Goering and Wehrmacht spheres of influence." He then went on to state that there must be "considerable treasures in the coal and steel industries."

Was Dr. Landwehr telling the truth? Almost certainly, says an official of the World Jewish Congress. "He has no reason to lie; on the contrary, the experience with these former German officials is that they were punctilious in telling the truth." Well, sometimes.

If the Landwehr interview gives an idea of the Nazis' long-term strategy in using Switzerland as a means of financing the war effort through relatively complicated methods such as the creation of the Ruhr coal fund, Safehaven report no. 11902 gives a more straightforward perspective. Dated Bern, 12 June 1945, this report, written after the Allied

victory, was part of the attempt to track deposits of loot remaining in
Swiss banks. Officials of Johann Wehrli & Co. in Zürich were involved
in channeling payments from an arms factory based in Austria to a Nazi
fund in which was deposited looted property, according to the document, stamped "Confidential."

Johann Wehrli's family was a centuries-old pillar of the Zürich establishment and even entertained the Kaiser when he visited the city in
1912. Wehrli was a close friend of Marcel Pilet-Golaz, the wartime Swiss
foreign minister, the man described as a "Swiss Quisling" by Sir David
Kelly, a British diplomat in Bern. Pilet-Golaz was largely responsible for
the Swiss government's policy of appeasement of the Nazis during the
war, a policy that, while supported by most of the seven-man ruling Federal Council and major industrialists and bankers, did not enjoy the
widespread support of the general Swiss public. In 1938 Johann Wehrli
served as intermediary in Goering's purchase of an Austrian munitions
factory, but by the start of the war Herr Wehrli senior was sixty-five and
did not want to be burdened with the day-to-day running of the bank.
His son ran its business in Latin America, while its activities in Switzerland were handed to Karl Kessler, an ardent Nazi. Not surprisingly, the
United States, after its entry into the war, was pushing hard for both
the Wehrli bank and Kessler to be put on the Allied blacklists that forbade those named from doing business in Allied territories.

"Wehrli is believed to be fairly neutral in his political views," wrote
one American official, "but perfectly willing to leave Kessler and [fellow
manager] Reutter in charge so that the firm works one hundred percent for the Axis countries, and he, Wehrli, without taking active part,
reaps large profits."

Kessler worked hard to promote the Nazi cause in Switzerland. Born
in Germany, with a German wife and a family estate near Hamburg, he
was on the boards of many companies in Germany and was a "very
close friend of von Ribbentrop," according to a report from the American consulate in Zürich. The report, by Leland Harrison, also accuses
Kessler of probably acting as Goering's private financial agent in
Switzerland, where his assets were estimated at $4 million. In 1943 the
United States placed Kessler on a list of people banned from Allied
business dealings because of Nazi connections. The United States also
recommended adding Johann Wehrli and his bank to the restricted list
unless Kessler was fired, but Wehrli refused to fire him.

However, Wehrli also had his friends among the Allies, who saw his bank as a valuable source of intelligence on the Nazis' financial dealings—friends such as Eric Cable, the British consul-general in Zürich. "It seems to me," he wrote, "that if we blacklist a firm like Wehrli and Co. on the flimsy material available, and in the teeth of arguments to the contrary, it is difficult to see how we can avoid blacklisting practically the whole of Switzerland."

Either way, the Allied officials who met with employees of the Price Waterhouse firm of accountants—who were trawling through the accounts of Johann Wehrli, the Safehaven report says, in order to glean information about the bank's wartime activities—had plenty to examine. By June 1945 the accountants had uncovered the role of the Gustloff Stiftung as a repository of property stolen by the Nazis and explained Johann Wehrli's role in moving Nazi money into the fund.

Wilhelm Gustloff, the head of the Nazi Party in Switzerland, was murdered in 1935. Always ready to exploit the death of one of their functionaries for its martyr-value potential, the Nazis put up statues to commemorate Gustloff and named one of their booty repositories after him.

The Gustloff Stiftung was "a fund in which were placed the assets and titles of property taken by the Nazis from Jewish businessmen in Germany and the occupied countries," the report says, quoting the findings of one of Price Waterhouse's examiners, who "has a personal knowledge concerning the background of this trust as a result of his many years residence in Germany before the war." The report goes on to say that Bank Johann Wehrli was to effect payments from the Hirtenbergerwerke, a munitions factory in Austria, owned by one Fritz Mandl, to the Gustloff Stiftung, in connection with the sale of the factory property.

Manufacturing arms for the Nazis was a lucrative business. In June 1945, when the Safehaven report was written, Fritz Mandl's account had a balance of approximately SF1 million ($220,000). Money had poured into Mandl's account at Wehrli in the buildup to the war, with credits of $1,500,000 and £492,000 in 1938. As well as detailing how the Third Reich used Switzerland as a staging post for its arms buildup, Safehaven report 11902 also examines the web of Nazi–Swiss financial connections in Mandl's arms business. During 1944 the Mandl account made quarterly payments of SF1,250 to Dr. Conrad Wespi and Dr.

Werner Von Arx—apparently directors' fees. Both were directors of the German-controlled companies Waffenfabrik Solothurn AG and Solita AG, both based in Solothurn, Switzerland. At the same time, Solita made a cash payment of SF2,200,000 ($482,000), which was credited to the Mandl account. Mandl also advanced SF500,000 to a company based in Surgdorf, Switzerland, in 1943, the report says.

For all his compliance with the Nazis, Johann Wehrli died a disappointed man. His hope that an American bank would entrust its business to his family concern came to nothing, and he liquidated his bank after the war's end.

In addition to monitoring the movement of looted Nazi gold and currency, Safehaven officials were tracking the transactions of European multinational companies with bases in Switzerland that they suspected of profiting from trading in war booty. Safehaven report no. 12179, written by American diplomats based in Bern, concerns charges that the Bally Shoe Factory in Schoenenwerd allegedly held a mountain of booty leather.

The chain of events that led to report 12179 show how a simple intelligence intercept of a family letter led to the uncovering of an international financial network, linking a Swiss company manufacturing something as mundane as shoes, into the continent-wide Nazi economic empire. The Bally Safehaven report had its origins in March 1945, when American intelligence agents based in Switzerland had intercepted a letter, dated 2 February 1945, from a Maurice Bossard in Geneva to his relative Daura Bossard, who lived at 152a Lauderdale Mansions, Maida Vale, London W9. In his letter Bossard claimed that millions of square feet of booty leather had been received in Switzerland during the war years. Writing about the Bally factory at Schoenenwerd he said Bally must also have "mountains of raw material stored up abroad, for immediate disposal, in any country, as soon as transport services are available."

In June 1945 Bossard's allegations that Bally was holding stocks of looted leather was referred to the American consulate in Bern. His letter was well timed as that month Bally had approached the consulate for permission to obtain approval to export a consignment of shoes, partly made from leather that had been purchased from the firm of S. A. de Tannerie in Lausanne. This company had been placed on the U.S. Treasury's list of companies that were forbidden to trade with the United States, but the leather was supposedly purchased before S. A. de Tannerie was blacklisted.

On 4 July 1945 Bally wrote back to the American diplomats, outlining its purchases of raw materials during the whole of 1944 and the beginning months of 1945. Regarding its imports from countries Bally described as "enemies of the United Nations," the letter said that no direct imports were made, apart from two hundred pounds of reptile skins bought from Germany. Bally had, however, purchased about 16.5 tons of various kinds of leather, mostly of German origin, from Swiss firms who had imported these skins. But what was the origin of Bally's leather imports from September 1939 to December 1943? About these Bally was silent, the U.S. diplomats noted; nor was reference made to the firm's leather stocks and those of its foreign affiliates. However much Bally fudged on this, it was now a matter for the Allied military missions in Frankfurt and Vienna, the report says, "where Bally is reported to have factories."

Meanwhile in Geneva, Bossard met with officials of the U.S. consulate on 17 July, to their continuing and considerable interest. "Mr. Bossard has been interviewed at length on the general subject of looted leather and the Bally-Trust," the American diplomats in Geneva wrote to their counterparts in Bern. "He is not in a position to prove any of the allegations contained in the letter, but he is as convinced as ever that the Bally-Trust has received millions of square feet of leather, particularly box-calf, from Germany."

Bossard's evidence was circumstantial but seemed convincing. The Bally shoe dynasty had German family connections and factories in two of the Third Reich's main cities. As the letter said, "Bossard pointed out that Bally himself is of German origin, his mother being German, and his father having been a German naturalized as a Swiss. Bally has two daughters, one married to an Italian count, and the other to a German. The firm has factories at Frankfurt and Vienna, and before the war employed a good many German nationals in their other plants abroad."

Looted gold was, of course, one of the main focuses of Operation Safehaven, but the movement of other war booty, such as leather, could also provide substantial pieces of the jigsaw of Swiss–Nazi economic collaboration, American officials believed. Like gold, leather was easily portable, had a high market value in relation to the amount of space needed to store it, and could be easily traded all over the world. With Bally apparently controlling most of the leather trade in Switzerland, the firm merited further investigation as part of Safehaven's mission, particularly in regard to Bally branches and factories abroad.

"Investigations made through German tanneries concerning exports, in addition to such records as may be available in the American zones relating to Bally enterprises, might well provide interesting leads for further investigation in Switzerland," the American officials in Geneva reported to their colleagues in Bern. "Leather is a commodity that can be stored for long periods of time without deterioration, and quantities of considerable value can be stored in relatively little space. It would seem necessary to start the investigation abroad, since Bally seems to control the trade and other associations in Switzerland."

Like many Swiss institutions, indeed the country itself, Bally too is engaged in a process of examining its wartime record. A team of historians has been engaged to trawl through the company's archives from the wartime era. "They are carrying out research, and they will have some news by mid-1997. It is difficult to comment on anything specific now, but we are absolutely open, because we want to know what happened," said a spokesman. Whatever the provenance of its leather imports, Bally's trade relations with the Third Reich were just one link in a long and very profitable chain. The full extent to which the Nazi economy relied on Swiss partners, bankers, insurance companies, and lawyers is revealed by Safehaven report no. 2969. Sent by the American legation in Bern to the Secretary of State in Washington, the six-page document is a long and detailed breakdown of Switzerland's role in oiling the Nazi war machine. The tradition of Swiss secrecy and concealment, and the inability of the Swiss government to provide an adequate record of foreign assets in the country meant the figures quoted in the report were a "refined guess," its author said.

The Third Reich participated in a total of 358 Swiss economic enterprises, the report says. Total Nazi capital in 263 of these was about $114 million; SF472,720,000, RM19,487,000 and 5 million gold marks; no information was available on the remaining 95. The tentacles of Nazi economic investment stretched across the whole of the Swiss economy, including wholesale and retail companies, manufacturing, and insurance. The report includes the following breakdown of the types of firms with German participation: textile manufacturing, 6; transportation equipment manufacturing, 6; insurance companies, 15; wholesale and retail, 67; banks, 9; chemical and allied products manufacturing, 15; holding and finance companies, 330; other machinery manufacturing, 11; and seven other types, each with less than 3.

The report quotes a Swiss banker as estimating that Swiss banks held a total of SF500 million ($110 million) worth of German assets, although they could range from SF400 million to SF700 million, Swiss banking secrecy precluding a more accurate estimate. In addition large amounts of valuables such as gold, currencies, jewelry, and other precious metals were sitting in safe deposit boxes or private safes, possibly registered in the names of German lawyers acting for their clients or of Swiss trustees. These assets, some of them almost certainly looted, probably totaled about an additional SF500 million. That did not include the piles of art looted by the Nazis that had been deposited in Swiss banks. British experts believed that looted art objects included fifty-three paintings, valued at SF2,200,000 ($484,000), while other sources estimated the value of ten other looted pictures as SF75,000 ($16,500), and yet other reports indicated that hundreds more looted paintings had been sent to Switzerland. The sum total of German assets in Switzerland, including everything from investment capital to looted paintings, was between SF1,770 million ($390 million) and SF2,490 million ($548 million), the report concludes.

But while the Germans had no difficulties bringing Nazi plunder into Switzerland, and while Nazi businessmen traveled freely in and out of Bern and Zürich to meet the Swiss middlemen who cloaked their often looted assets, for a very reasonable commission of 5 percent, Jewish refugees such as Anny and Kurt Kadisch were having trouble getting their money out. Just like their Hungarian coreligionists the Haraszti and Csillag families, and the Lódz millionaire Velvel Singer, the Kadisches had deposited their savings in a Swiss bank. Unlike those account holders, though, Anny and Kurt Kadisch got out in time, leaving their home in Graz, Austria, for sanctuary in the United States, and with them they brought the details of their account: no. 61879, held at the Schweizer Bankverein (Swiss Bank Corporation) in Zürich. The account contained 2,000 British War-Assented Loan shares at 3.5 percent.

Understandably, once they had reached the United States the Kadisches wanted to transfer their funds to their new home. This was to prove a troublesome quest. That the Swiss bankers have refused for decades to hand over the assets of Holocaust victims without the requisite paperwork is now common knowledge. That even in 1939 Swiss bankers, such as the officials of the Schweizer Bankverein, were refusing to hand over assets to Jewish refugees who had fled Europe is less well known. The Kadisches turned to their lawyer, Samuel J. Roberts, for help to try to recover their savings. It was the start of a chain of pressure on the Schweizer Bankverein that stretched to the U.S. cabinet. Roberts wrote to his congressman, Robert L. Rodgers, to ask for his assistance in recovering the assets of his client. From Congressman Rodgers's office the Kadisch case traveled along the corridors of power in Washington. Rodgers went a step up the ladder of government and wrote to Frederick Livesey at the Office of the Adviser on International Affairs at the Department of State. Eventually Secretary of State Cordell Hull himself became involved. Letters flew back and forth among Roberts, Hull, Rodgers, and Livesey suggesting everything from sending copies of their birth certificates to the State Department to proposing that their lawyer contact the American consul in Zürich, who could provide a list of local lawyers to act for Anny and Kurt Kadisch. The Kadisches were turning into an international incident.

On 23 May 1939 Roberts wrote to Albert Marti, director of the Swiss Bank Corporation in Zürich. He provided details of the account and asked: "Will you please be kind enough to give us whatever information you have concerning this account and forward to us forms, or documents, which may be necessary to prepare an order to effect a transfer of said account?" The reply came just over a week later on 2 June 1939: "Dear Sir, We are in receipt of your letter of May 23 and regret being unable to give you the information desired." The Kadisches, two Jewish refugees from Austria, far away in the United States, were stonewalled by the Swiss Bank Corporation. The Kadisch case is one of the earliest documented incidents—the records are held in U.S. State Department files—in which the same banking secrecy laws the Swiss had introduced supposedly in part to protect their Jewish clients from the Nazis were then turned against them, although apparently in accordance with Swiss law.

But when it came to dealing with the Nazis and their mountains of lucrative plunder, the Swiss played by a different set of rules. The German businessmen who held assets in Switzerland worth between SF1,770 million and SF2,490 million; the Reichsbank officials who channeled looted gold through the Swiss National Bank and the Bank for International Settlements; the Third Reich's financiers who transferred funds through Zürich and sent gold bars to Sofindus, the Nazi agent in Madrid, to buy tungsten—they all got as much information as they needed.

6

The Art of Economic Camouflage

It seems advisable to exercise control directly through foreign trustees, or, for instance, give majorities of shares to a trusteeship, because the trustee can be questioned under oath about the owner-ship situation of his property.

> Extract from a secret Nazi economics ministry memo, dated 9 September 1939, on how Nazi-owned businesses abroad must camouflage their connections to Germany

A new Tropical Institute has suddenly sprung up at Basel in Switzerland, which has neither ports nor tropical possessions. Notorious Nazi medical authorities are amongst the advertised collaborators in their new official journal, Acta Tropica, *which is a review of tropical science and medicine.*

> Extract from a report delivered to the Royal Society by Brigadier N. Hamilton Fairley, on 7 February 1945

The logistics, as well as the financing, of the purchase of sufficient foreign currency to keep the Nazi war machine rolling was a difficult and complicated task—much more so than it would be today, because banking in the 1940s was a far slower and more cumbersome process than in the 1990s. Functionaries of the Reichsbank president, Walther Funk, had to work out both where to buy Swiss francs and how to move them across Europe—for, questions of cash supply aside, the wartime procedures for moving large amounts of money were long and complicated.

There were no computers to zip millions of dollars around the world at the touch of a button. Instead there were reams of forms to be filled in, sealed with franks and stamps and shunted from desk to desk before the money started moving. Most countries operated some form of foreign exchange regulations to control the flow of cash, and every transaction in neutral countries' banks would be seen and noted by bank employees—natural targets for recruitment by wartime intelligence services.

The Third Reich's economic taskmasters set up a complicated web of financial chicanery to achieve this, as Safehaven report 2969—detailing how the Nazis took part in 358 Swiss economic enterprises—relates. Before, during, and after the war, the Nazis shifted money back and forth between Swiss banks and their foreign-owned front companies, and from dummy corporations based outside Germany back to the Reichsbank, in an attempt to disguise its provenance. The Reichsbank's aim was to prevent both Allied intelligence and the local authorities of neutral countries from discovering the true ownership of the Nazi network of shadow firms that on paper were legally owned and controlled by foreign nationals—but in reality were totally under the control of Berlin.

Every possible financial avenue was to be used in the drive to obtain hard currency and set up a Nazi economic base in neutral states, from small family firms to the giant industries that helped run the German war economy. The sick too were exploited to service Nazi greed. After Hitler took power in 1933, Davos, the Swiss health resort town where tuberculosis patients came to recover in the clean mountain air, was systematically turned into a Nazi economic enclave. The bank accounts of German sanatoria were used to channel Swiss francs back and forth to Germany. Even the International Red Cross, famed symbol of Swiss humanitarianism, was infiltrated by Nazi spies and used to smuggle gold back to Switzerland, according to recently declassified U.S. intelligence documents. And the massive Nazi chemical combine IG Farben, whose scientists invented the patent for Zyklon-B gas used in the gas chambers, and whose employees also ran a slave-labor camp at Auschwitz, operated in Switzerland as a nominally Swiss company.

Much thought went into the Third Reich's financial camouflage operations. A secret memo from the Nazi economics ministry, dated 9 September 1939, detailed how German businesses based abroad needed to disguise their operations, preferably through neutral countries such as Switzerland, once war broke out. The information within the memo was to be treated as a "state secret," it warns; such was the priority given by the Third Reich to establishing and maintaining channels for the acquisition of foreign currency through neutral countries.

German businesses with export claims against enemy countries would be permitted to transfer them to neutral trustees for collection, before the money was sent back to the Third Reich, the memo said, "for security purposes if it can be taken for granted that these claims are saved by such transactions and not lost for German exchange control. Care is to be taken that expenses and delays are kept to a minimum, but the instructions are to be carried out generously."

At the same time, the cumbersome economic bureaucracy was to prioritize the necessary paperwork to save Nazi assets in enemy countries or countries likely to join the war. These holdings would be saved by transferring them to neutral foreigners: "If German participation, real estate, shares, and other assets in enemy countries and endangered countries can still be saved by sale, transfer to neutral foreigners . . . I request that the necessary authorization be granted without delay, if an appropriate equivalent in foreign exchange is paid immediately or within a reasonable period to the Reichsbank."

Economics ministry officials gave a high priority to ensuring that German trade could carry on abroad after the outbreak of war. The preferred techniques for using foreigners, preferably citizens of neutral countries, as camouflage for Nazi financial affairs were dealt with in section two of the economics ministry secret memo, under the heading "Bridgeheads for German Trade Abroad." Nazi-owned companies with foreign subsidiaries must, if necessary, even sever their legal relations with their branches abroad, so that no legal links could be proved between the parent company in Germany and its foreign offices, which would then go under deep cover. These maneuvers, though, would be pure deception, because the German head office would instead use underhand methods and subterfuge to ensure its continued control, as the secret memo outlines:

Companies and enterprises subject to the provisions of RE 152/36 of the German Foreign Exchange Control will have to be camouflaged in consideration of the present international situation. It is of great interest that camouflage be effective and successful in order to enable these companies to act as far as possible as bridgeheads for German trade in the future. The camouflage the companies must undergo is to be carried out in such a manner that they can be *authenticated as independent foreign enterprises* [emphasis in original].

Converting, for example, the Zürich office of a German car manufacturer into a fully authenticated Swiss economic entity would be a lengthy and complicated procedure, the Nazi bureaucrats recognized. As well as satisfying the Swiss that the new company rising phoenix-like from the ashes of its Nazi predecessor was the genuine article, the rebirth would also have to deceive the many Allied intelligence agents in Switzerland monitoring German businesses and their Swiss frontmen. The economics ministry memo gives further guidance on dealing with this tricky situation:

It has to be expected that companies unable to prove their independence from Germany will have difficulties carrying out their functions. In many cases, it would therefore be advisable to renounce formally and legally these firms from all connections with their German parent companies if the latter's actual influence, established by other means, remains strong enough to guarantee their interests. Therefore it seems advisable to exercise control directly through foreign trustees, or, for instance, give majorities of shares to a trusteeship, because the trustee can be questioned under oath about the ownership situation of his property.

The foreign front firms would have to ensure that their new personnel had the correct political and, of course, racial, backgrounds to be able to properly carry out Berlin's wishes on neutral territory. Every new employee must be thoroughly vetted and rigorously interviewed to check that he or she met the high standards of the Nazi economics ministry. Firms could choose their own new workers, but it would be on their heads if they made a bad choice. Needless to say, no Jews could be entrusted with this vital war work, the memo explains:

The actual influence in the new foreign firms must be secured by effective economic and personnel measures. Special attention is to be paid to the selection of persons for appointment as managers of the newly created foreign firms. Selection of personnel, which as a rule should have foreign nationality, must be entrusted to the discretion of the German firms. Nevertheless, I request that you emphatically inform the firms that they will be held responsible in case bad choices result in damage not only to their own interest but also to those of German National and War Economy. Of course any participation of Jewish foreigners in camouflaged German firms has to be avoided.

There was no time to waste, for the Wehrmacht had poured across the Polish border on 1 September, and the Second World War had begun. The local Devisenstellen (foreign exchange offices) were given a free hand to ensure the rapid implementation of the economics ministry's plan in their own areas. "Applications must be attended to with the greatest speed. The danger exists that foreign exchange will be withheld from the Reich through promotions of new companies abroad," the memo concludes.

EACH January the Alpine town of Davos, Switzerland, plays host to hundreds of senior executives from the world's multinationals as they network with their contacts and colleagues. Together with a battalion of politicians, presidents, and prime ministers, they spend six days munching canapés and quaffing champagne at the annual World Economic Forum, taking occasional breaks on the snow-covered slopes before retiring to their plush hotels. The town, which lies just sixteen kilometers from the Austrian border in the German-speaking region of eastern Switzerland, was once part of Austria, from 1477 to 1649, and has always maintained strong economic and cultural links with the German-speaking lands. During the nineteenth century Davos—actually composed of two villages, Davos-Platz and Davos-Dorf—was developed into a health resort for tuberculosis patients, largely by German businessmen keen to exploit its natural setting and clean mountain air. Thomas Mann even set his sanatorium saga *The Magic Mountain* there.

But Davos has not always enjoyed such a prosperous and genteel reputation. For over fifty years ago, as the Second World War drew to a close and the Nazi exodus of cash, gold, and valuables reached new heights, much of that loot was sent to Davos, to be deposited in the network of German-owned hotels and sanatoria, which had been comprehensively infiltrated and then taken over by Nazi officials and party members.

Months after the war ended in Europe, the flight of cash and loot was in full swing, according to the American intelligence document dated 5 September 1945, entitled "Nazi Activities in Davos-Dorf and Davos-Platz." Swiss customs noted the shipments of money but did nothing to halt or hinder them. The report notes:

> During the last few days mail trains arriving from Nuremberg and Munich have contained large sums of money, jewelry, assets, etc., thought to belong to Nazi leaders, and destined for Davos. Swiss customs officials report that each wagon containing such money shipments arrived at the Swiss frontier guarded by not less than three police officials. One consignment from Nürnberg was addressed to the German sanatorium in Davos where several conspicuously large sums of money are said to have been sent during the last few months. The last two shipments from Munich are reported to have been destined for two banks in Davos where much German money is said to have been deposited.
>
> Rumors circulate, chiefly in Reichsbahn trainmen circles, in Baden, concerning secret convoys of money, gold, and other Nazi party valuables from Reich into Switzerland. Davos is named as the chief destination of these transports.

Hitler's supporters had for years targeted the Swiss health resort as a forward base in neutral Switzerland, both as a recuperation center for sick and wounded German soldiers and as a potential Nazi enclave. They even set up schools and children's homes in Davos, where sick youngsters could be thoroughly indoctrinated in the warped tenets of the Third Reich. Needless to say, they also established a network of holding companies and front firms to disguise their business interests, just as in Spain, Portugal, and other neutral countries, paying their Swiss frontmen and -women a 5 percent commission on the deal.

But, while the ownership of a German company could be disguised, the physical presence of over 1,000 Nazi soldiers and airmen was harder to cover up. The town was jammed with Nazi soldiers recuperating from their wounds during the war, as well as Allied airmen sent to Switzerland to recover. Many of the local Swiss were angry that their quiet streets were full of strutting Nazis, the report adds, quoting a source from 21 August 1944: "The loyal Swiss fear that incidents might take place between the Americans [200 American airmen] and the

more than 1,200 Germans living in the twelve or more German sanatoria. . . . Davos is full of enemies of the Allies."

The Swiss press was also angry at what it described as a Nazi citadel
at Davos. Many Swiss journalists and their newspapers were staunchly
anti-Nazi during the war and vociferously opposed Hitler. Swiss newspapers' reporting of public anger against the 13 August 1942 law that
sealed the border against Jewish refugees, for example, helped ease the
law's restrictions. An article in *Die Nation,* dated 30 May 1945, quoted
in the 5 September intelligence report, shows the depth of public feeling, asking that Davos be purged of Nazi elements, and includes a list of
alleged Nazi Party members active in the resort. Under the title "The
Citadel Davos" it claims: "The most important [pro-Nazi] organizations
continue to work undisturbed: the Fridericianum, the Konsul Burchard
Haus, the German Sanatorium Davos, the German Warrior's Hotel, etc."

The bankers of Zürich and the politicians of Bern took a more expedient view of relations with the Third Reich, but *Die Nation* was
valiantly fighting the good fight against the Nazis. "The Citadel Davos"
was part of a series of articles attacking the German takeover of Davos
and listing a total of forty-five people as acting in the interests of Nazi
Germany.

Allied intelligence too was monitoring the Nazi presence at Davos,
and the British and American embassies in Bern began to put pressure
on the Swiss government to clean its house out. Soon after the articles
appeared in *Die Nation,* twenty Germans were either expelled from
Davos or scheduled to leave the town. They included three employees
of the Third Reich's consulate, Wilhelm Dietz, director of the Konsul
Burchard Haus—a holding company for German interests, which Allied
intelligence believed was the center of Nazi activity in Davos—and the
director of the Fridericianum School.

Just over two months later, on 28 July 1945, the *Gazette de Lausanne* reported that the Swiss Federal Council had issued a decree
immediately dissolving a pro-Nazi organization, the Deutsche Tuberku-
lose Hilfswerke in der Schweis, in Davos, as well as all the enterprises
operated by it in Switzerland, particularly Konsul Burchard Haus,
which had its property seized. The article reported that the company
would be liquidated, effective from 20 July 1945.

By then the Allies had won the war in Europe, and negotiations were
about to start about the return of looted gold held in Swiss banks and

the unfreezing of Swiss assets in the United States. Ever attuned to the changing global realities around their borders, the Swiss authorities were completing a rapid about-face over their attitude to the Allies and Operation Safehaven, which was monitoring the movement of looted Nazi assets.

DURING the war years, though, the Swiss authorities took a more lax view of the Third Reich's attempt to take over Davos. Doubtless agents in the networks run by Col. Roger Masson, head of Swiss military intelligence, were watching with concern how the resort town was turning into an outpost of the Third Reich, but there seemed little political will in Bern to stop Berlin's growing influence there.

At first glance a small Swiss mountain resort, famed for its healthy air, seems an unlikely target for hijacking by the Third Reich, but Davos's geographical position—inside Switzerland, yet just a few minutes' drive from the Reich's Austrian border—meant there could be rich pickings there for the Third Reich, even among its sick inhabitants. In fact, its history as a convalescence home for sick Germans provided perfect cover for Nazi business interests, and espionage ones as well. In Davos too, just as in Bern and Zürich, Swiss banks were ready to channel funds for the Nazis. And Nazi totalitarianism meant that everybody, no matter how ill, who could serve the interests of the Third Reich had to be exploited for any possible advantage.

No avenue of possible power and influence was too small for the Third Reich to take over. Even tubercular patients had to be recruited and converted to the creed of *Mein Kampf* to serve Berlin. Just as Hitler and his economics minister, Schacht, pumped personnel and resources into the Bank for International Settlements in Basel as a means of keeping financial channels open to the Allies, Nazi doctors focused on Davos and its sanatoria to recruit both institutions and personnel to the Nazi cause.

The American intelligence report details how German doctors flocked to the Nazi banner, and how they made sure to send Nazi supporters with tuberculosis to the sanatoria in Switzerland, where they would recover in comfort, while others would be allowed to die. The Reichstuberkulose-Auschuss (Tuberculosis Committee) even had an SS officer as its president, one Dr. Walter, who, Allied intelligence believed, traveled between Bern and Davos after the war's end. There were twelve German-owned controlled sanatoria at Davos. At the same time, almost every one of the committee's senior officers was a Nazi Party member, and several of its twenty-eight regional district leaders were holders of the party's gold insignia for honored members.

An earlier intelligence memorandum, dated 10 June 1945, quoted in the 5 September report, details how the Nazi Party took over the Tuberculosis Committee, a necessary prelude to establishing the Third Reich's presence in Davos:

> Like everything else, the ancient German institution founded to combat TB was transformed after Hitler's accession to power into a Nazi instrument. While innumerable tubercular Germans, opponents of the Hitler regime, were permitted to perish without adequate medical assistance, the supporters of the regime, irrespective of the seriousness of their illnesses, benefited by excellent care, and many of them were sent to the German-supported sanatoria in Switzerland.

The takeover of the committee could never have happened without the active help of German doctors, who, although members of a supposedly humanitarian profession, proved themselves curiously ready to support Nazism.

> This was possible only through the cooperation of a great many German physicians, the majority of whom willingly "coordinated" themselves with the regime and joined the Nazi Party. It may be noted that, with the exception of the teaching profession, none of the liberal professions showed such a large participation in the Nazi Party as the German physicians.

The German takeover of Davos predated Hitler. German officers suffering from respiratory complaints were sent to the two mountain resorts after the First World War, part of a connection with Germany that dated back to the nineteenth century when a Dr. Spengler founded two hospitals in Davos, after discovering that the town's mountain air would cure TB. Long before 1933 the town had hosted one of the largest German colonies in Switzerland, and, as German society became comprehensively Nazified, it was simple for the Third Reich to merely take over existing German structures and organizations and pack them with Nazi place-men, whether at home or abroad.

There were Nazi societies for everyone, from hikers to filmmakers. Suffering from TB offered no respite from the officials of the Third Reich. "Dr. Spengler's hospitals were the beginning of Davos's connection with Germany," says the Swiss historian Gian Trepp, author of *Banking With the Devil.* "The Germans invented Davos, and it was already in their hands when the war started. It was integrated into the Nazi war machine as a hospital for wounded German officers, and they paid money to the Swiss government for it. The Germans said it was a civilian clinic for TB patients, but even now old people in Davos remember how the Germans would greet each other with the Hitler salute. There were plenty of Nazi sympathizers in the German colony there."

Davos was also home to the Swiss Nazi leader Wilhelm Gustloff, before his assassination by the Jewish student David Frankfurter. As well as being the Nazi Gauleiter-designate in case of a successful invasion by the Third Reich, Gustloff was the head of the Auslanderorganisation, the organization for Nazi Party members living outside the Reich, until it was banned by the Swiss authorities before the outbreak of the war. Those two qualifications, plus his history as a former TB patient, made Gustloff ideally placed to turn Davos into a Nazi citadel, says Trepp. "He was living there, and he made Davos the center of Swiss Nazism, and the plan was he would take over when the Nazis invaded."

The Nazis did not invade Switzerland, and they did not need to capture Davos. They took over the resort town either through expanding their existing network there or setting up front companies to purchase hotels to convert them into sanatoria. So important was Davos for the Third Reich that it even maintained a consulate there, although the total population barely reached five figures. As well as controlling, or having a substantial interest in, over a dozen sanatoria, the Nazis also had fifty-nine business interests in the town, according to the document "Nazi Activities in Davos-Dorf and Davos-Platz." The Nazi Party had its headquarters and meeting place at one of the sanatoria, and the town also had its own "German Aid Association" run by Otto Schmidt, who Allied intelligence believed was an active Nazi supporter. One of the sanatoria was also connected to an espionage ring, and in 1943 a secret radio transmitter was discovered there, and its operator arrested.

JUST as in Spain and Portugal, in Davos the Nazis shifted money from institution to institution to try to disguise its provenance and the complicated financial web that always lay behind the Third Reich's financial dealings. Money from the TB association was channeled to the German-run schools in Davos, according to its president, Dr. Walter, who was interviewed by Allied intelligence on 21 August 1944. Allied intelligence labeled one of the schools, the Fridericianum, the "Nazi Reich's Training School," while another was called the "Führer's School," where schoolage Nazis were brought in under the guise of being TB patients. A contingent of young Nazis arrived at Davos as late as February 1945, according to the 5 September intelligence report. One Allied diplomat received a letter from an Austrian friend asking his advice on preventing his son, who was being sent to the Führer's School, from being indoctrinated with Nazi ideology.

The influx of Nazi money, personnel, and ideology into Davos eventually made the Swiss authorities nervous. Accepting looted Nazi gold and selling the Third Reich the foreign currency it needed could be justified as part of a delicate geopolitical balancing act, but there was much less enthusiasm for allowing Berlin to establish its own economic enclave on Swiss soil. A Swiss government decree declared that hotels could no longer be purchased, and nor could land, which could only be leased. But for the Third Reich's agents in Davos and their Swiss associates, this new law was easy to get around, as the case of the Savoy Hotel illustrates. Renamed the Konsul Burchard Haus, the Savoy hotel was a TB sanatorium for about a hundred patients, all German civilians, paying half rates. It was also, Allied intelligence believed, the meeting place and headquarters of the Nazis in Davos. The hotel was owned outright by the Tuberculosis Association in Berlin, although two of the four principal shareholders were Swiss, says the intelligence report. The third shareholder was a Luxembourger, and the fourth a Herr Schmid, manager of the German Aid Association. Allied intelligence also believed that the hotel's director, a former German military officer named Wilhelm Deitz, was involved in smuggling and hiding Nazi funds; he was eventually expelled from Switzerland.

The ownership of the Deutsche Krieger-Kurhaus (German War Hospital) in Davos-Dorf was more straightforward. It was established in 1918 with German money, Allied intelligence believed. The Swiss newspaper *Die Nation* reported that both the medical head of the DKK and the bookkeeper were ardent and active Nazis according to the 5 September intelligence report:

> Dr Nasser, chief doctor of the German Krieger-Kurhaus at Davos, is even today 100 percent Nazi. He succeeded in bringing into Switzerland his doctor son from Innsbruck where he felt he was no longer safe from the Nazi-phobes there.
>
> Ernst Ruthardt, bookkeeper at Deutsche Krieger-Kurhaus, German Warrior's Sanatorium. He wears the German Party Insignia, has operated as party official and was released from military service.

Allied intelligence had found over a dozen sanatoria with German links, nearly all with owners and managers based in, or connected to, Germany. Most sinister of the establishments listed is the Pichert Schwestern on Davos-Platz. *Die Nation* described this children's home, established in 1927, as being owned by "fanatical partisans of the Nazi Party. They influence the children in this sense in every possible way." The report also calls for investigation into fifteen hotels in Davos and neighboring St. Moritz as possible centers of Nazi activity.

As well as a network of buildings, the Nazi movement in Davos also needed money. Allied intelligence believed that Ernst Risch, one of the officers of Konsul Burchard Haus—named as the headquarters of Nazi activity in the resort—was a banker with an interest in the Bündner Privatbank, a local financial institution, which was probably channeling Nazi funds into Davos.

"The greatest suspicions of receiving German money appear to be directed toward this bank, although this statement in no way precludes that the others have not acted in the interests of the Germans," the report says, naming the Graubündner Kantonalbank and the local branch of the Schweizerische Kreditanstalt [Credit Suisse] as other possible conduits for Nazi funds. This latter institution, whose main office was in Zürich, was also named in the Red House document detailing the plans for launching an economic Fourth Reich.

Money was reportedly channeled to the banks in Davos from Berlin, via Zürich. The Verrechnungskasse in Berlin instructed the Swiss National Bank in Zürich to pay the Kantonal Bank in Davos SF70,000 in favor of the Deutsche Krieger-Kurhaus as well as SF62,500 to the directors of the German sanatoria in Davos and Agra. At the same time,

Velvel Singer, with one of his sons, probably Sruel Moishe, in prewar Łódz. His nephew Ron Singer is now pursuing a legal claim for funds Velvel deposited in Swiss banks. The writing, in Yiddish, on the photograph says: "I was not feeling well, but I'm better now." (Photo courtesy of Ron Singer)

Gyorgy Haraszti, principal of a Budapest Jewish school, displaying documents detailing his grandfather's land and property which was nationalized by the Communists. Haraszti's grandfather deposited $600,000 in Swiss banks but was killed in Auschwitz. (Photo © Katalin Szephegyi)

Switzerland's financial nerve center, downtown Zürich, where leading banks have their headquarters. Jewish groups say the banks are still sitting on funds deposited by Jews killed in the Holocaust. (Photo © Hulton Getty)

Walther Funk, the Reichsbank director, on trial at Nuremberg, 21 September 1946. Funk, who received a life sentence, helped direct the Nazi sales of looted gold to the Swiss National Bank. (Photo © Hulton Getty)

German civilians forced to look at those killed in Auschwitz. The Nazi network of extermination camps proved a rich source of gold, extracted from the teeth of dead Jews. (Photo © Hulton Getty)

A cave at the Merkers salt mine jammed with Nazi loot. By war's end the Nazi leaders had accumulated so much stolen wealth they didn't have enough time to sell it and send the proceeds on to Switzerland. (Photo © Hulton Getty)

Henry Morgenthau, wartime U.S. Secretary of the Treasury, one of the leaders of Operation Safehaven, which monitored the passage of Nazi wealth to neutral countries, particularly Switzerland, during the war. (Photo © Hulton Getty)

Allen Dulles, wartime chief in Bern of the Office of Strategic Services, forerunner of the CIA. OSS agents helped supply information to Safehaven officials in Washington, D.C., about the movement of Nazi assets to Switzerland. (Photo © Hulton Getty)

Thomas H. McKittrick, president of the Bank for International Settlements, 1939–1946.

Isabelle Riff (right), as a six-year-old child, together with her sister, Charlotte, aged two. During the war the Riff sisters had to leave their parents in France. They crossed illegally into Switzerland with the help of the Jewish resistance. (Photo courtesy of Isabelle Silberg)

Isabelle Riff, now married to Rabbi Sydney Silberg and living in London. (Photo courtesy of Isabelle Silberg)

Raoul Wallenberg, Swedish diplomat who saved thousands of Jews in wartime Budapest and vanished into the Soviet gulag. Wallenberg worked with his Swiss colleague Charles Lutz and Friedrich Born, the representative of the Red Cross. (Photo © MTI)

Marcus Wallenberg of Sweden's Enskilda Bank and Raoul Wallenberg's uncle. Safehaven officials believed that Enskilda was trading heavily with Nazi Germany. (Photo © Hulton Getty)

SVÁJCI KÖVETSÉG
IDEGEN ÉRDEKEK KÉPVISELETE

KIVÁNDORLÁSI OSZTÁLY
V., VADÁSZ-UTCA 29.

SCHWEIZERISCHE GESANDTSCHAFT
ABTEILUNG FÜR FREMDE INTERESSEN

ABTEILUNG AUSWANDERUNG
V., VADÁSZ-UTCA 29.

2542/CX.
1944.

Die Schweizerische Gesandtschaft, Abteilung fremde Interessen, bescheinigt hiermit,
dass

C S E R H Á T   Z O L T Á N

im schweizerischen Kollektiv-
pass zur Auswanderung einge-
tragen ist, daher ist der (die)
Betreffende als Besitzer eines
gültigen Reisepasses zu be-
trachten.

Budapest, 23. Oktober 1944.

A Svájci Követség, Idegen
Érdekek Képviselete, ezennel
igazolja, hogy

C S E R H Á T   Z O L T Á N

a svájci csoportos (collectiv)
utlevélben szerepel és ezért
nevezett érvényes utlevél bir-
tokában levő személynek tekin-
tendő.

Budapest, 1944. október 23.

A certificate, issued by the Swiss embassy in Budapest in 1944, stating that the holder, a Hungarian Jew, is under Swiss protection. Charles Lutz, a Swiss diplomat based in the wartime Hungarian capital, managed to place 50,000 Hungarian Jews under Swiss diplomatic protection, saving them from both deportation by the Nazis and from being killed by Hungarian Arrow Cross Nazis.

Adolf Eichmann, hanged as a war criminal in Israel in May 1962. In June 1944 Eichmann arranged with Budapest wartime Zionist leader Rezso Kasztner for 1,685 Jews to escape on a special train to Switzerland, for a price of $1,000 a head. (Photo © MTI)

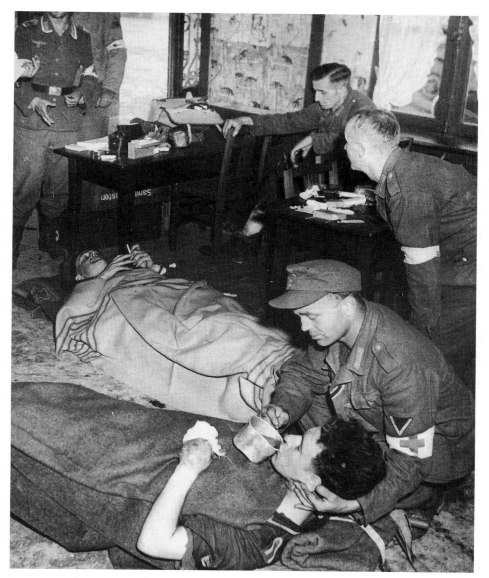

American and German Red Cross workers in the town of Avranches. Some Red Cross offices in wartime North Africa were infiltrated by Nazi agents, according to declassified U.S. intelligence documents. (Photo © Hulton Getty)

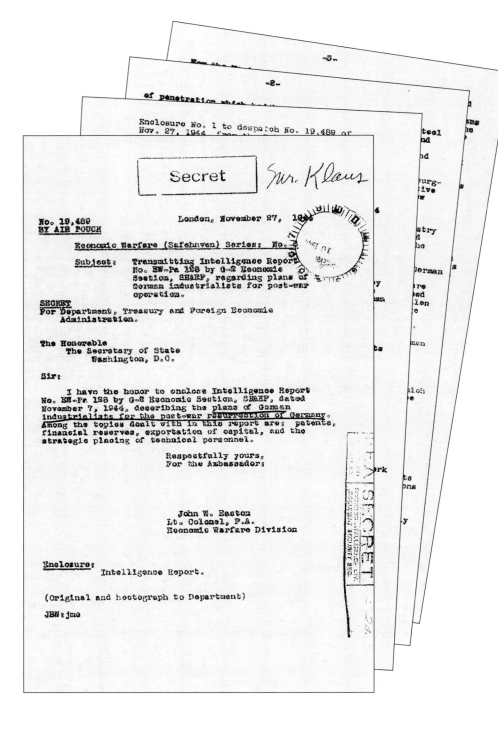

Enclosure No. 1 to despatch No. 19,489 of
Nov. 27, 1944 from

Mr. Klaus

No. 19,489
BY AIR POUCH

London, November 27, 1944

Economic Warfare (Safehaven) Series: No.

    Subject: Transmitting Intelligence Report
No. EW-Pa 128 by G-2 Economic
Section, SHAEF, regarding plans of
German industrialists for post-war
operation.

SECRET
For Department, Treasury and Foreign Economic
    Administration.

The Honorable
    The Secretary of State
        Washington, D.C.

Sir:

    I have the honor to enclose Intelligence Report
No. EW-Pa 128 by G-2 Economic Section, SHAEF, dated
November 7, 1944, describing the plans of German
industrialists for the post-war resurrection of Germany.
Among the topics dealt with in this report are: patents,
financial reserves, exportation of capital, and the
strategic placing of technical personnel.

               Respectfully yours,
               For the Ambassador:

               John W. Easton
               Lt. Colonel, F.A.
               Economic Warfare Division

Enclosure:

        Intelligence Report.

(Original and hectograph to Department)

JBW:jmc

I have the honor to enclose Intelligence Report
No. EW-Pa 138 by G-2 Economic Section, SHAEF, dated
November 7, 1944, describing the plans of German
industrialists for the post-war resurrection of Germany.
Among the topics dealt with in this report are: patents,
financial reserves, exportation of capital, and the
strategic placing of technical personnel.

SOURCE: Agent of French Deuxieme Bureau, recommended by
Commandant Zindel. This agent is regarded as
reliable and has worked for the French on German
problems since 1916. He was in close contact
with the Germans, particularly industrialists,
during the occupation of France and he visited
Germany as late as August, 1944.

6. After the defeat of Germany the Nazi Party
recognizes that certain of its best known leaders will
be condemned as war criminals. However, in cooperation
with the industrialists it is arranging to place its less
conspicuous but most important members in positions with
various German factories as technical experts or members
of its research and designing offices.

For the A.C. of S., G-2.

WALTER K. SCHWINN

G-2, Economic Section

Prepared by

MELVIN M. FAGEE

Distribution:

Same as EW-Pa 1.
U.S. Political Adviser, SHAEF
British Political Adviser, SHAEF

(Left) The Red House report, an intelligence report of a meeting at a hotel in Strasbourg,
France, in 1944, reportedly attended by representatives of German industry and Nazi offi-
cials. Allied intelligence believed that German industrialists were planning an underground
Fourth Reich after Germany's defeat, using Swiss banks as a forward economic base.
Excerpted passages appear above. The full text can be found in the appendix.

Allied Claim Against Swiss for Return of Looted Gold

1. It has been determined from available ledgers of the German Reichsbank that a total of at least 398 million dollars worth of gold was shipped to Switzerland by the German Reichsbank during the war. This figure does not include the following which, when verified and amounts definitely determined, should also be taken up with the Swiss:

    (a) one additional shipment known to have taken place after these books were closed and evacuated from Berlin;

    (b) other shipments believed to have taken place early in the war and to have been recorded in earlier ledgers of the German Reichsbank which are not now available;

    (c) an amount of approximately 12 million dollars worth of gold which the Germans seized when they looted the Italian gold but delivered directly to the Swiss.

2. It is perfectly possible that the entire amount of 398 million dollars (or more) worth of gold received by the Swiss from the German Reichsbank was looted gold because of the following facts:

    (a) the large amounts of gold known to have been looted by the Germans from the countries which they occupied in Europe before and during the course of the war. It is known that at least 579 million dollars worth of gold was looted by the Germans and made available to the German Reichsbank. This figure represents a conservative tabulation based upon the estimates of the countries from which gold was looted and upon a careful examination of the records of the Germans.

    (b) The relatively small amounts of legitimate gold available to them.

    (c) the very small proportion of the looted gold which appears to have remained in Germany at the end of the war or to have been disposed of in countries other than Switzerland. The amount of such looted gold now identified as being in Germany at the end of the war or disposed of to foreign countries other than Switzerland is only 169 million dollars. These figures have been derived from a complete inventory of the gold found in Germany at the end of the war and a thorough examination of the records of the Reichsbank, including a detailed tracing of the processing and disposition of more than half of the gold originally looted.

Subtraction of the loot thus traced to German war-end stocks and to third countries (169) from the total loot (579) leaves 410 million dollars worth of loot or more than the entire amount of the known shipments to Switzerland still to be accounted for.

...every ounce of non-looted gold available to the Swiss from Germany that Switzerland.

---

1. It has been determined from available ledgers of the German Reichsbank that a total of at least 398 million dollars worth of gold was shipped to Switzerland by the German Reichsbank during the war. This figure does not include the following which, when verified and amounts definitely determined, should also be taken up with the Swiss:

The intelligence document "Allied Claims Against Swiss for Return of Looted Gold," reveals how Nazi booty found a ready welcome in Switzerland and how the Swiss National Bank washed looted gold, reexporting it to neutral Spain and Portugal. Its detailed figures, the document says, are based on "a complete inventory of the gold found in Germany at the end of the war and a thorough examination of the records of the Reichsbank, including a detailed tracing of the processing and disposition of more than half of the gold originally looted." (The full text can be found in the appendix.)

GERMAN GOLD MOVEMENTS (ESTIMATE)
From April, 1938 to May, 1945 (In Millions of U. S. Dollars)

INCOME		OUTGO	
Germany started the war with estimated gold reserves of . . . . (Published gold reserves were only 29)	100	Sold to Swiss National Bank . .	275 to 282
Taken over from Austria	46	Possibly sold to Swiss Commercial Banks before 1942	20
" " " Czechoslovakia .	16	Washed through Swiss National Bank depot account and eventually re-exported to Portugal and Spain (larger part by far to Portugal) . . .	100
" " " Danzig	4	Rumania	32.5
" " " Poland	12	Sweden	18.5
" " " Holland	168	Found in Germany (including 64 earmarked for Italy and 32 earmarked for Hungary)	293
" " " Belgium	223		
" " : Yugoslavia	25	Sold to or used in Balkan countries and Middle East—mainly Turkey	10
" " " Luxembourg . . .	5		———
" " " France	53		752
" " " Italy	64		
" " " Hungary	32		
	———		
	748		

- -

SWISS GOLD MOVEMENTS (SWISS OFFICIAL STATEMENT)
From January 1, 1939 to June 30, 1945 (In Millions of U.S. Dollars)

Purchased from Germany	. . . .	282.9	Sold to Germany	4.9
" " Portugal	. . . .	12.7	" " Portugal	116.6
" " Sweden	. . . . .	17.0	" " Spain	42.6
			" " Turkey	3.5

Conclusions: (1) All gold that Germany sold after a certain date, probably from early 1943 on, was looted gold, since her own reserves, including hidden reserves with which she started the war, were exhausted by that time; (2) out of $278,000,000-worth of gold that Switzerland purchased from Germany, the larger part was looted gold; in addition, Switzerland has taken $100,000,000 looted gold in deposit, which later on was re-exported to Spain and Portugal for German account; (3) among the gold that the Swiss sold during the war to Portugal, Spain, and Turkey, there could have been looted German gold; (4) the gold that Switzerland bought from Sweden during the war could theoretically be German looted gold; monetary experts all over the world (Switzerland has monetary experts at her disposal) knew, or ought to have known, roughly the figures and movements as contained in the above estimate—certainly they knew the gold holdings and gold reserves of the German Reichsbank. Switzerland therefore was lacking good faith. In addition, she was warned that all Germany's own pre-war gold stocks had been used up by mid-1943 at the latest and therefore all the gold then in the possession of Germany must be presumed to be looted gold.

ES:CWFletcher:jd
2/5/46

Marcel Pilat-Goldz, wartime Swiss foreign minister, together with Army Chief General Henri Guisan. Pilat-Goldz was a driving force behind Swiss policies of accommodation with Nazi Germany. (Courtesy of Swiss Federal Archives, Bern)

Colonel Roger Masson, head of Swiss military intelligence in wartime. Masson met several times with SS General Walter Schellenberg, chief of Nazi foreign intelligence. (Courtesy of Swiss Federal Archive, Bern)

Allied intelligence officers believed that the Nazi groups in Davos were preparing to mortgage properties owned by the Germans in exchange for ready cash. Allied diplomats believed that any such arrangements would contravene the agreement of 16 February 1945 to freeze German assets.

UNDER pressure from the Allies, the Swiss eventually began expelling key Nazis from Davos in the summer of 1945. But the Third Reich's network in the town had decades-old roots, and merely throwing out a few functionaries would not close down the Nazi enclave. And if the Germans were no longer allowed into Switzerland, their Swiss colleagues and middlemen were still allowed out to Germany to take care of their friends' business interests, to the anger of Allied officials working on Operation Safehaven. Safehaven's aim was to evaluate and track German assets, and Allied officials feared that the Nazis' Swiss business partners would shift German assets into Swiss economic entities or transfer them into Swiss holding companies, as a means of evading the Safehaven officials. A letter from W. A. Brandt at the Economic Warfare Department of the Foreign Office, dated 19 December 1945, to Lt. Col. Dendy of the Control Office for Germany, details how Swiss nationals were acting for the Nazis in occupied Germany:

> We are constantly receiving evidence from Switzerland that Swiss nationals manage to gain entry to Germany, chiefly to the French and American zones. There they contact their old friends, and we do not doubt that the principal object of these journeys is to find ways of conniving with their German principals to efficiently hide German assets in Switzerland.

Swiss nationals should be forbidden from entering Germany, argued Brandt.

> It is obviously in the interests of our Safehaven activities that until we are satisfied that German assets in neutral countries are well under control, nationals of neutral countries should not be allowed entry into Germany, nor, of course, should Germans be allowed to enter neutral countries. We should greatly appreciate it if this could be brought to the notice of the competent authorities, with a view to a coordinated policy being decided upon in conjunction with the United States and French authorities.

While a few United Nations nationals were allowed into Germany to inspect their property, there was no reason to extend this scheme to citizens of neutral countries. "We are not at all satisfied that the neutrals' interests in going to Germany are identical with ours. . . . It is only natural that the neutral satellite of a German master will do his very best to arrange that these German assets, which are still hidden, shall permanently escape the tentacles of the Allies."

British Foreign Office files, now available at the Public Records Office in London, reveal how, after the war, Swiss citizens working for local subsidiaries of German enterprises traveled in and out of Germany, partly to try to coordinate a joint campaign to conceal the real extent of German business interests in neutral countries. A confidential note from the Commercial Secretariat of the British legation in Bern, to the Black List Section of the Economic Warfare Department in the Foreign Office, reveals how a Herr Moser, of the Ruhr & Saar Kohle AG in Basel, visited Germany in early autumn 1945. Herr Moser met with one Russel, who, the note says, formerly worked for the Basel firm but was now managing director of the Ruhr Coal Syndicate. "Russel's wife is said to be still in Switzerland and to be maintained by the Swiss firm. Furthermore, Moser is stated to have been assured by Russel of coal deliveries in the near future." Communications and visits to colleagues in Germany by employees of Swiss firms with German links or participation should be forbidden, at least until a proper policy was decided on this question, the note suggests, and continues: "The attention of the Control Commission for Germany and other competent departments [should] be drawn to the importance of ensuring that their activities do not run counter to Black List and Safehaven policy."

Coal was the glue that helped hold the Swiss–Nazi economic network together. Allied officials kept a close watch on any links between Switzerland and German coal suppliers. For, while the Germans needed Swiss banks, Switzerland needed German coal, upon which it largely depended to provide energy and heating. Without German coal Swiss industry would probably have had to shut down. "The Germans blackmailed Switzerland into cooperating by supplying the country with coal," says Gian Trepp.

Could Switzerland have bought its coal from other countries? Certainly, purchasing the fuel would not have been a problem, as there was money enough to buy it, but importing the necessary massive amounts of such a heavy material would have been more difficult and costly. After the German invasion of France in May 1940 Switzerland was surrounded by Nazi, or Axis-controlled or Axis-allied, territory. It is unlikely that Axis officials would have let coal purchased from, say, neutral Sweden pass smoothly across their frontiers.

Through Germany's sale of coal to Switzerland it virtually controlled much of its energy supply and so could help to ensure Swiss economic cooperation with Berlin. That said, Switzerland too had a card to play, for while its industry needed German coal, the Third Reich needed the Swiss francs with which the Swiss purchased their fuel. Just one more example of the ambiguity of neutrality.

Coal, and the supply of it to Switzerland, was also used by the Nazis to disguise their holdings in Switzerland, as we have seen. The February 1946 interview by an Allied intelligence officer with Dr. Landwehr, former head of the foreign exchange department of the Nazi economics ministry, outlined how the Third Reich created war chests in Switzerland by underinvoicing goods exported from Germany, leaving the unpaid funds as a pool of Swiss francs to draw on as need be. Dr. Landwehr singled out coal as a commodity especially used for this. A special Ruhr fund was even created to cloak German economic interests in Switzerland, he told his interrogators.

Back at the Economic Warfare Department W. A. Brandt knew all about Nazi–Swiss coal deals, and he was deeply unhappy that Herr Moser was allowed into Germany to meet his colleagues. "Frankly I cannot understand on whose authority these people were admitted to Germany. In this particular instance the position may prove very awkward indeed, as we have grave suspicions that the Ruhr & Saar Kohle AG are very closely connected with the Ruhr Coal Syndicate," he wrote to his Foreign Office colleague J. M. K. Vyvyan. "It may well prove that the real reason for the visit was to enable the parties concerned to conspire together about the evidence to be supplied to our people on the German interests involved. It is quite likely that Mr. Moser is a Swiss national, but I should have thought that neutrals applying for permits to enter Germany would come very low in the list of priorities."

THE WARTIME paper trail that implicates so many Swiss financial and government officials as aiding the Third Reich also names Swiss diplomats and the country's most important humanitarian institution, the

Red Cross, as helping to channel Nazi loot. A Safehaven report dated Istanbul, 21 May 1945, shows how Swiss diplomats were deeply involved in secret financial deals with German nationals living in Turkey, by hiding their property for them and sending Nazi assets on to Switzerland in the international Red Cross pouch. After diplomatic relations were broken off between Germany and Turkey, the Swiss took charge of German interests and assets, even setting up a special bureau for the purpose, says the report, which also credits British economic and military intelligence with providing Safehaven information to U.S. agents. The report says:

> When the bureau began to operate, rumors—some of which have since been confirmed—began to circulate to the effect that:
>   . . . Numerous nonofficial Swiss nationals in Turkey, sometimes in the capacity of temporary employees of the bureau, were in contact with the interned Germans and were secreting property for them (confirmed in part) . . .
>   Smuggling of concentrated forms of wealth from Germany into Turkey and from Turkey into Switzerland was being accomplished by the aid of Swiss couriers and via the International Red Cross pouch (confirmed).

The Geneva-based International Committee of the Red Cross (ICRC) was a natural target to be infiltrated by intelligence agents. It was an international relief organization that operated across wartime Europe, able to cross frontiers and work on both Axis and Allied territory, and with its mandate to collect information, its officials could interview both prisoners of war and military officers on both sides. The everyday work of an ICRC delegate, as he or she traversed Europe, could provide reams of intelligence reports for any intelligence service, from the OSS to Gen. Walter Schellenberg's Department VI of the RSHA, the Reich security organization that combined the Gestapo, the criminal police, and the SS security services.

Under the cover of the Red Cross, a spy who had infiltrated the organization could note everything from transport conditions, availability of food and power, movement of troops and material, and the destruction caused by bombing raids to the morale of the senior officials charged with helping the ICRC's work on both sides as he crossed the war zone. Red Cross documents were the perfect cover for an undercover intelligence agent, and the legal cover they provided to ask questions and travel unhindered were a wartime spy's dream.

Consequently, American intelligence officials were deeply suspicious of the ICRC local branches, believing them to be thoroughly infiltrated by Nazi agents and others working for German intelligence. U.S. agents believed that Red Cross officials were involved in smuggling Frenchmen to North Africa to work for German intelligence; that German military intelligence had infiltrated the French Red Cross in Madrid; that the ICRC delegate in Naples was in touch with enemy intelligence agents; and that the head of the Belgian Red Cross in Portugal had even helped to finance the purchase of minerals for the Third Reich.

A U.S. intelligence report dated 4 February 1944, entitled "Enemy Agents and the Red Cross," provides more details and outlines the extent to which OSS and other U.S. agents believed the Red Cross had been penetrated by the Nazis. "Information from many sources points to the conclusion that the International Red Cross is being used as a cover for German agents. While no one bit of evidence is irrefutably proved, the total leads to the conclusion that the ICRC has been penetrated by enemy agents," the report says.

Based on reports by U.S. intelligence agents, Allied intelligence sources, letters and cables sent by ICRC officials, and confessions of two arrested enemy agents, the six-page document covers eight areas, both in the theater of war and on neutral territory: Spain; French North Africa and Spanish Morocco; Italy; France, via Portuguese sources; Switzerland, via North Africa sources; Cairo; Denmark; and Portugal.

Frenchmen who were Nazi agents used the cover of being refugees under Red Cross protection when they reached Spain, en route to North Africa, the document says. The agents traveled down a chain of handlers based in Marseilles, Figueras, and Barcelona, run by "known German agents," including, in Barcelona, a former employee of the Red Cross, who used its services to ship the German spies into North Africa as refugees. The report provides further details:

> From two sources we learn that young Frenchmen are taken out of France to North Africa via Spain for intelligence work for the enemy so regularly that this is called the "normal route." Two Red Cross officials are active in this work. . . . In Madrid also, the French Red Cross seems to function as cover for agents posing as

refugees. French agents entering Spain via St.-Jean-de-Luz and San Sebastian, rather than via the eastern route, present themselves to M. Mattei of the French Red Cross in San Sebastian. From San Sebastian they go on through Spain under cover of an American or Canadian. There is a member of the German military intelligence service among the personnel of the French Red Cross in Madrid.

Secret escape routes to smuggle enemy agents, Nazi infiltrators posing as humanitarian workers, clandestine border crossing, fake identities—at first glance this appears to be the stuff of spy novels rather than history. Present-day ICRC officials have legitimately questioned the accuracy of the information on which some of the above report was based. But whatever the methods U.S. agents used to gather their intelligence—and those outlined in the report are fairly standard espionage techniques—it is a fact that wartime Spain, Portugal, and North Africa were crawling with spies, refugees, and the seedy peddlers of information that every war seems to throw up. The Red Cross offices were a natural target for their attentions. It is also a fact, attested to by present-day ICRC officials, that Jean-Roger (or Jean-Robert) Pagan, a former wartime Red Cross employee, was arrested in Algiers in October 1943 on charges of espionage for the Nazis. The U.S. report gives more details:

> On October 14, 1943, while flagrantly collecting information, Jean-Roger Alfred Pagan, an enemy agent, was arrested in Algiers. According to Pagan's confession, one C. Pasch, said to be general supervisor for the night shift at the International Red Cross Geneva (PO Box 2003), put Pagan in touch with Von Engelbrechten, German representative of the Red Cross in Geneva, and also, to the best of our information, engaged in intelligence work.

Pagan had three contacts in Switzerland for his espionage work for the Nazis, through whom he passed the information he gathered about the situation in Algiers—wartime capital of Free France—and communicated with his German spymasters. This trio, dubbed X, Y, and Z in the report, were a German man, aged about thirty, attached to the German embassy in Bern, whom Pagan met through his contact Von Engelbrechten; a Russian woman living in Geneva, Von Engelbrechten's secretary; and finally, Z, also known as "the Professor," who taught Pagan how to use invisible ink. The Professor, about forty years old, was also connected to the German embassy in Bern, Pagan believed. In the end, none of Pagan's connections, either with the ICRC or Nazi intelligence, could save him, and in December 1944 he was executed by firing squad.

Pagan also named another ICRC delegate working in North Africa, George Graz, as operating for Nazi intelligence. Graz had supplied military information to Pagan, the latter told his interrogators, and while it was not initially accurate he told Pagan that he would correct it. Graz was arrested several days after Pagan but escaped with expulsion from Algiers as "a known German agent," according to the intelligence report. Graz's secretary also worked for the Red Cross, it noted.

U.S. intelligence reports also implicate a wartime ICRC employee based in Turkey, another neutral country that was the focus of much attention from both Allied and Axis intelligence services. They accuse one Guiseppe Beretta of smuggling that may have helped the Nazis. Beretta began work for the Red Cross in February 1943, charged with organizing food supplies for the Greek islands in the Aegean, then hit by famine. In August 1943 he was transferred to Istanbul, to forward relief supplies to Italian POWs in Turkey. An ICRC report, dated 15 September 1996 and published in response to growing media attention on the evidence of Nazi infiltration of the Red Cross, gives more details of the Beretta case:

> In January 1945 he was placed under investigation by the Turkish police, on suspicion "of having acted against the provisions of the law on the protection of Turkish currency and having imported certain goods without declaring them to customs" (letter of March 12, 1945, from Turkish embassy in Bern to the ICRC).

After he was forced to hand over to the Turkish police 710 gold coins deposited in a strongbox rented in his name at the Deutsche Oriental Bank in Istanbul, Beretta was at once recalled to Geneva, arriving on 12 February 1945. On the following day, he tendered his resignation, which was immediately accepted.

Beretta then gave a complicated explanation of how he became involved in the strange affair of the 710 gold coins.

> Beretta declared that the 710 gold coins had been given to him by a Hungarian journalist named Willy Goetz-Wilmos, residing in

Istanbul. According to a report filed by a U.S. intelligence agent, Goetz-Wilmos was in fact a German working for the Gestapo. Beretta denied all the charges leveled against him, and at the present stage of our research there is no proof that he did indeed use the ICRC mail to transfer funds or valuables to Switzerland, although this absolutely cannot be ruled out.

A curious footnote to the case of Guiseppe Beretta was the letter written to the Red Cross in his support by Colonel Roger Masson, head of Swiss military intelligence, after Beretta's resignation from the service of the ICRC. Colonel Masson requested that the Red Cross treat Beretta with "benevolent understanding," possibly because he was an agent, or at least an asset, of Swiss intelligence.

News reports about the extent of Nazi infiltration of the wartime ICRC first broke in the autumn of 1996. They were part of the ongoing media battle—fought with leaked Allied intelligence documents—between the Swiss Bankers' Association on one side and the World Jewish Congress and Senator Alfonse D'Amato's office on the other. When the teams of researchers trawling the U.S. National Archives found the Red Cross mentioned in reports of Nazi smuggling of loot, the ICRC was immediately caught in the crossfire. Many Jewish activists were glad of an opportunity to lambaste an organization they believed had responded both feebly and inadequately to the Holocaust, although it was information transmitted in 1942 by Carl J. Burckhardt, a senior ICRC official, that helped first alert the world to the Nazi genocide of the Jews.

The Red Cross launched an immediate investigation into the accusations that some of its wartime staff either collaborated with the Nazis or were Nazi agents, and on 15 September it published a detailed preliminary report, part of which is quoted above. The IRC report said: ". . . it is already possible to refute the majority of the allegations and even the infiltration of the ICRC by German agents; moreover the author or authors of the recently published documents show total ignorance of the role and mandate of the ICRC and describe as espionage perfectly regular activities exercised openly, with the agreement or at the request of the Allied authorities."

While admitting that some of the intelligence documents contained more or less accurate information, as in the case of Pagan, it also pointed out several errors. For example, of the twenty-one people named in the documents as representatives of the ICRC, only sixteen were permanent or temporary staff members of the Red Cross. In addition the Red Cross argued that the information and accusations in the American intelligence wartime reports were not taken seriously enough by the U.S. government to affect its relations with the ICRC. "We have no evidence that any highly placed U.S. authorities have attached to these reports the importance that certain organs of the press are seeking to ascribe to them. In any case, neither the U.S. nor the French government has shown any lack of trust in the ICRC," the report concluded.

As well as monitoring the Red Cross, as we saw earlier, American intelligence agents in the Spanish protectorate of Tangier, Morocco, were closely watching the wartime business activities of Samuel Reichmann and his wife, Renee. U.S. officials believed that Reichmann was using Red Cross parcels to smuggle goods into Nazi-occupied countries, according to declassified documents. The Reichmanns, Hungarian Jewish refugees, went on to live in Canada, where they founded the multimillion-dollar property empire Olympia and York and built Canary Wharf, in part with the money Samuel Reichmann had made in wartime Tangier, according to his son Edward. Edward Reichmann told me that his father took "several million" to Canada from Tangier, a "big part" of which he had made there.

Safehaven report no. 534, dated London, 5 November 1945, accuses Samuel Reichmann of smuggling goods in Red Cross food parcels into Nazi-occupied countries and quotes reports that he had been trafficking in forged banknotes, stamps, and gold. "This Hungarian Jewish refugee family has always aroused a certain amount of suspicion, partly owing to the fact that Samuel, the father, has been reported as trafficking with the Germans, and partly on account of the frequent journeys throughout Spanish Morocco and Spain made by Samuel, Renee, his wife, and Eva, their daughter."

The report also notes the refugee relief work carried out by Renee and Eva, in sending relief aid to Jews in Europe and tracing and evacuating former concentration camp victims. Point two says: "It is now revealed that Eva, assisted by her mother, began sending food parcels to relatives in Hungary, and because she was so successful in getting them through she became eventually representative in Tangier for the Vaad Hahatzala Relief Society, 540 Bedford Avenue, New York, and sent a large quantity of food parcels to occupied countries on its behalf."

Point six adds: "Eva Reichmann gave this information, which is confirmed by Curt Albert Geiershofer Reinhard, of the Tangier Jewish Joint Distribution Committee, but adding that he holds no brief for Samuel Reichmann, who has no part in this refugee activity and has 'become very rich by other means.'"

Point seven provides more details: "Frequent suggestions have been made that Reichmann smuggled goods in Red Cross food parcels into occupied countries, and also he has been reported as trafficking in forged notes, and stamps and also gold." Renee, the report adds, was even able to travel in and out of Hungary in 1941–42, although she was a Jewish refugee, with visas issued by the Italian and French consulates.

What were these "other means," and how had this family of Jewish refugees ended up in North Africa, their activities monitored by Safehaven agents tracking the movement of cash and assets across neutral countries? As the war progressed and the danger for Jews increased, the Reichmann family fled Hungary westward, arriving in Paris. But then the French capital, also, became too perilous, and the family moved on to Biarritz, where they arrived in the early summer of 1940. Samuel Reichmann had made his fortune in eggs before the war; while he had bank accounts in the United States, Britain, and Switzerland, "he always carried ten to twenty thousand dollars in his pockets," Edward says. "He had a lot of money in America and England. He was very wealthy, and he was a pessimist."

From Biarritz the family moved to Bayonne, and from there, after a complicated series of arrangements involving visas for Spain and Haiti, the Reichmanns arrived in Tangier sometime around July 1940. There Samuel Reichmann set up as a money-changer. "We saw there were more than twenty money-changers in the market, some with tables, others with little stores," Edward recalls. "American soldiers would come in on the boats, and change ten or twenty dollars, and the money-changers lived from it. In a day they bought one hundred to two hundred dollars, and bought pesetas at the bank. My father discovered the banks made eight percent to ten percent and the changers made whatever they could."

The money-changers bought their pesetas from the banks before selling them on. Samuel Reichmann decided to buy pesetas himself in bulk and undercut the bank rates. Edward says, "The difference between the changers and the banks was substantial, so he undercut the banks. He opened an account and took every day, say, a thousand dollars. He bargained with [the banks]. He was a middleman." In 1943 Samuel had made enough money to open his own bank, and seven years later Edward opened the Tangier Stock Exchange.

A rich Jewish refugee who traded in foreign currency, and whose wife traveled in and out of Axis territory, was an obvious target for surveillance by Safehaven agents. U.S. agents were also monitoring the movements of the Reichmanns after the war as they traveled in and out of North Africa. A confidential memo from U.S. officials in Tangier, dated 18 October 1945, to the American embassy in Madrid, lists passengers on Iberia Airways who had been issued air certificates. Both Samuel and Eva Reichmann were included on the list, together with Samuel's passport number and his daughter's Swedish identity card number.

So why, I asked Edward, did U.S. intelligence believe that his father was engaged in black-market activities? In his reply he strongly denied that his father had ever been engaged in any questionable activities. "It is just a fantasy. There wasn't a black market in Tangier. In Budapest in the war, or before the war, you can say there is a black market, but in Tangier everything was legal. It is nonsense. Everyone has not only friends, but enemies."

These enemies, says Edward, included one Hollander, another Hungarian Jew, who was on the Allied blacklist for selling tuna fish to the Germans. Edward believes that Hollander had probably denounced Samuel to the Americans. He also argues that, if there had been any valid evidence against his father, "he wouldn't have got a valid visa to go to America." Anti-Semitism was also a motivating factor in writing the Safehaven report, Edward believes.

In his book *The Reichmanns,* Anthony Blanco investigates and debunks allegations that the Reichmanns were war profiteers, according to one review.

As for his mother's journeys across wartime Europe, Edward argues that, although Renee was Jewish her passport was not marked as such, and she was a Hungarian national, Hungary then being an ally of the Axis countries. Renee Reichmann's extremely effective wartime relief work for Jews is well documented in contemporary accounts. As well as sending food parcels to concentration camp inmates, she also persuaded J. Rives Childs, chargé d'affaires of the U.S. legation in Tangier, to use his good offices to persuade the Spanish high commissioner, General Orgaz, to arrange for visas to be issued to 1,200 Hungarian Jews in Budapest, who were each then issued with Spanish documents, probably the most useful of the various passes being handed by foreign legations at the time, as Franco was Hitler's ally. The Jews survived. In a letter to Renee Reichmann, dated Tangier, 13 June 1945, J. Rives Child wrote: "I think you give me too much credit to attribute their saving to my efforts, because I would never have known about them if it had not been for you."

A FEW months before the defeat of the Third Reich a new medical research facility opened in Basel, the Tropical Institute. Allied intelligence thought this an institution worth investigating, as Switzerland lacked both a seacoast, through which tropical diseases might be transmitted, and colonies in the Southern Hemisphere, where its citizens might contract tropical illnesses. Germany, though, had several major ports, such as Hamburg and Bremen, from where ships sailed all over the world, including the German colonies in Africa and South America, as well as links to Japan and China.

The Tropical Institute was, of course, a Nazi front, using Swiss facilities to further the aims of the Third Reich, according to a report given to the Royal Society by Brigadier N. Hamilton Fairley on 7 February 1945. Nazi doctors were heavily involved in the institute's work and it was almost certainly setting itself up as forward base for German chemical and pharmaceutical concerns to resume their work once the war was over, Fairley believed:

> Notorious Nazi medical authorities are amongst the advertised collaborators in their new official journal, *Acta Tropica,* which is a review of tropical science and medicine. Is anything more probable than that German tropical scientists, backed by big chemical industries in Germany, are already planning ahead so as to lose no time in reestablishing their dominant position in the control of chemotherapy of tropical diseases? Such foresight would be entirely in line with part German policy.

Indeed nothing was more probable. The institute's officials included a Dr. P. Peiser, formerly of IG Farben until he left Germany in 1938, and a Dr. R. Geigy, of the family who produced the insecticide DDT, according to records in British Foreign Office files. Basel was rapidly turning into a home away from home for fleeing Nazi chemists as the Allied advance proceeded, British intelligence believed. A letter from Lord Winster to Lord Hankey, dated 16 February 1945, includes the following: "I heard yesterday that the firm of Bayer . . . has moved from Hamburg and established itself at Basel. Also that a good many Nazis connected with pharmaceutical research have likewise made their appearance in that city."

Many of the Nazi scientists would have found a ready welcome at IG Chemie. IG Chemie was a front corporation, based in Switzerland and run by IG Farben on the lines outlined in the Economics Ministry secret memo of 9 September 1939. IG Farben is most notorious as the holder of the patent for Zyklon-B, the poison used in the Nazi extermination camps' gas chambers.

"IG Chemie was set up as a cloak for IG Farben. It was nominally in the hands of Swiss and Dutch stockholders," says Marc Masurovsky. "But when the U.S. Treasury Department investigated IG Chemie during the 1940s they found all sorts of unusual goings-on, such as stock buy-backs and strange events at shareholders' meetings. The whole setup was a glaring example of how German industry used financial and industrial devices to shield its activities and interests."

IG Farben's complicity in Nazi genocide goes much deeper than perfecting the formula for Zyklon-B, for scientists working for the giant chemical concern also provided the Third Reich with two essential products needed to keep the Nazi war machine going: synthetic oil and synthetic rubber. Much of this was manufactured at the company's slave-labor plant at Auschwitz, where inmates were worked to death. For William Shirer, author of *The Rise and Fall of the Third Reich,* IG Farben was a kind of metaphor for German national complicity in genocide. He wrote:

> It is not without significance for an understanding of the Germans, even the most respectable Germans, under Hitler, that such a distinguished, internationally known firm as IG Farben, whose directors were honored as being among the leading businessmen of Germany, God-fearing men all, should deliberately choose this death camp as a suitable place for profitable operations.

Although during the late 1920s the Nazis attacked IG Farben as serving the interests of international finance capital, as the Nazi Party's strength grew, its directors, such as Georg von Schnitzler, were among the earliest backers of Hitler. So was the German banker Baron Kurt von Schroeder, who also sat on the board of the Bank for International Settlements. Together with a couple of dozen other senior German industrialists, IG Farben's von Schnitzler met with Hitler and Goering in Berlin on 20 February 1933 to pledge their support, both political and financial, for Nazism. There would be no more elections, troublesome trade unions, or subversive liberals to bother German industry, promised Goering, when he and Hitler came to power, and the industrialists donated RM3 million to the Nazi cause.

The Swiss–IG Farben connection had other murky undertones. IG Farben's subsidiaries and allied companies stretched across the globe, and these connections continued during the war, argue John Loftus and Mark Aarons in *The Secret War Against the Jews*. IG Farben had strong links with American businesses, particularly with Standard Oil of New Jersey. The two combines signed an agreement before the war to share information on synthetic rubber and gasoline technology. IG Farben's prewar lawyer in the United States was Allen Dulles, the wartime OSS station chief in Bern, who is now often portrayed as a valiant fighter against Nazism, controlling a network of dedicated secret agents in the fight against the Third Reich. But both Allen Dulles and his brother John Foster Dulles were deeply entangled in the web of financial connections that linked Nazi Germany with the United States. Allen Dulles was a former director of the German Schroeder Bank, owned by Baron von Schroeder; Allen's brother John even sat on IG Farben's board before America entered the war.

The brothers helped run a cosy little clique of Wall Street lawyers and Washington power brokers, whose international influence and power was, if anything, boosted by the conflict with Nazi Germany. In London, British intelligence tried to cut the links between IG Farben and its trading partners. During the war British intelligence ran several covert operations to try to manipulate the American press to expose the continuing connections between Nazi and American companies. The Dulles brothers fought a rearguard action to protect IG Farben, record Loftus and Aarons, quoting declassified British intelligence documents:

As the British intelligence file shows, the Dulles boys wasted no time in pressuring the British to call off their pet dogs in the American press. Here is the classified British version of how they were blackmailed into silence: "Dulles and a colleague expressed their desire to have propaganda action in the USA, as far as IG Farben is concerned, discontinued. Their explanation of this was that, in their opinion, this might involve large American companies like Standard Oil of New Jersey, etc., thus impairing the war effort."

From the Schroeder Bank to the BIS, from the OSS office in Bern to the Schroeder Bank, from IG Farben to the OSS, this malevolent old boys' network stretched across wartime Europe. Small wonder, then, that so many Nazi officers and scientists found a ready welcome for their skills and research in the offices of the American intelligence services after Germany's defeat. Nor did the Dulles brothers' Nazi links hinder their postwar careers: Allen went on to run the CIA, while his brother became secretary of state.

7

The Boat Is Full

That Switzerland is the haven of the dispossessed is our proud tradi-
tion. This is not only our thanks to the world for centuries of peace but
also and especially our acknowledgment of the great enrichment that
has been brought to us by homeless fugitives since time immemorial.

Inscription on a mountain road to the 1939 Swiss National Expo-
sition

The German government intends to mark all passports issued hence-
forth to German and Austrian Jews with a special symbol, a circle
on the first page, in which the letter J will be imprinted . . . we have
a special interest in having the symbol entered as soon as possible in
passports of such persons already outstanding.

Extract from a letter from the Swiss Federal Council to its legations and consulates, dated 4 October 1938, instructing that
German Jews applying for Swiss visas must be told to get their
passport stamped with the J symbol

He was a true hero of the Holocaust, someone of whom Switzerland could—and should—be justly proud, but he died in poverty a broken man, shamed and rejected by the country that he planned to spend his life serving.

The story of how Switzerland punished a frontier police officer who saved thousands of Jewish lives began in the summer of 1938. That was a few months after the March Anschluss (union) when Wehrmacht troops, SS and Gestapo officers following in their wake, had marched into Vienna, bringing about the historical joining in Nazi bliss of Austria and Germany. Paul Grueninger was then a career police officer, com-

mandant of the Saint Gall canton on the Austrian frontier that, after
the Anschluss, became Switzerland's border with the Third Reich.

His border post was a magnet for fleeing Austrian and German Jews.
Slowly crushed and bleeding as the first cogs of the Holocaust machine
ground into action, for them the very word "Switzerland" represented
a kind of paradise. It was an island of peace and stability in a sea of
war. Safe behind its borders, they believed, they would be free at last
from the terror of the SS, the Gestapo, German policemen, the whole
panoply of Nazi officialdom, as its functionaries began to implement
the final solution, they believed. Not only was Switzerland safe, it was
also near. The desperate Austrian and German Jews flocked in their
thousands to the border of the country that was the home of the Red
Cross and proudly boasted of its history as a refuge. And Grueninger
took the simple, humanitarian option that seems so obvious now, with
almost sixty years' hindsight, but was then by far the exception rather
than the rule—and not just in Switzerland: he let the Jews in.

But just like Swiss wartime neutrality, that humanitarian tradition
was a flexible commodity, liable to be bent on the altar of political expediency. Bern was too near Berlin, and Swiss-German relations, both
economic and political, were too important to allow them to be disrupted by streams of Jews. Germany was one of Switzerland's most
important trading partners, and two mainstays of the Swiss economy
had substantial German customers: the private banking system and
Swiss precision manufacturing industries, turning out items such as
watches—whose mechanisms were used in Wehrmacht shells and Luftwaffe bombs. Bound to Germany by ties of language, finance, and, in
some regions, culture, Switzerland was also locked into the German
economy to a substantial degree. The ministers of the Federal Council
believed that a mass influx of Jewish refugees would only disrupt
Swiss–German financial relations.

The Swiss policy of economic collaboration with the Nazis, shaped
by the interlocked elites of the ruling Federal Council and the boards
of directors of the Swiss banks, directly affected its attitude toward
admitting Jews. For where there were jobs and profits at stake, people
came second. Floods of refugees, especially Jewish ones, with their different religion and culture, could disrupt these vital financial connections—or such was the view of the Federal Council. Hadn't quiet,
tranquil, Switzerland always traded, and traded very profitably, on its

reputation for rock-solid social and economic stability? An influx of tens of thousands of Jews, all needing to be fed and housed, could only disrupt that precious peace and quiet, Swiss officials believed. On 18 August the instruction came down from the Federal Council: close the border. Grueninger, like every frontier policeman, was told to refuse entry to Jewish refugees.

Unlike the Nazis arraigned in the dock at the postwar Nuremberg trials, Commander Grueninger refused to follow orders. Daily facing at his border post waves of Jewish families clutching suitcases into which they had packed a few meager possessions before fleeing their homes, he kept the frontier open. Not only did he defy Bern's ruling, he repeatedly broke the law to help the Jews enter Switzerland. It was easy enough to throw open the border gates, but once inside the country the Jews had to deal with officialdom, and the first thing any Swiss bureaucrat would demand was their passports. Without the right stamps they were liable to be thrown out, back into the hands of the Nazis. As late as August 1942 a thousand Jews who believed they had reached sanctuary inside Switzerland were forced back over the border into Vichy France.

The answer, Grueninger decided, was to falsify the official seals in the Jews' passports, to deceive Swiss officials into believing that the Jews had entered the country before the August ruling. Between that month and December 1938 Grueninger allowed 3,600 Jews entry into Switzerland and altered their papers. Grueninger was a policeman who was paid and trained to uphold the law. But his new role as temporary savior of Jewish refugees meant it was more important to break the law than observe its rulings that, in effect, ultimately helped condemn tens of thousands of Jews to death. The lifesaving open gate, though, was shut in just a few months, for Grueninger's actions were being monitored by German diplomats in Bern, who alerted the Swiss government that one of their frontier officials was letting in Jews. Dancing to Berlin's tune, Swiss officialdom swung into action.

In December 1938 Grueninger was suspended from his post, which he would never regain. Not only was he removed from his job, but in January 1939 the Swiss government opened an inquiry into his activities and filed charges against him of forging documents and abusing his powers. In 1941 he was found guilty of insubordination and sentenced to losing his job, a stiff fine, and forfeiture of all retirement and severance payments. His punishment lasted the rest of his life, until he died in 1971. Paul Grueninger never found another suitable position and drifted from job to job. But even that wasn't enough, and Grueninger was hounded by a smear campaign alleging that he took money from Jews or demanded sexual favors to let them in. They were lies, and in 1971 the former police commander was recognized by the Jerusalem-based Yad Vashem Holocaust Memorial Foundation as "Righteous Among the Nations," an honor given to non-Jews who saved Jews during the Holocaust.

The criteria are strict for anyone proposed as "Righteous Among the Nations"—and nobody may propose himself—demanding testimony from survivors and exhaustive cross-checking, but still the Swiss government refused, time and time again, to fully rehabilitate the man of whom they should have been so proud. It took five attempts by his family to properly clear his good name, although he was politically and morally rehabilitated by the cantonal government in St. Gallen in 1993 and by the Federal Government in 1994.

As the campaign to legally rehabilitate Grueninger grew, it was even joined by the then American ambassador to Switzerland, Larry Lawrence. In a letter to the Swiss government he wrote, using quite undiplomatic language, "It is my personal conviction that nothing short of the full legal rehabilitation of Mr. Grueninger would be sufficient to remove this unfortunate stain on Switzerland's reputation as a champion of human rights." The then Swiss justice minister, Arnold Koller, replied that Grueninger had already been "morally rehabilitated" and deserved respect for his actions. Eventually, a new court hearing was set, for 30 November 1995, to rule on whether Paul Grueninger should be acquitted of all charges.

By then, the verdict was never in doubt. On that day, finally, in the same courtroom where, fifty-five years earlier, Grueninger had been stripped of his post and humiliated, his name was cleared. Grueninger had been justified in faking the entry documents to allow the Jews in, said the court president, Werner Baldegger. The former police commander was acquitted of all charges.

LONG BEFORE Hitler took power, Switzerland had enjoyed a reputation of being a haven for refugees, and of providing political asylum to those persecuted at home for their political beliefs. Democrats, Republicans,

Marxists, even Lenin himself had taken refuge there to plot the Bol-
shevik revolution in the cafés of Zürich, before the Germans put him
on a sealed train to Russia, to bring down the tsar and build the workers' paradise. But while a handful of Russian revolutionaries plotting
over coffee was one thing, even good PR for liberal, humanitarian
Switzerland, a mass influx of fleeing Jews was another. So unhappy was
the Swiss government about even the prospect of their arrival that it
refused to host the conference that President Franklin D. Roosevelt
called in 1938 to discuss the problem of Jewish refugees. Representatives of thirty-two countries met on the shore of Lake Geneva, but on
the French side of the lake, in the resort town of Evian-les-Bains. Not
only Switzerland but virtually every country was unwilling to adequately
open its doors to persecuted Jews. The conference failed to come up
with any concrete answers for the problem of the coming waves of
Jewish emigration, and many historians argue that the West's unwill-
ingness at Evian to provide for refuge for the Jews gave a green light to
Berlin to proceed apace with the organization of the Holocaust.

Why was the Swiss government so reluctant to let the Jews in, or
even host a conference where other nations might decide to? A key
reason, given at the time, was that waves of Jewish immigrants would
increase anti-Semitism among the Swiss population. As the Jews were
not let in en masse, it is impossible to say whether this would have happened. Probably not, as much of the Swiss public found the Nazis'
racial mania quite abhorrent and had little sympathy for the Third
Reich.

But either way this argument was a political feint, for the real reason
to close the gate of sanctuary was, in fact, anti-Semitism, pure and
simple, combined with a fear of offending Berlin. The Federal Council
feared that even the simple, humanitarian act of hosting the Evian conference would send the wrong message out to persecuted Jews, that
Switzerland was a place of sanctuary for them. Switzerland was a transit country for Jews, and no more. That the Federal Council specifically singled out Jews, and Jews alone, for exclusion is shown by the
events surrounding the introduction of the J-stamp in the passports of
German and Austrian Jews, to enable Swiss border guards to distinguish them from Christians, about which more follows in this chapter.

The latest investigations by Swiss researchers in the federal and cantonal archives of Bern, Zürich, and Geneva have demolished the myth

that Switzerland offered a safe haven for Jews who managed to travel across wartime Europe to the country they imagined would provide a sanctuary. Like much of Swiss wartime history, its reputation as a refuge for fleeing Jews is the stuff of myth and legend, which shrinks and withers under historians' scrutiny. For years Swiss historians had believed that a maximum of about 10,000 refugees had been turned back from the border by Swiss frontier police, but new research reveals that the true total is three times that: 30,000 refugees, the vast majority of them Jews, were refused entry, most of them during and after 1942, when the Holocaust was in full flow.

But this dark part of Swiss history began several years before the war. For while Jews' money was always welcome at Swiss banks, Jews themselves received a more ambivalent welcome from the Swiss, their coreligionists included; some of them, like the Federal Council, feared that a massive influx of Eastern European Jews, who did not share the rigid Swiss cultural mores, would incite anti-Semitism. Still the Swiss Jewish community combated anti-Semitism, taking legal steps in 1933 against two Nazis who were distributing in Switzerland the notorious anti-Semitic work *The Protocols of the Elders of Zion,* a forgery concocted by the tsarist secret police that purported to outline the mechanics of the mythical international Jewish conspiracy. Some Jews took more than legal steps against Nazi agitators, and in 1936 a Swiss Jewish student, David Frankfurter, assassinated the Swiss Nazi leader Wilhelm Gustloff.

Two years after the assassination, the Federal Council took a decision for which, fifty-seven years later, its successor members would apologize. As well as triggering the August 1938 order to close the borders, the Anschluss also led to the rapid implementation of Switzerland's most shameful prewar policy decision: the introduction of the J-stamp. Fearful of a mass influx of Jewish refugees, Switzerland arranged with Nazi Germany for the passports of Jews living in the Third Reich to be stamped with the telltale *J. J* was short for the word "Juden"—German for "Jew"—which was later written across the yellow Star of David worn by Jews across Eastern Europe who languished, and died, under German rule. The J-stamp was a German measure that affected German and Austrian citizens, but its provenance was purely Swiss, and it was introduced by Berlin only after sustained and persistent pressure from Bern.

The J-stamp was introduced in October 1938, but it had its genesis as early as the spring of that year, when Swiss authorities began requesting that the passports of German Jews be changed so that they would be readily identifiable to Swiss border guards and consular authorities. On 13 April 1938, a month after the Anschluss, the Swiss Federal Department of Police and Justice wrote to the Swiss legation in Berlin, asking that German passports not be issued to Austrian emigrants—shorthand for Jews—in the same way as those issued to German Austrians who enjoyed a "normal relationship" with the state, meaning Christians.

The answer, suggested the Swiss officials, was for Jews to be given Austrian passports or, alternatively, passports of shorter validity. Aryan Germans would not have to apply for Swiss visas, but Jews, holding the proposed shorter passports, or Austrian ones, would have to. The main thing was to be able to distinguish between those Germans who worshiped at a synagogue, who would not be allowed in, and good Christian, Aryan, churchgoers, who would be. The spirit of the Nazi Nuremberg Laws, which restricted Jewish life and institutionalized the Third Reich's anti-Semitism, sat quite well in Bern, as well as in Berlin.

"We hope that the German government will be receptive to a solution that will enable us to limit the entrance of such emigrants by means of visa inspection, and we are prepared to propose to the Federal Council the measures that will limit this control as much as possible to such foreigners alone," the Swiss officials wrote to their colleagues in Berlin. All of which was shorthand for "No Jews wanted here."

"In August 1938, a few months after the Anschluss, the Swiss closed the border and introduced a visa requirement for all Austrians. This was a specific measure aimed at Austrian Jews: they had to prove they had a visa for another country, or a lot of money," says the Swiss historian Guido Koller, who has extensively researched Swiss wartime refugee policy. "As long as Austrian passports were valid it was easy to detect Jewish refugees, because almost everyone trying to get in was Jewish. Then Germany announced that all Austrian passports would be replaced by German ones, and a lot of Jews were leaving Germany. The authorities wanted to control immigration, but didn't want to introduce a visa requirement for Germans, because of economic reasons, because it would have disrupted trade relations."

Nazi officials were not as keen on the J-stamp proposal as might be expected. At this stage of the Holocaust mass emigration of Jews, rather than their extermination, was still an option in Berlin for dealing with the Jewish problem. But who would want to give sanctuary to German Jewish refugees when their passports were so clearly marked with the J? It was the bureaucratic equivalent of a leper's bell, for not only Switzerland but much of the rest of Europe and the Americas had virtually closed their doors to Jewish refugees. German foreign ministry officials such as Privy Councilor Roediger were not happy that Switzerland was introducing such restrictions on German Jews. Paul Dinichert, the Swiss minister to Nazi Germany, reported on their discussions about this tricky issue and on Roediger's views that "Germany had a direct interest in the emigration of these people provided that on the other hand no one would be damaged by accepting them. On the other hand it would hardly be possible to identify them in advance through their passports and thus make it more difficult for them to leave. There was also a fear that the Swiss precedent might establish a trend."

The problem for Switzerland was that if Bern introduced a visa requirement for all Germans, of whatever religion, Germany would reciprocate with a similar measure, which would be very inconvenient for Swiss businessmen, whose interests in Nazi Germany were a vital component of the Swiss economy. Paul Dinichert's report to the Federal Council suggested a visa requirement be applied to non-Aryan Germans, i.e., Jews.

> The simplest solution, of course, would be to restrict the requirement for a visa to non-Aryan German citizens. This is admittedly repugnant to our principles, but it could easily be justified in that it is also to the interests of Swiss Jews to be protected against any further influx of foreign Jews. Inasmuch as other countries, such as Hungary and Romania, are enacting more and more special restrictions on Jews, which are bound to lead to a new upsurge in the Jewish tendency to migration, it might prove worthwhile to give closer consideration to such a regulation.

Such measures of extraordinary cynicism in a country that prided itself on its supposed humanitarian traditions did not prove "repugnant" at all. The suggestion that Jews' passports be stamped with a J was first voiced at a meeting in the Nazi foreign ministry in Berlin, by Hans

Froelicher, successor to Paul Dinichert, after Swiss authorities had protested against illegal shipments across the Swiss frontier by German authorities, writes Alfred Haesler in his book *The Lifeboat Is Full*, an examination of Swiss refugee policy in the 1930s and 1940s. Dinichert's colleague, one Dr. Kappeler, pushed for even more stringent measures. In his report to Bern dated 20 August, Dr. Kappeler stated that the German foreign ministry was inclined to reach a compromise with Switzerland. Thanks to his request, German passport offices in Vienna, Cologne, Aachen, and Trier, and the German consulate in Rome, were ordered not to grant passports valid for foreign travel to Jews, unless it could be absolutely established that the passports would not be used to enter Switzerland. German officials even promised that they would instruct passport offices not to grant passports to Jews who Nazi officials suspected might intend to travel to Switzerland, unless the Jewish applicant could prove that he had right of entry there.

So tightened the bureaucratic web of Swiss restrictions that would trap German and Austrian Jews in the Nazi genocide machine. In fact, the bureaucrats at the Swiss embassy in Berlin were out of step with many of their fellow Swiss, who took a far more critical attitude to the Nazis' anti-Jewish policies. Relations between the two countries had become strained following Frankfurter's murder of the Swiss Nazi leader Gustloff, and the Federal Council had even banned the German Nazi Party from organizing and propagating Nazi doctrines in Switzerland. At the same time, the Swiss press, much of which was fiercely anti-Nazi throughout the war, was stepping up its harsh criticism of the Nazi regime.

A range of possible measures designed to keep Jews out of Switzerland were batted back and forth between Berlin and Bern that summer of 1938, as both countries' legal minds exercised their best bureaucratic talents over this tricky diplomatic problem and its possible consequences. For if Switzerland introduced visas for German Jews, then would not Germany have the right to introduce visas for Swiss Jews? But how to tell which Swiss citizens were Jewish, and which Aryan? Would the passports of Swiss Jews, living in their happy humanitarian refuge, have to be marked with a *J* also? This last proposal, that Switzerland mark the passports of its own Jewish citizens, was too much even for the Swiss diplomats in Berlin, who appear to have gone completely native on the Nazi approach to the Jewish question.

But on the matter of how to keep German Jews out of Switzerland there was, finally, good news, wrote the Swiss diplomat Dr. Kappeler. The Nazis had come up with two ideas to aid Swiss border guards in filtering out Jewish refugees. The first was that the passport holder's name be underlined in red ink, much as the report card of a naughty schoolboy might be, although the consequences of this marking would be more serious; the second, that the first page of the passport be imprinted with a circle about three-quarters of an inch wide, containing the letter *J*. Finally, then, a solution—part of a larger and also final one. Dr. Kappeler was bubbling with enthusiasm as he wrote to his superiors in Bern:

> It is my opinion that the German government's suggestions represent a very substantial compromise and that the solution proposed by Berlin is acceptable to us. It achieves the desired one hundred percent control over the entry of non-Aryan emigrants and makes it possible to settle every case quickly at the border, where the presence of the stamp on the first page, and in appropriate cases, of the visa, must be verified.

This then was the genesis of the J-stamp requirement for German and Austrian Jews, as formalized in the Swiss–German agreement of October 1938. Or, as Guido Koller says, "Switzerland asked Germany what could be done to control the influx of Jews, and the Swiss authorities threatened to introduce a visa for all Germans, so the German authorities came up with the J-stamp idea. It was a German idea, but it was introduced because of Swiss demands. Switzerland asked Germany to do something, and Germany came up with a solution. It was clearly racist, it broke international law, and that is to the shame of Switzerland."

BUT THE J-stamp was not enough for the Federal Council. In August 1942 a new law was passed that, in effect, hermetically sealed off the borders to fleeing Jews, just as the Holocaust was going into overdrive. This legislation was not passed in isolation; rather it was the ultimate step in a policy of excluding Jews that stretched back for years before the outbreak of the war and was the logical consequence of the J-stamp agreement.

The 1942 law, which was immediately denounced by Swiss churches and refugee and humanitarian groups, said that Jews were refugees for reasons of race, not politics. They would be sent back to Germany or Vichy France, even at risk to their lives. In fact, there was no doubt at all about the risk in sending the Jews back, as their fate was virtually assured: the gas chambers and the crematoria.

And even more sinister currents run underneath the decision to seal the borders: the driving force behind the legislation was Heinrich Rothmund, head of the police division in the Federal Department of Police and Justice, who had worked there since the 1920s.

Rothmund made stringent efforts to keep Switzerland a *through* country for refugees, rather than a place of permanent sanctuary. Would-be entrants had to show either that they had enough funds to support themselves and any dependants, or have the necessary transit visas, generally for France, Spain and Portugal, to exit Europe, as well as a full entry visa for another country, to show they would not be staying too long. "Rothmund was the central figure shaping Swiss policy on foreigners and refugees," says Guido Koller. "He prepared all the decisions and carried them out. He knew everything."

The August 1942 law came a month after the Federal Council received a report from the police outlining how Jews in the Third Reich were being deported en masse, shot as hostages, or sent to camps where the conditions were, it said, "terrible."

For the new generation of Swiss historians trying to discover the murky truth about their country's wartime past, such as Koller, the 1942 law is "one of the most shameful episodes in Swiss history." That law sealing the border was passed by the Swiss Federal Council just as accurate reports about the full extent of the Holocaust were reaching Swiss officials and, almost certainly, members of the Federal Council. By then gas chambers and mobile gas vans had been in use for nearly a year, and many of the 6 million Jews killed in the Holocaust had already been slaughtered, mainly in Poland and Russia, although it is not clear if the Federal Council knew of the mass killings by Zyklon-B.

August 1942 was also the month that Gerhard Riegner, Geneva-based representative of the World Jewish Congress, sent his telegram to London and New York, alerting the world of the Germans' plans to exterminate European Jewry and the use of prussic acid as a poison gas. Whether or not the Federal Council knew the full extent of the horrors of Auschwitz, its members certainly knew that dreadful events were occurring to the Jews under Nazi rule, says Koller.

"Information came through in the summer and autumn of 1942 about what was happening the Jews. The people in authority [the government] knew about the deportations, they knew that French and German policemen took Jews hostage, and they knew the deportations ended in the camps, where the situation was terrible. In July 1942 the police compiled a report on what was happening to the Jews in relation to Switzerland and refugee policy."

The public outcry over the August 1942 law led to its rapid amelioration and ten days later, on 23 August, a telephone order was issued to border police that they should accept Jews under sixteen, anyone with connections to Switzerland, families, and old people. Others were handed back to the Gestapo.

The true total of those who made it over the border and were sent back, or were merely refused entry by the frontier police, will never be accurately tallied; not every name was recorded, and many records of refugees refused entry were destroyed in the 1950s. Either way, the legend of Swiss wartime humanitarianism is shattered, says Koller. "We can say through our research that Switzerland refused over thirty thousand people entry who tried to find refuge there in the war. These thirty thousand were not only Jews, although the majority were. There were also Poles, Russians, men and women who had escaped from forced-labor camps, Italian and French young men. Swiss history is full of myths and legends. One of them is that Swiss policy to refugees was positive, humanitarian, and was a legitimation of neutrality. Now this legend is broken, and the public has to face reality."

And the reality of Switzerland's prewar and wartime refugee policy is shameful, says Thomas Lyssy, vice-president of the Swiss Federation of Jewish Communities. "Switzerland has lost its shiny and bright façade, and I think it is good. The J-stamp was the first thing. Now they have found out what we thought a long time ago: that there were more than thirty thousand refugees sent back, not only ten thousand, like they said. In my opinion Switzerland could have taken these people. Other people are saying if they had taken them, then maybe Hitler would have invaded, but this is hypothetical—there was space for all of them. Switzerland was the last safe haven, but it didn't take them: it sent them back, and they knew exactly what happened to them. This is a very dark part of Swiss history, the question of refugees. Darker than today with the banks."

Could Switzerland really have taken more Jewish refugees? That Switzerland could have taken at least those 30,000 refused Jews is evinced by the fact that on one day in April 1945 there were over 100,000 refugees in the country, says Guido Koller. If there was room in April, then there was room during the war years. "The only thing we can say is that in the summer of 1942 the boat was not full. . . . It is clear that Switzerland could have taken them: there were enough places for them and enough food."

THE Swiss Federal Council could issue reams of orders to the border police to fortify its frontiers against Jewish refugees, but even fortress Switzerland was not impregnable in August 1942, as the Swiss policemen interrogating eight-year-old Isabelle Riff were discovering, to their growing annoyance. Together with her four-year-old sister, Charlotte, Isabelle was held in the Bern main police station, where police officers were trying to make her reveal where and how she had crossed the border, and who had helped her. Their tactics varied from using persistent questioning to bringing in piles of cream cakes, but even at eight years old Isabelle knew not to talk about the underground resistance network that had brought her in from southern France, where, together with their Nazi allies, French policemen were rounding up Jews for deportation to Auschwitz, and where she had been forced to leave her parents, who were in hiding.

Now living in Hendon, in northwest London, and married to Rabbi Sydney Silberg, Isabelle still recalls every detail of her interrogation by the police. "Everybody looked at us in disbelief, that two children could cross into Switzerland, reach Bern, and not be detected. The police took me into a room. They kept me there the whole day. There was a big map the size of the wall, and they gave me a bamboo stick in my hand to point out where we had crossed. They wanted me to tell them the names of the people who helped in France and tell them where I crossed into Switzerland. They brought in eclairs for me to eat—they tried to bribe me with cakes. They didn't threaten me, but they insisted. They interrogated me the whole day. They wanted to get the names of the people in Switzerland who helped me. I said I didn't know, or had forgotten. I said I couldn't remember where I crossed."

The two little Jewish girls' arrival in Bern was the culmination of a two-and-a-half-year journey from their family home in Antwerp, Belgium, that saw them made homeless and bombed, and their father wounded by shrapnel. The Riffs made their way across wartime Europe on a seemingly endless trek through a series of temporary refuges, where the family could, for a time, try to stay together.

But it was a journey that would ultimately separate the sisters from their parents for the rest of the war. Isabelle Riff was six and a half years old when the Nazis invaded Belgium in May 1940, and two days later the family was packed and ready to leave. They traveled for days, sitting on the floor in cattle wagons. From Antwerp they went to Abbeville, in France, when an order came over the loudspeaker that all passengers must disembark immediately.

"The train stopped there in the middle of some cornfields. It was beautiful: there were flowers everywhere. They told us to run for shelter because there was an air raid. We ran through the cornfields and lay down and covered ourselves with leaves and tried to cover ourselves with branches," she says. "The German planes came right down over us, and when we looked up we could see the pilots in the cockpits, shooting and strafing us and dropping bombs. Most of us were civilians, but there were a lot of soldiers. After the air raid there were dead people and wounded people. My father was hit by shrapnel in the base of his head and his shoulder. My uncle threw himself on top of me. I remember him whispering in my ear, 'Now say the *Shema* [the most important Jewish prayer] because we are all going to die here.' He was also hit by shrapnel, which went right through his shoulder, but it remained in his shirt, and that is how I was saved. I was six and a half, but I remember as if it happened yesterday. We had to leave my father and my uncle there, because they were wounded and bleeding. There were a lot of people dead, wounded, wailing, waiting for the Red Cross."

Miraculously, the Riffs were reunited at Rouen station, where Isabelle and Charlotte found their father and uncle sitting on a bench, covered with bandages and still wearing the hats worn by Orthodox Jews. From Rouen the family traveled to Beziers in the south of France, where they stayed for over two years, until her parents decided after a visit from her uncle, who was in the resistance, that the German advance across Europe meant it was too dangerous to stay.

"My mother's brother was a student in Montpellier and in contact with the underground," says Isabelle. "He came to Beziers to see us, and he told my parents that times were very hard, very dark, and the only way for the children to survive was to give them away to Christians. He knew about the concentration camps and the extermination camps. There was a big discussion, with the argument that my parents shouldn't give away their children, because with children people would have pity on us, have *rachmanas* [mercy]. But in those days there was no pity. Somehow my mother understood the situation better than my father. She told my uncle to make whatever arrangements he needed. He told my parents that the only way for them to survive for the time being was to go into hiding."

Then came the letter from the Beziers town council to the Riffs' home, instructing them to assemble at a certain time, at a certain place, with a suitcase. Forewarned by Isabelle's brother, the Riffs split up and the children fled. Their landlady agreed to hide Isabelle's parents, but said the children must leave, because they would not be able to keep silent.

Isabelle and Charlotte moved to a nearby village, where their aunt was staying, but there was no safety there. Isabelle recalls, "As soon as we arrived, very early in the morning, we heard a lot of commotion, shouting, screaming. We looked out of the window, and we could see French gendarmerie and German Gestapo, with two large vans standing outside. They were shouting '*Raus, raus, alle Juden, raus, raus*' [Out, out, all Jews out]. The French gendarmerie also came into the house, and we were all sent out into the street. I got hold of my sister, and I was holding her by the hand, and we watched our friends and neighbors shoved and pushed into the vans. For some unexplainable reason, I don't know why, only my sister and I were left standing on the pavement. Until today I don't know why we remained there. The people who were deported in the bus, we never heard of again. Everything went quiet after that."

From then on nowhere in France could be safe for the two little Jewish girls. Their uncle in the resistance arranged for them to be taken across the border into Switzerland. But before they left, there was to be a tearful goodbye to their parents, still hiding in Beziers.

Isabelle remembers that "it was very hot, a tropical climate, when we returned. We walked through the streets—it was very quiet, siesta time—until we reached the place where our parents were hiding. We had to take off our shoes and be very quiet so that nobody should notice us. We reached the top floor, and my parents were standing there in their socks, overwhelmed to see us. They had heard about the roundup in the village, so it was a great relief to them to see us.

"My mother insisted we had to sit down and have a meal, and somehow she had bought us two long summer dresses. She gave me a little leather handbag with a strap and put two hundred and fifty French francs inside. She said that I had to be very careful with it, because she didn't know when she would be able to give me some more. She put a little comb, a nail file, nail scissors, into my handbag, and she wanted me to show her how I would look after my sister, how I would cut her nails. I was eight and a half, my sister was four. She kept on repeating to me, 'Never forget that you are Jewish.'

"We didn't stay long, because the landlady was anxious that people shouldn't hear that anyone was in the attic. My father blessed us, as a Jewish father blesses his children on a Friday evening. There is no need to say—it was a painful separation. We went down into the street, in the blazing sunshine, and the landlady took us by the hand, and said, 'From now on, you are no longer Jewish. If anybody asks you if you are Jewish, you deny it.' A minute before, my mother had told me never to forget that I was Jewish. The next minute, the landlady was telling us that we didn't look Jewish: we were fair, we were blond, we are not Jewish.

"We walked through the park where we used to play, and there were monkeys there in a cage, and I remember, even as a child, thinking: I wish I was an animal behind the cage, because then I wouldn't have to run. It was difficult to understand what was the reason why I had to hide and run away from people, what was the big crime I had committed, that we had to run, and fear people."

In Beziers the two sisters were handed over to the resistance. Together with a French student, they traveled through the night to the town of Thonon on the French side of Lake Geneva, not far from Evian-les-Bains, where four years earlier thirty-two countries had met to agree on how they didn't want to take in Jewish refugees.

"My sister and I sat in one corner, and the student sat in the other corner. We were not supposed to talk to him. He was accompanying us, but if something happened we were not together, because we had no papers. It was night when we reached Thonon, and I looked out of the window. I could see the passport control outside, with French gen-

darmerie and German Gestapo—they always worked hand in hand.
They got onto the train together, and when I saw that I got hold of my
sister's hand and told her that we were going to the toilet. Fortunately,
somebody opened the door of the train. The gendarme outside must
have been in a happy mood, and he lifted her off the train. Somehow,
I don't know how, we ducked the control and we were out. The student
was with us; he had papers."

Together with the student, Isabelle and Charlotte stayed in Thonon
for a week, waiting for their contact. After seven days without news
from the resistance, the student became anxious and telephoned their
uncle in Montpelier. But the telephone was tapped, and within an hour
the Gestapo arrived at the hotel, looking for the sisters. "When the
Gestapo turned up, the windows were open, so I got hold of my sister
and we walked out into the street. At that moment there was a performance going on, with a dancing bear and somebody singing. We min-
gled in the crowd of the people watching. We were children and we
forgot ourselves, and just stayed and watched."

Isabelle and her sister returned to the hotel and quickly moved on
to the next way station on the underground network that smuggled
Jewish refugees into Switzerland: a cellar in the house of a Protestant
priest. "We said goodbye to the student, and of course we were sepa-
rated from our parents, so we had got terribly attached to him. The
separation was painful, but you grow mature overnight, and we knew
there was no time for crying, for hysterics. The priest had a lovely
house, with a garden where the vines were full of grapes, and they
made us welcome."

The endless moving, running, and hiding, though, was taking its toll
on the little girls, who just wanted to stop running. "In the evening we
had supper in the cellar, where there were other Jews hiding: men,
some with beards, and women. All of them wanted to go to Switzerland. My first reaction when we arrived was 'Can I stay here?' "

But here too there was no sanctuary. "After about a week, we were
woken in the middle of the night: the priest's daughter came in and
said, 'Get dressed. The Gestapo are coming.' She took us to a friend of
hers, a very fat, jolly old lady. The next day the priest's daughter arrived
at her house and told us she was taking us to an orphanage high up in
the mountains, very close to the Swiss border. We arrived there in the
evening, after a long journey, and she warned us not to speak to the

staff, although we could talk to the children. It was a Thursday evening, and she said if the weather was fine on Sunday morning we would all go out into the woods to gather mushrooms in little baskets, but at a certain time she would tell us when to leave the group, and she would show us the way, where to cross into Switzerland.

"The Sunday came, and the whole orphanage climbed into buses, and we went into the mountains. It was so quiet, so serene, and I couldn't understand why I couldn't stay. We got a little basket. The teachers showed us which mushrooms to gather. Then we got the signal, and the priest's daughter walked with us. She showed us the green pasture going down into the valley, where there was a wide road, and she showed us the guards, in their huts. She told us exactly when they go out patrolling, and told us, 'We want you to go now, because that is in between the time they go out and come back.' She told us to walk always between the trees and watch the main road. There in the woods, at a certain distance, she said, there would be somebody waiting for us. She hoped that by the time we met that man we would be in Switzerland. There was no crying, no argument. She said, 'Now you go.' And we went.

"We started walking. It must have rained very heavily the day before. There were a lot of leaves on the floor—the ground was really sodden. My mother had given my sister a new pair of shoes, and the sole became undone. She wanted me to carry her, but she was too heavy. I kept on pulling her behind me, and suddenly—I can't remember how long we walked, it seemed an eternity—in the distance I saw something moving in the woods. I realized it was a man, and I left my sister on the floor, and I started running after the man. I had an uncle in Switzerland, and in my wild imagination I thought it would be him. I hugged him, and he calmed me down and told me he wasn't my uncle."

The two sisters had successfully crossed the border, where the Swiss section of the underground railway was waiting for them. "The man had a sandwich box, and he took out some Swiss chocolates to eat, and they tasted so heavenly. We followed him into a village, into a house. They made us welcome. Everywhere they were very warm and welcoming people. Again, my first reaction when I got there was 'Can I stay here?' They said we couldn't stay there, though, because they knew that the Swiss border patrol handed back Jews to the Germans. So to make sure that we could stay in Switzerland we had to reach Bern, before the authorities knew about us. From there [at the border] another student turned up, and took us on the train to Lausanne, from there to Bern. There my uncle was waiting at the station."

For the two little Jewish girls, who had been bombed, made homeless, left their parents, and escaped the Gestapo, who had been shunted from stranger to stranger, who had walked across an international border on their own without an adult, who had come from wartime France with its food shortages and Nazi persecution, Switzerland seemed like a paradise. It was hard to believe that this peaceful country bordered a continent at war.

"Switzerland was so beautiful, so manicured, I couldn't get over it. Coming from wartime France, Switzerland was like a toy town to me, with the cleanliness of the train and the railway station. I just couldn't believe it. That night we wrote a card to my parents, which my parents received. My parents tried to follow us on the same route, but they were arrested and taken to a camp."

The next morning Isabelle and her sister went to the police station in Bern, together with their uncle. As children they would be allowed to stay, so the authorities had to be alerted to their presence, to arrange shelter and schooling. Their uncle, though, had refugee status and so could not look after the little girls himself. Hours of relentless questioning failed to persuade the little girl to talk, and in the evening the two sisters were given permission to stay.

A month after their arrival they stayed with a Jewish man who was waiting for his family, but once the family arrived there was no more space for the two girls, and they had to leave. Another family offered to take Isabelle, but without her sister. "The Swiss officials threatened me that if I didn't go without her they would send me to a [refugee] camp. I told them, 'All right, send me to a camp, but I promised my mother that I wouldn't leave my sister.' Then the family said they would take both of us."

The sisters stayed with the family, who lived just outside Bern, for more than three years, until the war was over. From there they wrote to their parents, who had been interned in a French concentration camp after being captured while trying to cross into Switzerland. Isabelle Singer still has copies of the letters she wrote to her parents in the Gurs camp, in her childish hand, full of carefully inscribed good wishes and exclamations of love. Letters to camp inmates could be no longer than twenty-five words. One of hers was thirty words long, and on it the German censor stamped, "We do not have time to read novels. Letters of this length will be destroyed."

Life with the Swiss family was the next best thing to being at home. The sisters were well treated, although their presence went unnoticed by the local Jewish community. Isabelle says, "My personal experience is that, wherever we went, people were bending over backwards to be kind to us. I can't complain about anybody in Switzerland, apart from the interrogation when I arrived. I went to school. If I needed medical help they looked after us, and we went to the *cheder* [Jewish religious school] in Bern. But I didn't meet any other refugee children. The Jewish community made no special effort, although you would think that if a Jewish refugee child came they would organize something. I don't think they were really aware of what was going on outside Switzerland."

Thanks to the senior Riffs' indomitable landlady, Mme. Dessus, who had hidden Isabelle's parents in Beziers, they survived the war. After they were put into the Gurs camp, Mme. Dessus traveled to Vichy France, where somehow she managed to obtain release papers for them, and they were freed, escaping deportation to the East, and Auschwitz.

Hermann and Gizelle Riff passed the rest of the war in a small village in southern France. In January 1945, six months after the liberation of France by the Allies, Isabelle's mother came to fetch her daughters. But the years on the run, the loss of the family home, her time in a concentration camp, and the separation from her beloved children had all taken their toll, says Isabelle. "She wasn't the same person as the elegant woman I remembered. She was a broken person."

Isabelle and Charlotte Riff were two of about 22,000 Jewish refugees who found sanctuary in wartime Switzerland, included in the total of 230,000 who passed through the country. Those 230,000 refugees all found safety in Switzerland, but few found comfort. Many were held in camps, behind barbed wire and guards, that for some were all too reminiscent of the Nazi concentration camps from which they had escaped, although the refugees were not in danger of being killed or tortured. The camp system was set up in the autumn of 1942, after the August law sealing the border was relaxed, following a public outcry. The first camp was set up at the frontier near Geneva, initially as a collection point to hold refugees before they were sent on to other camps being built across the country. The general rule was that fit young males were held behind the wire and put to work, often at tough manual labor, while women and children were hosted by Swiss families, many of whom wrote to the authorities offering a place for a refugee.

Conditions in the Swiss refugee camps were certainly much better than being under Nazi rule, but they were not holiday resorts. The diet was basic and medical attention often cursory at best. Children, too, sometimes spent time at them before being sent on to hosts, and some remained there, often without any special provision being made for their educational and social needs.

For Betty Bloom, originally from Berlin and now living in London, the poor conditions at the camps in Switzerland—where she passed much of the war as a Jewish refugee and fell seriously ill—almost certainly cost her the chance to have children. Just like Isabelle Riff, Betty Bloom was brought to the border by the underground, in her case the Jewish resistance operating in that southwestern sector of France where she had fled. Together with another family, but without her parents, she sneaked across the border when she was thirteen, into the arms of the Swiss police, who interrogated her before sending her on to the refugee camp at Champery.

"We couldn't leave the camp," Bloom recalls. "To me it was like a concentration camp: there were guards around, there was barbed wire. We had nothing, we had no change of underwear, because I couldn't take anything from France."

They were long and empty days behind the Swiss barbed wire, Bloom says. "I didn't do anything, because there was no schooling. We all had jaundice because of the conditions in France where we had been, but the conditions in Switzerland were no better. I used to get food parcels from a godparent in Switzerland, sardines, and to this day I cannot eat sardines. We couldn't leave the camp. One day they didn't give us any food, because somebody had done something wrong. I was in three camps, and I was ill in one, but nobody took any notice. I had TB, TB of the fallopian tubes, and that is why I never had children. . . . There was no medical attention."

Switzerland gave Betty Bloom sanctuary, but even now she is bitter at the conditions in which she lived. "A lot of women are childless, for very many reasons. But various doctors I went to [after the war] all came to the same conclusion. They asked me about my background. Obviously I was undernourished in the war—there were all sorts of things wrong. But when I told them the symptoms, they said it was TB of the fallopian tubes. I was thirteen. I was very, very sore about that. What can I say?"

To the extent that they held the funds of organizations such as the Geneva branch of the World Jewish Congress and other groups that ran rescue and relief operations, some Swiss banks aided Jewish refugees. But of all the accounts in Swiss banks opened to hold funds to help persecuted Jews, the most extraordinary was the one in the name of Albert Goering, whose brother was Hermann Goering, head of the Nazi Luftwaffe. One of the prime architects of the Holocaust, Hermann Goering escaped the hangman's noose by committing suicide.

Unlike his brother, Albert Goering wanted to save, not kill, Jews, and he opened an account at Bank Orelli in Bern to do so. The money was made available to his Hungarian Jewish doctor, Ladislao Kovacs, according to declassified British intelligence documents. Albert Goering's humanitarianism is one of the most remarkable footnotes of the Second World War. Not only did he donate his own funds to help Jews, the report says, but he also used his position as Hermann Goering's brother to extend his personal protection to Dr. Kovacs once the Germans occupied Rome, where they both lived.

This astonishing story, like so many previously unreported episodes of the war, lies in the faded piles of paper in the archives that still hold so many wartime secrets—in this case, the British Public Records Office files on the activities of the Special Operations Executive (SOE) in wartime Hungary. The SOE's mission was to operate behind German lines, gathering intelligence, disrupting communications, sabotaging transport, killing Nazi officials, blowing up ammunition dumps, and generally wreaking havoc. In short, SOE operatives were to do as much as possible to "set Europe ablaze," as Churchill had instructed. Every SOE agent knew there was a high chance that he or she would never return. They worked alone or in small groups on Nazi-occupied territory, often operating among a hostile, or at best ambivalent, population.

Born in Papa, Hungary, in 1908, Kovacs studied medicine in both Vienna and Würzburg, until his prescient professor warned him in 1930 that, because he was a Jew, his position there would soon be impossible.

Kovacs went to live in Pisa, where he completed his studies and married a German refugee in 1933. The next year he moved to Rome, opening a private practice with patients mainly from the Hungarian émigré population in the city. His younger brother was an antifascist who fought with the Republican army during the Spanish Civil War, after which he was interned in France before returning to Hungary, the SOE file records.

In June 1944 Dr. Kovacs was interviewed in Rome by a Major Dunlop about general conditions in Hungary. This was three months after the German invasion of Hungary in March, prompted in part by Admiral Horthy's increasing pro-Allies tendencies. He then proffered more information, records Major Dunlop. "This account is given voluntarily at the end of the first interview and was prefaced by the remark 'There is one other matter which I think I ought to tell you.' " This other matter, about Albert Goering, was of considerable interest.

In 1939 Dr. Kovacs was asked by a friend to attend a German and his sick wife, who were then staying at Frascati. "He was warned not to be surprised and to have no fear of the consequences," the SOE report says. But Dr. Kovacs was very surprised indeed when he saw who the husband of his new patient was: Albert Goering. As a doctor Kovacs was obliged to help anyone who was ill, but as a Jew he found he could not have anything to with Mrs. Goering, sister-in-law of Hitler's right-hand man, let alone treat her. The report provides more details:

> In spite of the warning and the particular request of his friend to help Goering's wife, Kovacs found himself quite unable to attend to her. He told Goering his point of view quite frankly, and begged to be excused. He said that he could not have any dealings with the brother of the man who had been directly and indirectly responsible for the sufferings of the Jews in Germany and the general consequences of the Nazi regime. Goering in reply asked him to sit down with him and to take some coffee, and at least get to know him a little better. At the end Goering asked Kovacs to return the following day.

Coffee, that great lubricant of Mediterranean social life, did its work. The two men, one the brother of one of the Third Reich's leaders, the other a Hungarian Jewish doctor, exchanged a few pleasantries. Dr. Kovacs calmed down and returned the next day. "When Kovacs went back, Goering explained that he was not interested in politics and burst out into a tirade against his brother, Hitler, and the Nazi regime, and said, '*Ich spucke auf Hitler, ich spucke auf mein bruder, auf die ganze Nazi Regierung.*' " (This translates as "I spit on Hitler, I also spit on my brother, and the whole Nazi regime.")

That angry outburst persuaded Dr. Kovacs of Albert Goering's sincerity, and he decided to treat Mrs. Goering. Over the next few weeks, the doctor got to know the Goerings quite well, as Mrs. Goering was severely ill (the report does not specify her ailment). The Roman climate was not aiding her recovery, and eventually she was sent back to Vienna.

So friendly did the two men become that Goering even invited his doctor's wife and two children to stay with him in Frascati for a fortnight. After that visit, Goering told Dr. Kovacs that he could not afford to keep up the residence in Frascati and wanted to move to a more modest apartment in Rome, which he asked Dr. Kovacs to find for him.

Six months later Goering informed Dr. Kovacs that he was receiving a salary of about 25,000 lire a month and needed much less than this sum for his own expenses. "The remainder he handed over to Dr. Kovacs and requested him to utilize it for the assistance of Jews and other refugees from Nazi tyranny. He required no receipt nor knowledge of who was helped," the SOE report says.

Sometime after he made his offer to Dr. Kovacs, Goering traveled to the Skoda arms factory in Czechoslovakia. While there he arranged for an account to be opened at Bank Orelli in Bern and deposited some funds in his account. Writing to Dr. Kovacs in Rome, Goering explained that, to get access to the funds, Dr. Kovacs merely had to write to the bank; he asked the doctor to use the money to aid Jewish refugees and help them escape via Lisbon.

With the German occupation of Italy in September 1943, Dr. Kovacs had his own personal safety, and that of his family, to worry about. Until then conditions for Jews in Italy had been tolerable, at least in comparison to those in the Third Reich. Mussolini, while a fascist, like Franco, was not himself anti-Semitic, and under Italian fascism, as opposed to Nazi occupation, Italian Jews had fared reasonably well. Fascism, at least in its original Italian form, was more concerned with the organization of the corporatist state than race or bloodlines, and some of the founding members of the Fascist Party were Jewish. Italian fascism at its outset was not anti-Semitic, and between October 1930 and November 1931 the Fascist regime passed three laws that reorganized the Jewish community under a new civil code, to improve its status. Mussolini even had a Jewish mistress and biographer, Margherita Sarfatti, as well as a Jewish finance minister, Guido Jung, from 1932 to 1935. Once Hitler came to power, Italy became a refuge for Jews, and by October 1938 over 10,000 had fled there, from Germany, Austria, and, like Dr. Kovacs, from Hungary. But in November 1938, Mussolini, under pressure from Hitler and pro-Nazis in his government, passed anti-Jewish race laws designed to bring Italy more into line with Nazi Germany. Still, even in wartime, the Italian flag represented a sort of sanctuary. Jews in Croatia, for example, fled en masse to the areas of the country occupied by the Italian army, to escape the bestial Ustase regime, whose Croatian troops outdid even the Nazi Einsatzgruppen in their brutality, killing their Serb and Jewish victims by hand, with knives and clubs.

For Jews in Italy, whether native-born or Hungarian refugees, the days of safe haven ended with the Nazi occupation in September 1943, and the transports to Auschwitz and other extermination camps soon began, where about 8,000 were murdered.

Even before the Nazis arrived, Rome was becoming less safe for Dr. Kovacs and his family as German occupation became more imminent. Albert Goering promised to help, by providing a personal laissez-passer. Signed by the brother of one of Hitler's most important associates, the document was enough to deter even the most ardent Gestapo agent from harassing Dr. Kovacs. "On his next visit to Rome Goering gave Kovacs a statement in writing to the effect that Kovacs was his personal physician, that he, Goering, visited Rome very often, required his regular attention, and desir[ed] that Kovacs not be molested [i.e., by the Gestapo]," the report details.

Goering even saved the Kovacs family's furniture. After the German occupation, Dr. Kovacs became worried that the contents of his home would be requisitioned by the Nazis. He mentioned his fears to Goering, who gave him a certificate to the effect that all the furniture in Kovacs's flat belonged to him, Albert Goering.

Increasingly amazed at Dr. Kovacs's account of Albert Goering's humanitarianism, Major Dunlop asked him why Hermann Goering's brother had gone to such extraordinary lengths to aid a Hungarian

Jewish family, and Jewish refugees in general. "He replied that he [Goering] was completely disinterested in politics, that he loathed all oppression and tyranny, and that he was doing, in some small way, everything in his power to atone for the evil and brutality of his brother and all the leaders of the Nazi regime." Albert Goering refused to speak about politics, his brother, or any other Nazi leader, Dr. Kovacs told Major Dunlop, except for his first outburst against the Third Reich, when he was asking for medical help for his wife.

PAUL GRUENINGER, a Swiss border police commander, and Albert Goering, the brother of one of the leaders of the Third Reich—these were just two of those with a Swiss connection who tried to aid Jewish refugees. The Swiss humanitarian tradition also lived on among much of the general population, while their country gave sanctuary to 230,000 refugees, including 22,000 Jews. The refugees included civilians from all over Europe and over 100,000 military refugees, including a large contingent of Poles. Many of this 230,000 were hosted by Swiss families, some of whom opened their homes for years, while the Swiss press kept up the pressure on the Federal Council to keep the country a place of refuge. Just as the Federal Council's policy of economic collaboration with the Nazis was opposed by a considerable part of the Swiss general public, so was its claim that "the boat is full."

The boat was not full, except for Jews. For the Federal Council, keeping the channels of finance open between Bern and Berlin was far more important than the fate of the tens of thousands of Jews who saw, wrongly, Switzerland as a place of sanctuary. The J-stamp and the 1942 border law specifically targeted Jews as unwelcome aliens who must be kept out. For fleeing Jews there was no neutrality, no policy of impartial dealing, at Switzerland's wartime borders.

8

A Nest of Spies

I only had relations with [the Nazi intelligence chief] Walter Schellenberg, and not with other chiefs of the SS. It is a monstrosity that you portray me as a friend of the Nazis, because I am not.

Letter from Colonel Roger Masson, head of Swiss military intelligence, to Federal Councilor Karl Kobelt, head of the department of military affairs, dated 3 October 1945

I knew Oberst Masson personally; I do not think I was wrong in thinking that there was a certain mutual sympathy on both sides, which had gradually developed through our political discussions.

Undated statement of Walter Schellenberg to his Allied interrogators, after his capture

If one man can personify a period in a nation's history, then Colonel Roger Masson, wartime head of Swiss military intelligence, is a perfect symbol of Switzerland's compromised neutrality. Between September 1942 and March 1943 Masson met three times with a leading war criminal, SS General Walter Schellenberg, to discuss matters of mutual interest. All of his meetings with the chief of Nazi foreign intelligence—two of which took place on Swiss soil and lasted several days—occurred with the knowledge and approval of the Federal Council, according to Masson.

Like Swiss–Nazi economic collaboration, the Masson–Schellenberg connection showed that Swiss intelligence officials were also prepared to trade with Berlin, when they believed it served their country's interest to deal with a criminal and genocidal regime. Like the Swiss National Bank, which asked the Federal Council for advice on whether to proceed with accepting Nazi gold and was told to go ahead, Masson was given the green light to meet with Schellenberg. On their third liaison he even took with him the Swiss army chief, General Guisan, who, pressed by Schellenberg, subsequently issued a declaration that any foreign troops on Swiss soil—including Allied forces—would be met by maximum force.

Like the bankers' deals with the Reichsbank, the Masson–Schellenberg connection was rationalized as a necessary move, predicated on the possible threat of a Nazi invasion, although by spring 1943 the Third Reich was barely capable of holding onto its remaining conquests, let alone of invading Switzerland. The Masson–Schellenberg connection was an integral part of the same policy of accommodation with the Third Reich that encouraged the Swiss National Bank to accept Nazi gold. And just as Colonel Masson's connection with the SS general would come to haunt him at the war's end, over fifty years later the shady network of underhand deals between Bern and Berlin has finally burst into the public eye, demolishing the myth that Swiss neutrality meant impartiality in its dealings with the Allies and the Axis powers.

THE TWO intelligence chiefs, the Nazi and his neutral opposite number, met for the first time on 8 September 1942, at the town of Waldshut in Germany, not far from the Swiss border. Colonel Masson was taken there by Schellenberg's assistant, Hans Eggen, a Brigadeführer in the SS, who, usefully enough, was also the representative in Switzerland of a company in Berlin with business interests in Lausanne. Switzerland's borders were by then sealed off to Jewish refugees fleeing Nazi terror, but there was still easy passage in and out for senior Nazi officers such as Eggen. The SS officer's frequent visits to Switzerland made him ideally placed to feed intelligence about that country to Schellenberg—especially as two of Eggen's principal business contacts were Paul Meyer-Schwertenbach and Paul Holzach, who were working for Swiss intelligence.

Both spymasters, Swiss and Nazi, had their own agenda for this unprecedented contact, but while Masson had several specific demands, Schellenberg's aims were more amorphous. Swimming in the dangerous and contradictory currents that swirled around the upper echelons of the Nazi leadership, he had begun to flirt with the idea of opening a channel to the West for a separate peace with Britain and America, to allow Germany to concentrate on its battle with the Soviet Union. This idea of splitting the Allies, which enjoyed Himmler's sporadic support, is a persistent theme of the several sets of clandestine meetings that took place in wartime Switzerland, whether between Masson and Schellenberg in the autumn of 1942, or between the Hungarian Zionist leader Rezso Kasztner, the SS officer Kurt Becher—who, like Schellenberg, was close to Himmler—and the Swiss Jewish leader Saly Mayer, two years later in Search.

As a Nazi whose beliefs were both flexible and grounded more in expediency than ideology, Schellenberg was perpetually planning for his own future position, working out a complicated series of strategies and counterstrategies, much as a chess grand master does—except that Schellenberg was playing a game in which the stakes were Europe's future.

"He was a very complicated personality, playing the game and looking out for his future after the war. Schellenberg was a careerist and would do everything for his career. He wanted to make connections, and the place to do that was Switzerland. He gave a lot of information to Roger Masson," says the historian Guido Koller.

Masson's immediate objective was the recovery of two boxes of files belonging to the French General Staff. The containers, which had been captured by the Germans in June 1940, contained secret documents on plans for Swiss–French military cooperation, if the Nazis decided to attack France by advancing underneath the Maginot line that stretched from the Swiss to the Belgian border. In the event, the Maginot line, for all its dense fortifications, gun emplacements, and tank traps, proved almost useless, for the Wehrmacht simply advanced on France from the north, by attacking through Belgium.

Colonel Masson wanted those boxes of incriminating documents back, for they severely compromised Swiss neutrality. But he decided at that first meeting to test the waters of cooperation with his new Nazi contact by requesting assistance on two minor matters. The first concerned an employee of the Swiss consulate in Stuttgart who had been arrested and was sentenced to death for spying. That Stuttgart was an important base for Nazi spies operating in Switzerland—in both the Abwehr (military intelligence) and Schellenberg's organization—was ironic but not much help to the young Swiss. Schellenberg promised to release him, upon which Masson also asked for his aid in muzzling a press agency in Vienna run by two Swiss pro-Nazis that was constantly attacking Switzerland. To this too Schellenberg agreed.

Buoyed by his apparent success in his meeting with the SS general, Colonel Masson arranged for a second rendezvous, to try to get the boxes of secret documents back and to further investigate this strange embryonic relationship. This time the meeting took place on Swiss soil. On 16 October 1942 Schellenberg and Eggen crossed the border into Switzerland and were driven by Colonel Masson's chauffeur to the house of Meyer-Schwertenbach, who lived by Lake Constance. Schellenberg had kept his promises: the young Swiss was released, and the Vienna-based press agency had stopped attacking Switzerland. He even promised that the compromising documents would be destroyed. But what did the SS general want for himself? More specifically, what did he want from Colonel Masson?

There were several possibilities. The first and most straightforward could be merely to bank a couple of favors with the intelligence service of the country that was neutral, neighboring, and the main foreign currency provider of the Nazi war machine. This was especially important to Schellenberg, who had to fund agents across the globe with hard currency. As the war ground on, he and other farsighted and intelligent German officials could see that the total victory promised so many times by Hitler was retreating into the distance and was more fantasy than reality.

Credit in the Swiss bank of good turns received was always a useful asset for forward-planning Nazis. Another possible benefit was a trade-off for information about Soviet-run spy rings operating in Switzerland such as the Rote Kapelle (Red Orchestra), which was forwarding information on to Moscow, and the OSS networks run by Allen Dulles. But these were mere chaff in the bigger harvest Schellenberg was hoping to reap: a separate peace with Britain and the Unites States that would split the Allies. There was probably nothing so crude as a direct request to Masson to approach the Allies, but the theme of such a conversation between two important players in the game of shadows that is intelligence and espionage need not be directly spelled out. Hints and allusions are enough to open the subterranean channels of communication and possible areas of cooperation.

Wartime Switzerland was a comfortable habitat for Schellenberg and his Allied opposite numbers. As a neutral country at the center of a continent at war, the country was crawling with spies, double agents, triple agents, and some who no longer knew for whom they were working, as long as they were paid. Many of the intelligence networks, such the Soviet spy rings, had been in place before the war. A hit team dispatched by the Paris station of the NKVD—forerunner of the KGB— had assassinated the Soviet defector Ignace Reiss after he had fled to Switzerland in 1937. The Soviet hit team had met Reiss in his favorite restaurant in Lausanne, before kidnapping and killing him.

Switzerland was the wartime base of both the Rote Kapelle and the Office of Strategic Services, forerunner of the CIA, run in Switzerland by Allen Dulles. The cafés of Zürich that once played host to Lenin were riddled with agents of every belligerent nation's secret service, from Britain to Bulgaria. They tapped each other's telephones, tailed each other from clandestine rendezvous to base and back again, opened letters, and intercepted the telegrams that clattered across the globe. Both the Allies and the Axis had extensive shopping lists of Swiss products needed for their war machines: jeweled bearings needed to manufacture aircraft instruments; precision machine tools to make armaments; timing devices for bombs and artillery shells—a by-product of the Swiss watch industry; pharmaceuticals; and industrial diamonds. Almost as important as the acquisition of these products was to know what the other side was purchasing, where from, and for what price.

The Nazis ran one of the most extensive intelligence operations in Switzerland, both from German consulates across the country and from the Abwehr base in Stuttgart. Berlin also made stringent efforts to spread Nazi propaganda inside Switzerland. As a German-speaking country, Switzerland was a natural target for the Third Reich's ideas of uniting all Germanic people in one superstate, but Hitler's ideas of racial supremacy did not find a particularly warm welcome among the Swiss public, who failed to share the bankers' enthusiasm for collaborating with the Nazis. Swiss police and intelligence also closely monitored Berlin's attempts to boost the pro-Nazi Swiss far right, which never enjoyed widespread support, despite the funds it received to propagandize Nazi ideas, especially in the early years of the war. German diplomats based in Switzerland agreed to dispatch SF3,000 ($670) to the far-right journal *L'Action Nationale,* according to a secret letter, dated 7 August 1940, from the consulate in Geneva to the legation in Bern.

More significant than Nazi propaganda was Switzerland's tolerance of Allied intelligence activities. Turning a blind eye to Allied intelligence agents aided the struggle against the Third Reich, says David Whipple, a former CIA station chief in Geneva. Civil courts tried almost 400 people for spying during the war, both Swiss and foreigners, but the machinations of Allied intelligence services such as the OSS and the British secret service were generally tolerated as part of the country's balancing act between the Allies and the Axis. Switzerland had plenty of reasons to expel Allied secret agents en masse, as almost all of their activities were illegal, but chose instead to help tacitly in the intelligence battle against the Nazis.

"The Swiss were careful not to offend the Germans," says Whipple, "but they did what they could to help the allies. They overlooked OSS activities; there was a certain amount of quiet collaboration with Allen Dulles. His whole operation was well known, and the Swiss did not find that so embarrassing that they had to ask for his departure. Any country who thinks that its sovereignty is being interfered with has the right to declare any official persona non grata. Technically all intelligence people are violating everybody's sovereignty when they engage in intelligence work. Intelligence work is by definition illegal. If it is very effective intelligence work, it is very illegal."

Switzerland's own intelligence strategy focused on containing threats inside the country's borders. Unlike the Third Reich, Switzerland had no need of an extensive intelligence service operating in foreign lands, whether newly conquered or still on a territorial shopping list, because Switzerland had no territorial ambitions, except to conserve its borders. Few resources had been spent on its intelligence services, although during the war the Swiss Viking Line intelligence network in Germany was given high priority. Mostly, though, Masson's organization, at least in its early years, was a makeshift affair that could never hope to compete with Schellenberg's operation. Masson had so little money that he even contacted the Büro Ha, a freelance intelligence-gathering outfit set up by Captain Hans Hausamann, a staunch anti-Nazi, who had started out in the shadow world by collecting press clippings about the rise of the Nazis in Germany. As a Swiss businessman with extensive foreign contacts, Captain Hausamann was well placed to bring in information from his friends across Europe. Once the war began the Büro Ha was transferred to a village just south of

Lucerne, where it worked with Masson's intelligence station in the city, although it stayed independent.

When it came to foreign intelligence operations, Switzerland was genuinely neutral. Masson and Hausamann ran networks in Allied and other neutral countries as well as in Nazi Germany. That was both sensible and understandable, for any military threat would almost certainly come from Berlin, although some Swiss officials feared that Allied troops might transit Swiss territory to reconquer Italy and so violate its neutrality. But even if they had, London and Washington had no desire to actually annex Switzerland.

The key question, still debated by historians, that may justify in part Swiss economic collaboration with the Nazis is this: was there ever a real threat of a Nazi invasion of Switzerland? The answer is complex, predicated on a mix of factors, both economic and military. Just as important is the year during the war to which the question refers, because the Third Reich of 1939 was a much different beast from that of 1943, let alone 1945.

Understandably, the Nazi advance across Europe as the Panzers rolled across Belgium and France sent shock waves through Switzerland. In one month, May 1940, the Nazis invaded France, Belgium, Holland, and Luxembourg. The last three capitulated within days. That German guarantees of Belgian neutrality had proved worthless was well noted in Bern. Many Swiss believed they were next. Landlocked, surrounded by Axis-held territories that controlled access to its frontiers, Switzerland found itself in a poor strategic position. Certainly there were Nazis in Berlin who wanted to annex Switzerland: it was a neighboring country, strategically positioned in Europe's center; most of its population spoke German; and there was plenty of money there.

But Switzerland's position was stronger than it appeared. The country had money, technology, and mountains on its side. We have already seen how Swiss private banks' supply of foreign currency, and the Swiss National Bank's acceptance of Nazi-looted gold, helped keep the Wehrmacht rolling across Europe. Berlin needed Bern, and a Nazi invasion would have triggered an immediate collapse of the Swiss franc.

At the same time, as the war progressed, the Germans relied on Swiss high-tech exports of vital war equipment, which was another reason to keep good relations with Bern. Swiss industry turned out war material from light artillery to bomb-timing mechanisms and exported it to Nazi Germany. Swiss technological expertise aided the Nazi war machine, says the Swiss historian Jacques Picard, author of *Switzerland and the Assets of the Missing Victims of the Nazis*. "On a factual level, Switzerland worked in the interests of the Nazi war industry, in the way it made money by exporting highly technological products which could be used for the production of German weapons," he says. "For example, a watch. You can use a watch for many things, in the army, the navy, and the air force, as a timer for bombs. The Swiss watch industry also gave the same tiny watches to the Allies, but they smuggled them to them, because in the forties the Federal Council was pressed by the Germans, who completely surrounded Switzerland, not to give such goods to the Allies."

Third, and just as important, was the military reality of the costs in men, money, and material to the Third Reich of invading Switzerland. Invasion plans were mapped out by the Wehrmacht's planning units and logistics officers, but they were never implemented. In large part this was because subduing Switzerland would have been a far different and bloodier battle for the Wehrmacht than capturing the Benelux nations, which put up little resistance. Swiss military strategy was based on defense and maintenance of the country's neutrality, and the Swiss were ready to fight. Like the Israeli army, the Swiss army was a citizens' fighting force, and every able-bodied man was required to undertake military service. By May 1940 there were 450,000 soldiers armed and ready to defend the country. They were well trained, equipped with modern weaponry, and motivated.

The Swiss basic defense plan was to blow up all the bridges, tunnels, and viaducts that linked the Alpine country together and so cut off the invaders' lines of supply and communications. The Swiss army would then fall back to the country's heartland. The German blitzkrieg tactics employing waves of tanks and skies full of dive-bombers was well suited to the flatlands of Poland, for example, whose vastly outgunned forces never stood a chance against the Wehrmacht. They would not have worked as well in the Alpine passes, for even German Panzer tanks are not much use on a snowy mountainside. With virtually every Swiss male of fighting age armed and well trained, the Swiss army would have fought a highly effective partisan guerrilla war—every general's nightmare. The Yugoslav partisans kept the Nazis bogged down in the mountains of Bosnia and Serbia for years, and Tito's forces were far more poorly equipped—and diverted by a near civil war with rival groups—than the Swiss army.

Certainly some among Switzerland's military elite would have welcomed the Nazis, but, like the bankers and the ministers of the Federal Council, they were unrepresentative of the general population. Many junior officers and the lower ranks of the army were anti-Nazi, some even ready to execute their commanders if the Wehrmacht arrived, says the historian Gian Trepp. "In general Swiss people were antifascist. My father told me that the soldiers in his regiment had lists prepared of pro-Nazi officers whom they would shoot if the Nazis invaded. There was a strong pro-Nazi faction in the Swiss army. It was infested with Nazis, more among the officers. They wanted to join up with Hitler, and they thought the French were decadent. But Switzerland was not monolithic in its relations with Nazi Germany, and there was also a secret military contract with France that Switzerland would fight if the Nazis tried to cut under the Maginot line in Basel."

Even with over fifty years of hindsight we can never know when a Nazi invasion of Switzerland was no longer militarily feasible. But there is an almost unbeatable argument that by 2 February 1943 even the most voracious SS general no longer had Bern and Zürich in his sights. That was the day when the German generals surrendered the remnants of the Sixth Army at Stalingrad, after a siege of the Soviet city that had lasted since the previous summer. The Nazis and their allies lost 850,000 men at Stalingrad, and immeasurable quantities of equipment and material were destroyed. Stalingrad followed the Anglo-American landings in French North Africa and Rommel's defeat at El Alamein. In July of that year the Allies invaded Sicily and the last great German offensive was crushed by the Red Army at Kursk. The Third Reich was reeling. By then it was clear there would be no invasion of Switzerland.

But when did Colonel Masson's agents know that Germany was incapable of invading, and when did he communicate that information to the Federal Council, which as late as November 1943 told the Swiss National Bank to continue to accept Nazi gold? For Gisela Blau, a Swiss journalist who has for years researched Switzerland's wartime history, a Nazi invasion was no longer a threat by December 1940. "The question is, how soon did the secret service in Switzerland know that Germany was absolutely incapable of invading? By the end of 1940 the Nazis were preparing Operation Barbarossa, and they were not capable of any sidesteps. The Swiss secret service must have known about that, very early. The question is, how early? The fiction of the pressure [from Germany] I doubt very much."

Either way, Schellenberg, the youthful Nazi general, traded effectively on Germany's military might in his dealings with the Swiss. Even before he met Masson, Schellenberg's star was on the rise in the Third Reich. Schellenberg took over Department VI of the RSHA—the Reich security organization that combined the Gestapo, the criminal police, and the SS security services—in June 1941 at the age of thirty-one. Department VI was responsible for foreign intelligence, and Schellenberg ran both its headquarters in Berlin and all its outposts across the Third Reich. From his base in Department VI he quickly expanded his empire from foreign intelligence gathering to domestic as well. He established an economics intelligence unit to liaise with major German companies such as Dresdner Bank, which had foreign contacts, as a means of obtaining foreign currency.

A photograph survives of Schellenberg from 1938. It shows a pleasant, open-featured man with amiable eyes and a full mouth, who could be a bank manager or insurance salesman, although the dueling scar on his chin offers a hint of menace. His personnel report of March 1937, when he held the rank of SS master sergeant, evaluates his overall character as "Pure Nordic," although he did not look like the Aryan ideal of a blond-haired, blue-eyed giant. Schellenberg was a persuader and a diplomat, rather than an enforcer, who preferred to use the power of his arguments rather than the usual Nazi methodology of brute force. But, however smoothly he talked, as an SS general he was deeply implicated in the Nazi genocide, much of which was organized by his boss Reinhard Heydrich. Heydrich was the inventor of the Einsatzgruppen, the Nazi special extermination squads that stripped Jews of their valuables before shooting them into pits. Of the 6 million Jews killed in the Holocaust, about 2 million died at the hands of the Einsatzgruppen's guns.

Not every Wehrmacht officer was as keen as Schellenberg's boss on the bloodbath of Jews as the regular army advanced across Europe. Many objected to the Einsatzgruppen, although often more on grounds of military discipline and procedure than any real distaste for the killing of civilians. There were complicated questions of protocol and precedent to sort out between the Wehrmacht and the SS death squads, although their subtleties were lost on the Jews as they lined up for death. Here too Schellenberg was ready to use his skills of diplomacy to make sure the Holocaust ran smoothly, and he helped negotiate the necessary agreements between the rival Nazi military bodies. Schellenberg had plenty of blood on his own hands.

On 3 March 1943 Colonel Masson, together with General Guisan, the commander-in-chief of the Swiss army, met again with Schellenberg. The two men were nervous. In January of that year the Viking Line, a Swiss intelligence network in Nazi Germany that worked with anti-Nazi Wehrmacht officers, had forwarded to Colonel Masson the report of a meeting at Hitler's headquarters in October 1942, attended by Goering, Himmler, Goebbels, and Rosenberg, in which the Nazi leaders had discussed invading Switzerland. This was extremely alarming news, for the Viking Line's information had so far proved accurate, and it was one of Switzerland's most important intelligence networks. The answer, Guisan and Masson believed, was to meet again with Schellenberg.

In fact, by this stage in the war, the Nazi leadership was less concerned over invading Switzerland than over the possibility that the Allies might march through Swiss territory on the way to attacking Italy, which was anyway starting to lose its enthusiasm for the Axis. Would the Swiss army take up arms against Allied troops? asked Schellenberg. Guisan replied that he had recently given an interview to a Swedish journalist in which he emphasized that Switzerland would defend herself against any aggressor. He offered to supply a copy, but that was not enough for Schellenberg, who demanded a written statement, signed by Guisan, affirming Swiss neutrality. The document, with the general's signature, was handed over on 6 March and more than met the Nazi demands:

"Whoever invades our country is self-evidently our enemy. He will be confronted by a united army of the greatest strength and a nation imbued with a single accord. At such a time there exists only one militant Switzerland inspired by one will. Because of the topography of our country we are able above all to defend our Alpine front.

"Whatever may come to pass this assurance is immovable and unalterable. No doubt can arise about that either now or in the future."

Schellenberg stayed in Switzerland until 10 March, the longest of his visits to Masson. Eight days later, the Viking Line sent another message, that the Nazi leadership had again discussed an attack on Switzer-land, just when another agent reported to Masson that German para-chutists and mountain warfare divisions were being prepared for an attack. Seen in hindsight, this message could well have been organized by Schellenberg on his return to Berlin from Switzerland, with that country still fresh in his mind. For the cardinal axiom of intelligence work is to ask Lenin's question when deciding the protagonist of any event: "Who benefits?" And the March Alert, as the incident is now known, benefited Schellenberg most of all.

Masson acted very unwisely after the Viking Line message, records Jozef Garlinski in *The Swiss Corridor.* "Colonel Masson was shattered by this information and responded immediately, although very unwisely. Believing that Schellenberg was indeed sincerely disposed toward Switzerland, he asked Meyer-Schwertenbach to get in touch with Berlin by telephone and to arrange for him to go there for talks with General Schellenberg and Major Eggen in order to find out whether there really was any danger."

An understandable reaction, but a stupid one. By doing this he immediately alerted Schellenberg that Switzerland had an informant in the highest echelons of the Nazi leadership. A few weeks later, one of the main agents of the Viking Line was arrested. In the end the March Alert was a false alarm. Meanwhile, in Bern, Karl Kobelt, head of the department of military affairs in the Swiss Federal Council, was furious that Swiss military officers were meeting with high-ranking Nazis, with-out either liaising with the government or even properly informing Bern about their discussions. On 6 April General Guisan was repri-manded in a resolution passed by the Swiss government, which reminded him that the army should stay out of politics and stick to mil-itary matters.

MASSON'S secret meetings with Schellenberg came back to haunt him after the war's end. Under pressure from Swiss left-wingers, the Fed-eral Council launched an official inquiry into the relationship between the Swiss spymaster and his Nazi counterpart and described the meet-ings as "unauthorized." Masson fought hard for his reputation. On 3 October 1945 he sent a lengthy letter to Federal Councilor Karl Kobelt, defending his actions and arguing that the Federal Council had known exactly what he was doing in his relations with the Nazi intelligence chief. "I only had relations with Walter Schellenberg, and not with other chiefs of the SS. It is a monstrosity that you portray me as a friend of the Nazis, because I am not. I disapproved of the German attitudes, especially those of Hitler. I said to Walter Schellenberg that he shouldn't be surprised by the hostile attitudes of the Swiss, especially from the moment that the Germans found this term 'Herrenvolk' [master race]," wrote Masson. He also claimed that SS Officer Eggen, while imprisoned, had not been charged with any crimes and had even left Switzerland under the protection of the U.S. military attaché in Berlin.

Masson also claimed that Heinrich Rothmund, chief of the foreigner police and a key figure in the closure of Swiss borders to Jewish refugees, had found the Eggen–Schellenberg channel useful.

> The first beneficiary of this line was Dr. Rothmund, with the support of President Von Steiger, who had on a number of occasions to meet Eggen in Switzerland and was later received by Eggen in his private property in Berlin. He knew exactly who Eggen and Schellenberg were, and he knew also that they didn't alter their role during the war.
>
> Today as I am obliged to defend my honor as an officer, it is very important for me that people know that before I saw Walter Schellenberg for the first time I asked for the general's authorization, who not only gave his agreement but was also grateful to me for the results which we gained through this contact. . . . I ask you now very respectfully to take the attitude of the general to the chamber because I cannot protect myself.

As for Schellenberg himself, once in Allied hands he was more concerned with muddying the murky waters of Swiss–Nazi collaboration than clearing them, as extracts from his undated interrogation statement show.

"I knew Oberst [Colonel] Masson personally; I do not think I was wrong in thinking that there was a certain mutual sympathy on both sides, which had gradually developed through our political discussions," the SS general claimed. "Perhaps on Masson's part it was due to the fact that I was a real friend of Switzerland." Schellenberg said that his aim in his discussions with Masson was to open a regular channel for the exchange of information with him—in other words, make the head of Swiss military intelligence some kind of Nazi agent. By regularly meeting with Schellenberg, Masson had allowed himself to become, if not an agent, at least a de facto asset of the RSHA's Department VI, and while detailed records of their discussions are not available, there must have been some trading in information and intelligence taking place. There is no such thing as a free fact, especially in the shadow world in which the two spymasters moved.

"Masson and his colleague Dr. Meyer[-Schwertenbach] were the contacts with whose help I hoped to bridge the gap either to the British or American military attaché, as soon as I should have made progress enough in Germany. Above all last year I hoped to get into contact with Dulles," the SS general stated.

As the man charged with keeping a watching brief over Nazi Germany, Masson had no choice but to keep some kind of line of communication open with the Nazis. Ultimately he probably gained little from his and General Guisan's liaisons with Schellenberg, apart from a couple of minor triumphs, and he probably compromised the country's prime intelligence network in Nazi Germany, the Viking Line. He refused point-blank to supply direct military intelligence. His reward was obloquy in the eyes of some of his fellow countrymen for trading with the Nazi spymaster, and a perpetual question mark over his judgment in his dealings with Walter Schellenberg has forever marred his reputation.

As for Schellenberg, he admitted to his Allied interrogators that his prime motive in dealing with the Swiss was, of course, money and the acquisition thereof, particularly vital foreign exchange. The special intelligence department that he set up within the RSHA was also charged with procuring foreign currency, naturally focusing much of its energy on Switzerland. The SS general, like so many of his Nazi colleagues, needed Switzerland as a center for purchasing foreign currency, and any intelligence gathered there from Colonel Masson or his assistants was a useful but almost incidental fringe benefit. As a separate report of Schellenberg's interrogation dated 13 December 1946 says: "When Swiss–German relations grew worse, Schellenberg undertook trips to the Swiss border. Subject claims that he could not afford to lose Switzerland as a market for foreign currency and as a base for his secret service operations."

The acquisition of foreign currency aside, the final prize for Schellenberg was opening a channel to Bern OSS station chief Allen Dulles and, through him, communicating Himmler's hopes for a separate peace deal with the western Allies. For his part Dulles was certainly interested in communicating with Schellenberg, whether directly or through an intermediary, at least according to Roger Masson, who often met with the American spymaster. Masson wrote to Karl Kobelt, the head of the Swiss military department, "Finally I had on a number of occasions to talk with Dulles, who was representing Roosevelt in Bern, about Schellenberg. He had a good opinion about these conversations."

The OSS was set up in 1942. Allen Dulles arrived in Switzerland that November and received diplomatic status at the U.S. embassy in Bern as an assistant to the ambassador. His ostensible intelligence mission was to evaluate the extent of the anti-Hitler opposition within Nazi Germany and analyze its effectiveness, but that wide brief gave him plenty of opportunity to open links with the many spy networks operating in wartime Switzerland to build up his intelligence empire.

That the Americans sent a sharp Wall Street banking lawyer and not a soldier to run the OSS in Bern is very significant, says the Swiss historian Jacques Picard. "That tells a lot. They didn't send a military officer: they sent a lawyer—a smart, fast lawyer. He could look behind things; he had a clear picture of how finance and goods are the base for a war drive. He played games, like all secret services do."

Dulles was power-mad, says historian Marc Masurovsky, running intelligence operations that were so complicated it was sometimes difficult to see what lay behind them. "He was an egomaniac: he wanted to run the war out of Bern. He was a very successful corporate lawyer, and he had a tremendous amount of friends in the German business and legal community. He was not pro-Nazi, but he was pro-German. He supported the conservative resistance very heavily. He was trying to negotiate unconditional surrender; he was setting up deep-penetration operations all over Europe; he was lobbying and setting up networks of people everywhere, with a very clear antenna out for the Russians, paving the way for the postwar, Cold War era. He thought very highly of himself. He was devious and condescending, and as far as he was concerned anything that was good for international business was good for him and vice versa."

Dulles's contacts with Nazi Germany in his previous work as a lawyer proved most useful, although once war broke out they could not be maintained openly and had to be preserved through clandestine channels. His contacts included the Schroeder Bank, and he openly maintained his business links with Nazi Germany until hostilities broke out. Unlike many of his operatives, Dulles was not an antifascist with a hatred of Nazism. He had no great love for Jews, was tainted by anti-Semitism, and, as a former State Department official in the Middle East department, had extensive business dealings in the Middle East, particularly in the Arabian Gulf, where he had a network of connections with oil companies.

"Dulles had German clients before the war," says Masurovsky, "and kept legal relations with them, and once Dulles started work in the OSS he put these German connections to use. He knew German bankers and manufacturers who were politically conservative. He was very ingenious and used third parties such as the intelligence agencies of central European countries, where he also had contacts."

But first Dulles had to establish a modus operandi in the country where he was stationed. He cultivated Colonel Masson and was pleased to learn that Masson's bureau was also in touch with the Nazi and Italian intelligence services. He also liaised with Captain Hausamann of the Swiss Büro Ha. Both of these were receiving information, some channeled through the Viking Line, about the activities of the Schwarze Kapelle (Black Orchestra), the anti-Nazi German opposition movement rooted in the business and conservative circles of Germany, precisely where Dulles had his prewar contacts. Conservative anti-Hitler German circles probably even helped finance Dulles's networks, Masurovsky believes. "They wanted to be on the winning side, and so they helped his operation."

Like Schellenberg, who was in some ways—such as his duplicitous policy of pure self-interest—his Nazi mirror image, Dulles was planning for a postwar Europe. His aim was to build up a continent-wide intelligence network, both as part of his personal empire and as a means of laying the groundwork for the coming Cold War against the Soviet Union. Dulles knew, as did Stalin, that a defeated Germany would be the prime battleground for control of postwar Europe. Churchill and Roosevelt had adopted a policy of "unconditional surrender" toward the Third Reich at the 1943 Casablanca conference, although Stalin was taking a more conciliatory line. The Casablanca policy was not very encouraging to the Schwarze Kapelle, for it left no window of negotiation open with the anti-Hitler opposition to split the

German leadership—although with hindsight it is clear that the Black Orchestra was never playing a tune that could arouse the German masses into any kind of revolt.

But however useful, or useless, the Black Orchestra was as a base for an anti-Hitler German movement, it still had to be exploited by the Allies, both as a source of information and as a means of destabilizing the Third Reich. Bern was the place to do this, and Dulles's channel to the anti-Hitler Germans was Gero von Gaevernitz, of German origin, but an American citizen with a Jewish mother. Von Gaevernitz maintained contact with the Third Reich through his father, a teacher at Freiburg and Breslau universities. Through von Gaevernitz Dulles made contact with Hans Bernd Gisevius, a German diplomat based at the consulate in Zürich, who was connected with the German resistance and the anti-Hitler plotters in the group around Count Berthold von Stauffenberg, architects of the failed July 1944 bomb plot.

Gisevius, a former Gestapo official who was also an agent for the Abwehr (Nazi military intelligence), was deeply involved in the July bomb plot, as he had been in the feeble maneuverings of the generals in 1938 and 1939 to depose Hitler in a military coup. Part of Gisevius's wartime work in Search was to pass messages from the conspirators, such as Carl Goerdeler, the anti-Nazi mayor of Leipzig, to Dulles. Gisevius even brought Dulles a memorandum in May 1944 from General Beck, general chief of staff and a key figure in the July bomb plot, proposing a separate peace with the West. Ironically its basic outline was probably not that far from Himmler's conception of a deal with Britain and the United States, but that didn't save Beck and the other conspirators from capture by Himmler's officials in the Gestapo and SS.

Beck's proposal was that the German forces in Western Europe would be withdrawn to the German border after the Allied invasion. At the same time, the German anti-Hitler conspirators would take charge of Berlin, aided by three airborne divisions of Allied troops, who would also invade on the northern seacoast and from across the channel into France. Meanwhile anti-Nazi German troops would capture the area around Munich and Hitler's retreat at Obersalzburg. This plan, fantastic in its conception, is perhaps best seen as an indication of how out of touch with the reality of the war the plotters were. Dulles rejected it out of hand and told the Beck group that there could be no separate peace with the West.

The OSS chief in Bern was also visited by such leading figures in the conspiracy as Adam Trott zu Solz, in their—in hindsight—pathetic attempts to overthrow Hitler. Trott zu Solz, like thousands of his fellow conspirators, was captured and executed after the failure of the bomb plot. Himmler's interest in a separate peace with the Allies, to be negotiated through his Allied contact in Switzerland, could not save him, and Trott zu Solz was hanged on 25 August 1944. Thirteen days before this, Goerdeler was arrested in east Prussia. He survived in prison until 2 February 1945, surviving longer than many of his fellow conspirators because of Himmler's continuing hopes of splitting the Allies and replacing Hitler, argues the author William Shirer: "Apparently Himmler delayed the hangings because he thought the contacts of the two men, especially those of Goerdeler, with the western Allies through Sweden and Switzerland might prove helpful to him if he took over the sinking ship of state—a prospect which began to grow in his mind at this time."

There was no separate peace between the anti-Hitler plotters and the West. The late-night meetings, the secret memoranda, the plans, the discussions, the hints of deals to be brokered in Bern between Dulles and the anti-Hitler Germans—all these came to nothing. But for Dulles and the other Allied intelligence services based in Bern, the German contacts they made were extremely useful. They provided the nucleus of the intelligence networks in Germany that would be turned against the Soviet Union in the coming Cold War. Many senior Nazis, including Schellenberg, escaped serious punishment. Others were recruited by Allied intelligence agencies.

The Nazi war criminal Klaus Barbie, dubbed the "Butcher of Lyons" for his brutality was put on the books by the U.S. Counter Intelligence Corps. Schellenberg's work with Heydrich, organizing the Einsatzgruppen, would probably, in the normal course of postwar justice, have earned him a capital sentence at Nuremberg.

Instead, the extensive contacts and intelligence networks Schellenberg had built up as head of the RSHA Department VI meant the Allies decided he should escape the hangman's noose that claimed so many of his Nazi colleagues. Schellenberg was held in Allied custody and shunted from capital to capital to be interrogated and debriefed by Allied intelligence services. He even wrote a book about his wartime activities, *Labyrinth,* which, like his life in the service of Nazi genocide, was self-serving and riddled with lies. But justice, of a sort, prevailed in the end. In 1949 SS General Walter Schellenberg was sentenced to six years' imprisonment. The following year, chronically ill, he was released. He died in 1952.

As for Colonel Roger Masson, his career never recovered from the postwar scandal that erupted around his links with Schellenberg, and he retired, forever tainted by his connection to the SS general.

9

Dealing With the Devil

Anyone holding such a [Swiss] letter, and who could also get into a "Swiss protected" house, was not conscripted for labor service and was relatively safe from molestation by the authorities. Such a letter, therefore, was in effect a life insurance policy.

> Report by Dr. J. Goldin, of the Jewish Agency's Istanbul office, dated 16 May 1945, on the rescue work of Charles Lutz, Swiss diplomat in wartime Budapest

For the 1,685 Hungarian Jews in Budapest we paid $1,000 per head, and we undertook to pay $100 per head, for the 15,000 Jews to be driven to Austria. . . . The Swedes delivered steel to the Third Reich, the Turks chrome, and Switzerland issued a clearing credit of millions of dollars. We have paid less than that.

> Extract from a report by Rezso Kasztner, wartime Budapest Zionist leader, who arranged with Adolf Eichmann to send 1,685 Jews on a secret train to Switzerland

They were desperate scenes in Budapest that autumn and winter of 1944. Crowds of frantic Jews mobbed the apartment buildings on the streets near the Danube over which flew the flags of neutral nations. The banners of Switzerland, Sweden, and Spain all fluttered in the wind that blew over the river. Other buildings had a Red Cross plaque fixed to the wall. The emblems gave dozens of buildings extraterritorial status as areas under neutral sovereignty, and so provided sanctuary to tens of thousands of Jews. When the Red Army finally arrived in January 1945, there were so many Swiss flags flying that its commander wondered aloud whether he was liberating Budapest or Switzerland.

181

Conditions inside Budapest's middle-class Jewish quarter—dubbed the "International Ghetto" to distinguish it from the ghetto by the Great Synagogue that was not under neutral protection—were horribly overcrowded and unsanitary, for up to 30,000 people were jammed into living space designed for 8,000. But space was the least of the Jews' concerns. Entrance to one of the Swiss safe houses, which were spread across the Hungarian capital's district XIII, meant safety: safety from the squads of Hungarian Nazis in the Arrow Cross Party—who roamed Budapest, lining up Jews, tying them together with wire, and shooting them into the Danube at will—and conscription onto the SS-organized forced-labor death marches to the Austrian border.

The Swedish diplomat Raoul Wallenberg, who was captured by the Russians and later vanished into the Soviet Gulag, is the best known of the neutral envoys in wartime Budapest who saved tens of thousands of Jews by issuing protection papers. But the Swiss diplomat Charles Lutz, who initiated the technique of issuing documents that placed both individual Jews and whole buildings under the protection of neutral countries, saved more lives.

Lutz had arrived in Budapest in January 1942 to represent the interests of Allied countries, such as Britain and the United States, that had severed relations with Hungary. After the German invasion in March 1944, he worked with Moshe Krausz, the Budapest representative of the Jewish Agency in Jerusalem, to save as many Jews as possible. Lutz and Krausz's method was to issue entry certificates for Palestine. Palestine was under British rule, and Lutz was Britain's representative in Budapest, so Lutz was also Palestine's man in Budapest. There was virtually no way a Jew from Budapest could have reached the Middle East in the summer of 1944, but few who received the certificates, stating that the bearer would eventually receive Palestinian citizenship, ever intended to use them.

Under pressure from the Jewish Agency and the Swiss, Britain agreed that Lutz could issue certificates for immigration to Palestine to Hungarian Jews. As Palestine was under British rule, this meant that holders of the precious certificates were to be treated as potential British subjects. It was a well-timed maneuver. Under a barrage of international protests about the Hungarian Holocaust, Hungary's ruler, Admiral Horthy, had stopped the deportations to Auschwitz in July 1944 and even agreed that 7,800 Hungarian Jews could leave for Palestine. Lutz then issued Palestine certificates that were valid for a family, rather than an individual, and so about 50,000 Jews were eventually brought under Swiss protection. But however impressive were Lutz's Swiss papers, franked with the Swiss seal and all the panoply of officialdom that worked their magic with the Arrow Cross and the SS, they were still no match for a bullet. And of those there were plenty in Budapest in 1944.

Why did Hungarian officials take any notice of Lutz's papers? By spring 1944 Admiral Horthy was leaning far toward the Allies, so much so that in March the Nazis invaded and, while he remained technically in control, the real rulers were the German ambassador, Edmund Veesenmayer, and Adolf Eichmann, who oversaw the Hungarian Holocaust. Hungary was at war with Britain, but even the most ardent pro-Nazi Magyar official was not about to arrange the death of 50,000 potential British nationals—especially as many in Horthy's circle, including the admiral himself, were hopeful that American and British troops, rather than the feared Russians, would soon arrive and defeat the Germans. Horthy's planning for postwar Hungary necessitated good relations with both neutral countries and the western Allies.

But his plans came to nothing, for, once the Germans marched in, Horthy's days were numbered. In October 1944 the Arrow Cross regime of Hungarian Nazis took power, toppling the admiral in a coup with German support. He was replaced by the Arrow Cross leader, Ferenc Szálasi, who was later executed as a war criminal. It was a murderous and outlaw regime, but Szálasi was still desperate for international recognition. Szálasi didn't like what Lutz was doing, but he wasn't about to stop him by force. Lutz's continued presence in the Hungarian capital and ongoing negotiations with the Arrow Cross regime meant Szálasi's government had some kind of de facto international status. Together with Wallenberg and the papal nuncio, Angelo Rotta, Lutz dangled the prospect of full diplomatic recognition as leverage in his dealings with the Arrow Cross government. The Arrow Cross chief and his underlings fought a running bureaucratic battle with neutral diplomats such as Lutz and Wallenberg to restrict their operations, but it was a battle fought with paper and meetings, and the lifesaving work continued.

As for the Germans, as previous chapters explain, the Third Reich needed to maintain good relations with Switzerland for economic reasons. There was a personal debt to be paid by them as well, as Lutz had helped German nationals in Palestine. While serving as a Swiss diplomat in Tel Aviv at the outbreak of the Second World War, he had intervened on behalf of 2,500 German settlers there who were being deported from Palestine by the governing British as enemy aliens. This debt extended to German diplomats instructing the Arrow Cross—who at this stage in the war were far more enthusiastic about continuing to kill Jews than the Nazis themselves—that Lutz's protected houses must remain unharmed.

Other neutral diplomats followed Lutz's precedent. Thousands of Jews were put under Swedish protection, and Spanish as well—the Spanish connection organized by Renee Reichmann in Tangier. Unlike many of his bosses at the headquarters of the International Committee of the Red Cross in Geneva, Frederick Born, the ICRC's Budapest representative, took a vigorous approach to saving as many Jewish lives as possible. During the war many senior Red Cross officials took the view that intervening to stop the Holocaust would only jeopardize their work with prisoners of war. The POWs took priority. Many Jewish organizations and historians alike are extremely critical of the ICRC's poor record in publicizing and protesting against Nazi genocide. It was not until 1943, a full decade after Hitler had taken power, that the Red Cross set up its Special Assistance Division to aid victims of Nazi persecution, mainly Jews.

Spurred on by mounting pressure from the Swiss public to take a more vigorous approach to save the remaining Jews, in the summer of 1944 the Red Cross leaders in Geneva finally cranked into action. Born got the go-ahead to start work. He organized Red Cross safe houses with extraterritorial status, issued about 3,000 letters of protection, vigorously protested against the brutal treatment of the Jews, gave asylum to members of the Jewish Council, organized food supplies for the ghetto, and even persuaded the Hungarian ministry of the interior to issue a decree forbidding looting, so as to protect Jewish property, all the time working together with Lutz's and Wallenberg's staffs.

Those safe passes issued by neutral countries soon became more valuable than food or fuel. A simple piece of paper with an official frank meant the difference between life and death. The young activists in the Zionist and Jewish underground who ran armed hit-and-run raids against the SS and the Arrow Cross soon began their own citywide printing operation. A network of secret presses was set up in basements across the city, where the fighters would churn out forged protection papers. But the Hungarian authorities eventually realized that too many Jews were brandishing the lifesaving documents. Something had to be done to sort the real from the fake. And who would know better than Charles Lutz himself? The man who had saved so many Jewish lives was now forced to decide who would live and who would die. In his report to Jerusalem on Lutz's work, Dr. J. Goldin, the Jewish Agency's man in Istanbul, who met Lutz there, describes the scene when the Hungarian police raided the International Ghetto, together with Lutz's staff:

> This situation created terrific confusion and chaos. Instead of 50,000 letters there were about 100,000 in circulation, and all of the letter holders were trying to get into the protected houses. Mr. Lutz (who was chief of the Division for Foreign Interests) [i.e., in charge of Allied interests in Hungary] was placed in a very difficult and embarrassing position and was charged by the Hungarian authorities with overstepping his instructions. The authorities also charged him with responsibility for the entire situation and intimated that he was in a sense responsible for the issuance of the forged letters because he had no business to issue any such letters except to the group of 7,800, especially selected for emigration to Palestine.

Angry though they were at the forged papers, the Hungarian authorities were not about to invalidate Lutz's extension of Swiss protection to 50,000 theoretical British subjects. Relations with Switzerland and hopes for liberation by the Allies were more important than killing another 42,000 or so Jews. But for Lutz there was a nightmare price to pay for those 50,000 saved, as Goldin's report relates:

> The authorities indicated, however, that they would permit those people to remain in the houses who held genuine letters issued by the Swiss legation, but none of those who held forged letters. As a result, Mr. Lutz had no alternative, except to supply six members of the Swiss legation, who, together with twenty police officers, entered the house to check the validity of the letters. The situation was trying and tragic. Those persons with forged letters were forcibly removed from the houses and were compelled at

once to start their march on foot to the Austrian border, for work in labor camps.

That hundred-mile trek was known as the "death march." The Jews were allowed to take as much food and clothing as they could carry for the ten-day walk. Supplies ran out after a couple of days, the marchers slept in the open in a bitter Eastern European winter, and the Jews died in their thousands. Corpses lay at the side of the road all the way to the Austrian border in this, the final stage of the Holocaust's mass murder. It was a pointless exercise anyway because, by the time survivors reached Austria, they were far too weak and sick to work. But then logic was never one of the Third Reich's strong points.

At the end of 1944 Lutz and his colleagues began preparations to ship the 7,800 original Hungarian certificate holders to Palestine. Two collective Swiss passports were prepared, each containing about 1,000 names and photographs, together with personal details. The Swiss passports survived the war; one is held in the archives of the Yad Vashem Holocaust Memorial Museum in Jerusalem, the other at the Swiss Federal Archives in Bern. The Jews' faces still stare out from their pages, dressed in their best weekend suits and dresses, hopeful and a bit disbelieving, perhaps, that they will be saved from the Nazis and the Arrow Cross by Swiss officialdom.

Here are Mr. and Mrs. Josip Schmeizer, born in 1909 and 1911 respectively, numbers 426 and 427 on the lifesaving list. Before them come Dr. Tibor Czinner, born in 1906, and his wife, born in 1913, her hair drawn back in a bun, as they stare at the camera. Numbers 428 and 429 are Sabetaj Alteras and his wife, leaning toward each other with their heads touching. Sabetaj's hair is neatly combed, and his mustache is carefully trimmed in the manner of the Hungarian bourgeoisie. Three fading snapshots of a vanished world of central European Jewry.

Transport to Palestine through the Balkans for the 7,800 proved impossible to arrange, because of "war operations and other difficulties," as Dr. Goldin's report relates in the understated manner of officialdom. Instead, Lutz applied to Bern to bring the first 2,000 to Switzerland. With the Red Army at the gates of Budapest, the Arrow Cross government even provided five trains to transport the Jews and guaranteed safe passage. Even the German ambassador, Veesenmayer, a driving force behind the Hungarian Holocaust, suddenly got in on the act and guaranteed safe passage. By then, it was too late, for the Jews were saved anyway. The Red Army smashed its way through the Nazi and Arrow Cross lines, and Budapest was liberated. Even now Holocaust survivors remember how Russian soldiers used their bayonets to cut off by hand the Jews' yellow stars as the Red Army stormed into the ghetto. Over 200,000 Hungarian Jews lived through the Holocaust, the largest Jewish community to survive in any area under Nazi rule.

Lutz, like his colleague Wallenberg, refused to leave the city as the Russian advance progressed, although the head of the Swiss legation left in November 1944. When, in early 1945, the Soviet troops stormed his building, Lutz jumped out of the window and fled across the river to unoccupied Buda. He survived the war and earned the eternal gratitude of the Jews he saved. Lutz was fully supported by his boss, the Swiss ambassador, in his lifesaving work, but some of his colleagues at the Swiss foreign ministry in Bern took a different view of his activities in wartime Budapest. What was a Swiss diplomat doing, saving Hungarian Jews by issuing certificates for British-ruled Palestine? they asked, tut-tutting and shaking their heads. Instead of being hailed as a hero, Lutz was reprimanded by the Swiss foreign ministry for having overstepped his authority in his wartime work.

NEVER had Switzerland been the focus of so much united attention from both Jews and Nazis as during those months of 1944, while Lutz and Krausz were issuing their protection papers. The Nazi flight of capital to neutral countries was in full flow in this final stage of the Holocaust. As the defeat of the Third Reich appeared inevitable, Nazi leaders such as Himmler were wondering if Hungary's remaining Jews might not be worth more alive than dead, as a card to play in opening negotiations with the West, through Switzerland. In Budapest a Zionist leader named Rezso Kasztner was negotiating with Adolf Eichmann to transport Jews to Switzerland, the first link in a chain of controversial deals that would, in a few months, stretch from wartime Europe to Washington, D.C. In Bern, Recha and Rabbi Isaac Sternbuch, leaders of a rescue group, were working with former Swiss president Jean-Marie Musy, a pro-Nazi and friend of Himmler, to ransom Europe's surviving Jews.

Meanwhile, in Stuttgart, Andor "Bandi" Grosz, a Hungarian Jew working for Nazi intelligence, was preparing to leave for Switzerland on a mission to buy Swiss goods for the Third Reich and spy on the British presence there.

Why did the Jewish–Nazi negotiations in the summer and autumn of 1944 concern only Hungarian Jewry? The answer is simple: by then the rest of Eastern Europe's Jewry was virtually eradicated. Three million Jews were killed in Poland alone, and the Jews of Budapest were the last remaining Jewish community. At that time about 200,000 Hungarian Jews were still alive, while the once-flourishing communities of Warsaw, Vilna, Prague, Berlin, Vienna, Bratislava, Belgrade, and Salonika had all been wiped out. The cities were, in Nazi terminology, Judenrein, or "Jew-free." There was no one else left to negotiate over.

To start with, the Kasztner–Eichmann negotiations. On the surface at least, the two men sitting face to face in Budapest in June 1944 to discuss Kasztner's negotiating proposals had a lot in common. Both were supremely arrogant careerists, disdainful of their underlings, passionately interested in the Jewish question, and even shared a knowledge of Hebrew. The difference was, one wanted to kill as many Jews as possible, the other to save them. But those dog days of 1944, as the Allies advanced from the West and the Soviets from the East, and the Third Reich began its death throes, made for unlikely partners. Under Himmler's instructions Eichmann and Kasztner managed a modus operandi of sorts and arranged a secret deal that allowed Kasztner to choose 1,685 Jews and put them on a secret train to Switzerland. The VIP train, as it became known, would haunt Kasztner for the rest of his days and eventually cost him his life.

The Nazi leader, who was later kidnapped by Israeli agents, put on trial in Jerusalem, and hanged, was quite taken with Kasztner, as an interview he gave, published in *Life* magazine in November 1960, reveals:

> This Dr. Kasztner was a young man about my age, an ice-cold lawyer and a fanatical Zionist. He agreed to help keep the Jews from resisting deportation—and even keep order in the collection camps—if I would close my eyes and let a few hundred or a few thousand young Jews emigrate illegally to Palestine. It was a good bargain. . . . Except perhaps for the first two sessions, Kasztner never came to me fearful of the Gestapo strong man.
>
> We negotiated entirely as equals. People forget that. We were political opponents trying to arrive at a settlement and we trusted

each other perfectly. When he was with me, Kasztner smoked cigarettes as though he was in a coffeehouse. While we talked he would smoke one aromatic cigarette after another, taking them from a silver case and lighting them with a cigarette lighter. With his great polish and reserve he would have made an ideal Gestapo officer himself.

As a matter of fact, there was a very strong similarity between our attitudes in the SS and the viewpoint of these immensely idealistic Zionist leaders who were fighting what might be their last battle. As I told Kasztner: "We too are idealists, and we too had to sacrifice our own blood before we came to power." I believe that Kasztner would have sacrificed a thousand or a hundred thousand of his blood to achieve his goal.

Who then was this man whom Adolf Eichmann might have employed himself under different circumstances? Born in 1906—the same year as Eichmann—in the town of Cluj, now in Romania, Kasztner ran the Relief and Rescue Committee of Budapest (RRCB), under the aegis of the Zionist movement, one of many Jewish organizations active in the wartime Hungarian capital. A lawyer and a journalist, Kasztner ran a committee that was the hub of a clandestine network of Jewish rescue organizations that stretched from Hungary to Switzerland, Poland, Slovakia, and Istanbul. Even his defenders admit he was not a very sympathetic personality, but then these were not very sympathetic times.

"He was a very unpleasant fellow," says Yehuda Bauer, professor of Holocaust studies at the Hebrew University of Jerusalem. "He was ambitious, overweening. He wasn't too literal with the truth. He was very unpleasant toward some of his underlings, and he did things that are with hindsight utterly condemnable."

Kasztner's conceited personality was probably better suited to war than peace. When the Nazis marched into Hungary his committee contacted Eichmann. He believed, correctly as it turned out, that he could negotiate with the Nazis, exchanging lives for cash that the Nazis could then deposit in neutral countries such as Switzerland. The RRCB's model was the secret negotiations between Slovak Jewish leaders and the Nazi official Dieter Wisliceny, Eichmann's representative, that attempted to ransom Slovak Jewry for a payment of several hundred thousand Swiss francs, known as the Europa Plan. In the event, the

Europa Plan, to be financed partly through Saly Mayer, the Swiss Jewish leader and representative there of the Joint Distribution Committee, the American Jewish relief organization, failed to save Slovak Jewry. Seventy-five thousand Slovak Jews were annihilated, over four-fifths of the country's Jewish population. Even so, negotiating channels had been opened and the deportations delayed. The Slovak talks showed that the Nazis were ready to discuss deals. At this late stage in the war, even delaying tactics were better than nothing, Kasztner and his colleagues believed.

But Eichmann had no time for delaying tactics once he arrived in Budapest. His methods there followed the classic Nazi model in dealing with local Jewish authorities. It was, in essence, to force lay and religious leaders to organize the destruction of their own communities, through a combination of terror and threats, appeasement and cajoling, a poison brew sweetened by the false promise that better days were just around the corner. Even now, many Hungarian Holocaust survivors, such as Zoltan and Katalin Csillag, nurture a decades-old anger at the response of the Hungarian Jewish community leaders to the Nazi demands.

"Samu Stern, the president of the Jewish Council, had a lot of power, but he just kept telling people to relax, to be calm because nothing will happen to them, but he should have warned us," says Mrs. Csillag. "He knew a lot more than we did, and a lot of people would have left if he hadn't always been telling them to calm down, especially the Jews in the countryside. I have a copy of his memoirs, and he is trying to white-wash himself. I tried to read them, but I got too upset. He was very conceited and self-assured."

THE GHOST of the Kasztner train that rumbled out of Budapest on 30 June 1944 still haunts both Hungary and Israel. All its passengers were saved and eventually reached Switzerland, albeit after a lengthy stopover at Bergen-Belsen. Kasztner himself helped draw up the passenger list, which included his family, friends, and senior Jewish and Zionist leaders. But why did Eichmann agree to save Kasztner's friends and relatives? The price was high, more than any amount of money, some Hungarian Holocaust survivors charge: silence about Auschwitz and a quiescent Jewish population that would meekly board the cattle trains that left Budapest's Jozeftown station for "resettlement in the East" in exchange for safe passage to Switzerland for Kasztner's chosen VIPs.

Kasztner, and other Jewish leaders, knew full well what awaited Hungary's Jews in Poland. By the end of April 1944 Kasztner had received information about the contents of the "Auschwitz Protocol." Compiled by two former Auschwitz prisoners, Alfred Wetzler and Rudolf Vrba, who had escaped that month and made their way to Slovakia, it was an incredibly detailed report on the inner workings of the prime site of the Nazi genocide machine. Its authors had seen the preparations being made at Auschwitz for the annihilation of Hungary's Jews and hoped that, once alerted, Hungarian Jewish leaders would organize passive or active resistance, or even just encourage the Hungarian Jews to flee into the countryside. But Kasztner and his colleagues kept silent, and Hungary's Jews meekly boarded the cattle trains to their deaths.

Budapest-born Ernest Stein, a fighter in the Budapest Zionist resistance, well remembers Kasztner. During 1944 Stein, then twenty-one, frequently traveled to the city's Keleti (eastern) station, where for 100 pengös ($20) he would buy Luger pistols from Hungarian soldiers returning from the eastern front. "Kasztner was above us, a big shot. I heard a story about him. A witness told me in Israel that in Oradea [now in Romania], when people were being put into the wagons, and Kasztner was a personal friend to these people, he told this person's father that he could go into the train. He said, 'Nothing is going to happen to you. They are going to take you over the Danube and you will go to work,' " says Stein, now living in the United States.

"This man was a personal friend of Kasztner. That shows Kasztner was less than a rat: he was a liar, he was a thief, he did it on purpose to help the German cause. Kasztner received the Auschwitz Protocol, but he never showed it to anybody. I am sure that he did a deal with the Nazis to get permission to take that train out. He did everything for that train. For him the rest of the Jews were not important. He figured that if he took out the fifteen hundred or two thousand people the rest can go to hell—it was his friends, and his family."

Hearing rumors of the planned secret train to Switzerland, Stein attempted to get a place for himself and his family. "I could not get in: they had only people who were paying money, and their personal friends, major functionaries in the Zionist movement. Kasztner wasn't paying Eichmann off: he followed Eichmann's orders. The Jewish Committee followed Eichmann's orders because they were chicken. Kasztner was the same as the other families, the famous Jewish families, like the Weiss family, who the Gestapo took out to get the ownership of the factories."

Certainly, unlike Ernest Stein, Kasztner believed in negotiating with Nazis, rather than shooting them—so much so that when two Jewish soldiers were parachuted in from Palestine to Hungary, with British assistance, to help organize resistance against the deportations, Kasztner forced them to turn themselves in to the Gestapo. He argued that their presence endangered the whole community, although it is hard to imagine how much more perilous the situation of Budapest's Jews could get.

Kasztner's main ally in organizing his VIP train to Switzerland was an SS officer called Kurt Becher, who arrived in Budapest soon after the Nazis occupied Hungary in March 1944. Becher's official title was head of the "Commission for the Registration of Remount Horses," but his real role was to channel Nazi loot to neutral countries for his ultimate boss, Heinrich Himmler. As Eichmann himself said, as reported in *Life* magazine, "Becher was bartering Jews for foreign exchange and goods on direct orders from Himmler."

An OSS report on Nazi financial dealings in Switzerland, dated 6 April 1945, names an Obergruppenführer Becher as helping arrange a trip to Switzerland for a Hungarian businessman who had recently arrived in Zürich with a trunk containing securities. "Becher, who is one of the chief fixers in the Nazi Party, is suspected of being charged with the task of providing safe haven for Nazi funds," the intelligence document says. Becher, who had served at Dachau, was also implicated in looting goods and valuables from Jews in Poland.

The Hungarian Zionist leader and the SS officer got on so well that in early 1945, as Himmler leaned further toward the idea of a separate peace with the western Allies, Becher traveled across Germany to try to prevent the destruction of the camps as the war drew to a close and save the remaining Jews, working with SS General Walter Schellenberg under Himmler's instructions. He even took Kasztner with him. Becher's murky record on the eastern front before his arrival in Budapest did not dim Kasztner's admiration for the SS officer. After Germany surrendered, Kurt Becher was arrested by the Allies as a suspected war criminal, but Kasztner came to his Nazi friend's rescue and testified to his good character. The former SS officer was released and went on to make a successful career in business in West Germany.

Becher's business career in wartime Budapest was also quite successful, as he oversaw all the financial arrangements for the VIP train. With 1,685 passengers, each paying $1,000 a head in cash or the equivalent, the "Becher Deposit"—as the price for the Kasztner train became known—was worth over $1.5 million. It was paid in various forms, including foreign currency such as U.S. dollars, British pounds, and Swedish crowns; Napoleon, British, and Hungarian gold medals; jewels and platinum; gold and platinum watches, Hungarian shares and currency and diamonds. Rich passengers subsidized those who could not pay. What happened to the Becher Deposit? Some of it was returned to at least one Jewish organization after the war, the Jewish Agency in Jerusalem, according to files in the Central Zionist Archives, but a large part simply vanished, almost certainly into Becher's own pockets.

Kasztner is still remembered in Budapest, and not with affection. "He used to threaten his people with the Gestapo if they didn't behave well. He had the power standing behind him," says one Hungarian Holocaust survivor. "He deserved to die, but he should have been put on trial and punished legally. I think he made a deal with Becher because he was afraid Becher would frame him, and they had an agreement not to betray each other under any circumstances."

Kasztner's ambiguous relationship with Becher, the man he described in his postwar report as "cut from a different wood than the professional mass murderers of the political SS," eventually caught up with him. In August 1952 Malchiel Gruenwald, a Hungarian Jew living in Jerusalem, published issue 52 of his private newsletter. It accused Kasztner of stealing the wealth of Hungarian Jews together with Becher.

Kasztner brought a libel suit against Gruenwald, but the case soon turned into a trial of his wartime connections with Eichmann and Becher. In his summing up, the judge, Benjamin Halevi, accused Kasztner of having "sold his soul to the devil" by negotiating with the Nazis. In March 1957 Kasztner was shot dead outside his house. The Israeli Supreme Court eventually cleared Kasztner of all accusations except the charge that he had helped Nazis escape justice. His killer was caught and imprisoned, but some saw murkier undercurrents at work and blamed Israeli intelligence for his death. Dead men don't talk, and nobody knew more than Rezso Kasztner about the secret deals between Budapest's Zionist leadership and Adolf Eichmann.

As THE Allied armies marched toward Germany and Himmler schemed for a separate peace with the western Allies, the Nazis dreamed up ever wilder schemes to save themselves, using Jewish lives as ransom. The deal, Himmler believed, could be negotiated through Jewish groups in Switzerland, such as the Joint Distribution Committee, or through the Jewish Agency in Palestine. Himmler, like many Nazis, had fallen victim to his own propaganda and really believed that the mythical international Jewish/Zionist conspiracy existed, with branches in London, Palestine, and Switzerland, from where it controlled the world.

One of the most bizarre attempted deals between Jews and Nazis was the Joel Brand mission to Istanbul. In mid-April 1944 Eichmann summoned Joel Brand, a Hungarian Jew and former Comintern agent who had been smuggling Jewish refugees from Poland and Slovakia into Hungary, to his headquarters at the Hotel Majestic on Budapest's Schwab Hill. Brand worked closely with Kasztner. Eichmann, almost certainly under instructions from Himmler, offered him a deal: the Nazis would swap a million Jewish lives for goods to help the German war effort. The price of a million Jews was finally agreed as 10,000 trucks and large quantities of consumer staples such as cocoa, to be supplied by the western Allies. These goods, promised Eichmann, would only be used on the eastern front against the Soviet Union.

Brand was accompanied on his journey to Istanbul by the unlikely figure of Andor Grosz, the Hungarian Jew who was working for Nazi intelligence. Grosz was a sleazy figure, a convicted smuggler and black marketeer, an agent for the Abwehr (German military intelligence), the Hungarian secret service, and probably the Zionists as well.

Like Joel Brand, Bandi Grosz was soon arrested, once he left Turkey, and held by British authorities. His interrogation report, marked "Top Secret," has been declassified. Grosz's story shows how, for venal Nazis eager to shift their wealth to Switzerland, money took precedence over Nazi racial theories. A Jew too could serve the Aryan master race if there was profit enough for the Germans.

Grosz was supplying Austrian Jews with Hungarian passports as well as smuggling gold between Switzerland and Hungary. But his past was catching up with him, and the police were on his trail. Salvation, he believed, lay in the arms of the Nazis, who promised to deal with the Hungarian police for him. Early in 1942 Grosz was recruited by Nazi intelligence, by one Kleer, paying 10,000 pengös for the privilege to another Nazi agent operating in Hungary, Franz Szigli. Grosz did not have to spy exactly, his new Nazi taskmasters told him, just help in commercial activities, especially by using his many connections—by this time Grosz was known as the "smuggler king of Budapest"—to buy up goods in Switzerland and transport them to the Third Reich. Using a Hungarian Jew as a front for purchasing goods in Switzerland was not exactly what the Reichsbank officials had in mind when they issued their comprehensive instructions in September 1939 on how to camouflage Nazi financial assets, but then war makes for strange financial bedfellows.

In February 1942 Dr. Gustav Busse, the chief of the Stuttgart bureau that controlled Nazi espionage in both Switzerland and Spain, came to Budapest to visit his new recruit. Dr. Busse was well pleased with Grosz and promised both to sort out his local difficulties with the Hungarian police and even to issue him with a German passport. Grosz and Busse had a fine time carousing in Budapest, as Grosz's interrogation report says: "During the remainder of Busse's stay in Budapest, G. showed Busse the alcoholic sites of the Hungarian capital, usually paying his bills as a privilege for being guide."

Before he returned to Stuttgart, Busse gave a long list of instructions to Kleer for his and Grosz's mission to Switzerland. They were to purchase food for Germany, including chocolate, rice, and coca, devise a means of getting these to Germany, find out which transport firms were dealing with Britain, and discover which Swiss companies were selling bomb fuses to the Allies.

The two Nazi agents' trip to Switzerland did not go very well, at least for the German war effort, although Grosz and Kleer appear to have enjoyed themselves. Never one to waste a moneymaking opportunity, Grosz smuggled some platinum into Switzerland; he planned to sell it in Zürich and divide the profits among himself, Kleer, and Busse. Grosz met Kleer in Zürich, where Kleer outlined their mission in Switzerland. This was too much like hard work, especially as Grosz had language problems. He might have been a German agent, but he could not actually speak German, as his interrogation report details:

Kleer and Grosz, after probing the possibilities of carrying out Busse's mission, soon came to the conclusion that they could do nothing useful, particularly as the Swiss required goods and not money in return for their own goods. Moreover, G. spoke very little German at this time. Kleer proposed that the best thing they could do was to make as much money as possible in order to please Busse, who was not a rich man, and whose interests lay in money, women, and alcohol rather than espionage.

The two spies then spent a pleasant few days loafing and black marketeering in Switzerland, before returning to Stuttgart. There Dr. Busse did not seem too bothered at their lack of results, as he was drunk. As the report says: "They found Busse in a state of blissful intoxication. He showed no interest in whether they had carried out his instructions or not, and gladly assented to the formation of a smuggling society composed of himself, G., Kleer, and Scholz, for the purpose of filling out their own purses."

The Brand mission never stood a chance. Brand and Grosz were arrested by British authorities on their way to Palestine to meet officials of the Jewish Agency. The Allies rejected Eichmann's proposal out of hand, viewing it as an attempt to split Britain and the United States from the Soviet Union. Joel Brand died in Israel in 1964, a sad figure who never really recovered from the failure of his mission, although it was doomed from the start. He took revenge of sorts by testifying at Eichmann's trial in Jerusalem. As for Bandi Grosz, the Hungarian multiple-secret agent, he left Israel in the mid-1950s, probably with a payoff to keep his mouth shut about this murky episode in Zionist–Nazi relations, and died in Munich in the early 1970s.

WARTIME Switzerland was more than a dream of sanctuary: it was also a base for Jewish organizations that used Switzerland's role as an international financial center to aid and rescue Jews in the rest of Europe. Some Swiss banks too played a part in the relief effort to aid Jewish refugees. They held the funds of the Jewish organizations based in Switzerland, such as the Joint Distribution Committee (JDC), which ran clandestine operations to bring out Jews from Nazi-occupied Europe. They channeled money from the United States through the Swiss offices of the War Refugee Board to aid fleeing Jews. They held the organizational funds of the Swiss Jewish community leaders, such as

Saly Mayer, who tried to stall the final stages of the Holocaust by meeting in Zürich with Himmler's envoy, the SS officer Kurt Becher, who was based in wartime Budapest.

One bank, Intercommerz AG of Zürich, even offered to wipe out Hungarian debts of several million pengös to its Swiss clients if an equivalent sum would be paid instead to Hungarian Jews, documents in the Hungarian National Archives reveal. "Intercommerz AG made the following offer through the Hungarian Bank of Commerce: to cancel Hungarian debts to Swiss creditors if the countervalue of this amount in Hungarian currency would be paid to Jews in the following way: half to named Jews and the other half to assist poor Jews through the Association of Hungarian Jews," according to the Hungarian Government Protocol of 2 August 1944. Intercommerz's offer was treated favorably by both the government and the Swiss National Bank, says the document, and the ministry of finance asked for authorization to accept the offer.

While Joel Brand was languishing in a British prison, Rezso Kasztner was traveling to Switzerland to negotiate with the JDC representative Saly Mayer and SS officer Kurt Becher. After news reached Budapest of Brand's arrest by the British, Kasztner approached Mayer and suggested that the two of them negotiate with the Nazis to ransom the remaining Hungarian Jews. Mayer had also been involved in the Europa Plan, the abortive attempt to rescue Slovak Jewry by paying off the Nazis. The JDC said that Mayer could not represent them in any negotiations, while U.S. officials in Switzerland gave the go-ahead for the talks, on condition that he inform them in detail about the discussion, and instructed him to offer Becher neither goods nor money. With his hands so tied, Mayer's tactics were to procrastinate as long as possible and so save the remnants of Hungarian Jewry.

Mayer, Becher, Kasztner, and others met several times between 21 August 1944 and 5 February 1945. At first the Swiss authorities forbade Becher from entering Switzerland, and Mayer did not want to enter Germany, so the first meeting took place in the middle of the border bridge at St. Margarethen. There were five men that summer's day standing on the Swiss–German frontier: Mayer, Kasztner, Becher, and two more German officers, Max Grueson and Hermann Krumey. Becher again demanded the 10,000 trucks Joel Brand had failed to supply, and, to show their good faith, the Nazis brought with them from

Bergen-Belsen 318 passengers on the Kasztner train—or "pieces," as Becher described these Jews in his report to Himmler of that meeting on the bridge. Mayer did not have one truck at his disposal, let alone 10,000, but to tell Becher that would have immediately terminated the negotiations. Instead he offered to try to supply minerals and industrial goods. This would take time to arrange, he explained, for these were difficult and complicated times.

The bridge negotiations had an immediate result, one that highlighted Himmler's seriousness in his desire to open a channel to the West. On 24 August Himmler issued an order to the Nazis in Budapest not to deport the city's Jews. After the war Becher attempted to take credit for this by claiming that he had persuaded Himmler to stop the killings.

At the same time Mayer was negotiating with the Nazis, another group of Jews based in Switzerland was also trying to cut a deal with Himmler. This was the Montreux Committee, led by Isaac and Elias Sternbuch and Isaac's wife, Recha. They and Mayer loathed each other. The Sternbuchs saw the Swiss Jewish leader as a pedantic bureaucrat who wanted to operate only through official channels, while Mayer viewed them as uncontrollable radicals whose work threatened the delicate state of Swiss–Jewish relations.

Recha Sternbuch had been rescuing Jews from the Sternbuchs' base in Switzerland since before the war, by running a relief operation that supplied refugees with forged visas that she took into Austria or Germany. She also bribed diplomats in Bern to issue visas that she would then distribute. In the spring of 1939 she was arrested and charged with bribery. The case dragged on until June 1942, when all charges against her were dismissed.

Mayer had several run-ins with the Sternbuchs over Jewish refugees. When two Jewish refugee brothers named Blum were caught and were about to be sent back to France, Recha Sternbuch went to see Mayer. She asked him to intercede with Heinrich Rothmund, head of the foreigner police, in their favor. Mayer responded to her pleas with a lecture on Swiss patriotism, record the authors of *Heroine of Rescue*. "Frau Sternbuch, if you were a good Swiss citizen you would consider it your duty to take the two men who had crossed illegally by the collar and hand them over to the police," said Mayer, arguing that Jewish law ruled that the law of the land must be obeyed.

In the autumn of 1944 the Sternbuchs found help from an unexpected quarter. Jean-Marie Musy was a former Swiss president, a pro-Nazi, and a friend of Himmler. Aware, like every Swiss official, that the Germans had lost, Musy decided to restore his tattered reputation. He had already freed a Jewish couple from a concentration camp by using his connections. Recha Sternbuch, who must have been a truly remarkable woman, persuaded this admirer of Hitler to travel to Berlin and bribe Himmler into freeing the Jews held in the camps. Traveling through the Allied air raids in a new Mercedes with a large red cross painted on its roof, which the Sternbuchs had bought for him, Musy arrived in Berlin in autumn 1944. He met with both SS General Walter Schellenberg and his old friend Heinrich Himmler.

The price for the remaining Jews was SF5 million ($1.1 million), said Himmler, offering a bargain rate. Those were difficult times for senior Nazi leaders, who knew they would probably soon be put on trial as war criminals and wanted to improve their bloody reputations.

Musy made several trips to Berlin to see Himmler and Schellenberg as the Third Reich crumbled. They were extremely dangerous journeys for this seventy-five-year-old pillar of the Swiss establishment. His son Benoit, an officer in the Swiss air force, drove for hours through the bomb-scarred wreckage of the Third Reich, dodging Allied bombs, which on one occasion peppered the vehicle with shrapnel. Musy failed to persuade Himmler to open the camps and free all the Jews, but neither were they destroyed and all the survivors slaughtered, as many Nazis planned. Among the piles of dead stick-men and women at Bergen-Belsen and Mauthausen, Ravensbruck and Dachau, Allied troops found survivors as well. Probably his greatest achievement was Himmler's decision to release 1,210 Jews from the concentration camp at Thereisenstadt in Czechoslovakia. The "Musy train," as it was known, arrived in Montreux, Switzerland, in February 1945.

Isaac and Recha Sternbuch; Saly Mayer; Rezso Kasztner; Roswell D. McClelland, a representative of the U.S. War Refugee Board (WRB); the SS officers Kurt Becher and Walter Schellenberg; Jean-Marie Musy—this cast of the Swiss–Jewish–Nazi talks was growing ever larger. With two sets of simultaneous and overlapping negotiations going on in Berlin and Bern, it was no wonder that even Himmler himself got confused. Which Jewish group was demanding what from the Nazis, and what could they deliver in return? On 18 January 1945

Himmler wrote a note to himself asking who had the links to Washington that he so craved: "Who is the one with whom the American government actually maintains contact? Is it a rabbinical Jew [Sternbuch] or is it the Jioint [sic—Mayer]?"

While Musy was negotiating with Himmler in Berlin, Saly Mayer soon realized that he would have to offer the Nazis more than money. The time had come to arrange a meeting with a representative of the Allied powers. Mayer arranged for Kurt Becher to be granted a Swiss visa, and on 5 November Becher and Mayer met at the Hotel Baur in Zürich, together with Roswell McClelland. Mayer's trump card was a cable from the WRB, with the signature of Cordell Hull, U.S. secretary of state. The cable promised a credit of SF20 million ($4.4 million) for Mayer's relief work, although Mayer did not tell Becher that the money could only be used for relief work and not to purchase goods for Germany.

Becher was impressed by this telegram, Kasztner records in his postwar report. Here at last was a channel to Washington, opened, just as Himmler believed it would be, by international Jewry. "This telegram was of special importance for Becher. Although it was not said in the telegram that the $5 million (approx. SF20 million) was targeted for the delivery of goods for the Reich, he tended to assume that the business was developing, because it corresponded to his dreams rather than reality. . . . He was especially impressed by his discussion with McClelland and was able to notify Himmler that he had managed to contact Roosevelt's special commissioner. He connected this contact with vague and unexpressed hopes, and with a secret wish for the possibility of a political approach and for a personal alibi."

This discussion, among an SS officer, a Jewish leader, and an American official, was one of the most extraordinary meetings of the war. Yehuda Bauer writes:

> What happened at the Hotel Baur on that November day is quite amazing: an official representative of the U.S. government met with a high SS officer on neutral ground, ostensibly to discuss humanitarian issues. The meeting was in total contravention of official U.S. policy, according to which the only purpose of any negotiations with the Germans would be to settle the latter's unconditional surrender. Indeed, I know of no comparable action on the part of the Americans during World War II.

Considered in isolation, the discussion at the Hotel Baur achieved little, for the Nazis would not hand over Jews on Mayer's and McClelland's terms, and Washington would not allow Mayer to pay with money for Jewish lives. But, taken as part of a continuum, the discussion at the Hotel Baur was the culmination of a process of negotiations in Switzerland that had almost certainly slowed down the Holocaust and saved many Hungarian Jewish lives from the gas chambers at Auschwitz, in particular the 1,685 passengers on the Kasztner train.

After the war McClelland issued a statement, dated Bern, 6 February 1945, defending Kasztner. He stated that all the meetings among the Germans, Mayer, and Kasztner between the summer of 1944 and early 1945 had been conducted with the full knowledge of both the WRB and the U.S. State Department, with the British and Russian governments kept advised of any developments.

> I wish to add that, to the best of my knowledge, no charges could be made against those Jews on the spot who organized the release of these two groups [passengers on the Kasztner train] nor against those who were included in these transports either because of their activities as organizers or members of these groups. . . . In view of the desperate circumstances prevailing at that time, and the mentality of the Nazi leaders involved, the very fact of bringing these two groups safely to Switzerland was to be considered as an achievement of great importance.

While by late 1944 Budapest's Jews had been saved from mass deportations to Auschwitz, many thousands more would die on death marches to the Austrian border or shot into the Danube. But the Weiss family—wealthy Hungarian industrialists—were saved. The Weisses, who were of Jewish origin but had converted to Christianity, escaped the Holocaust to safety in Switzerland and Portugal by arranging a secret deal with the Nazis. As with the Kasztner train, the deal between the Weisses and the Nazis was completed by Kurt Becher, the SS officer charged with funneling Nazi loot to Switzerland.

Headed by Baron Manfred, the Weiss family, by the 1930s, ran Hungary's "largest and most important industrial establishment," according to an eighteen-page U.S. intelligence report, dated Lisbon, 23 May 1945. The Weiss empire manufactured everything from bicycles to armaments. In Berlin, the Nazis wanted the Weiss economic empire, which stretched around the world, and the struggle for it even triggered an intra-Reich power struggle between Himmler and Goering. In Washington, D.C., Safehaven officials watched nervously as the Germans prepared for an invasion of Hungary, for if the Weiss empire fell into Nazi hands the Third Reich would obtain the perfect economic cloak for shifting Nazi economic assets into neutral countries, not to mention the boost the Weiss factories would give the Nazi war machine. Operation Safehaven focused on Switzerland, as that was the Nazis' main refuge for looted gold, but that was just one link in the chain of Nazi financial chicanery that sought both to acquire looted assets and to find a means of disguising their provenance before sending them on to Switzerland. The Weiss family holdings became part of that chain.

The Weisses were active anti-Nazis, although part of Hungary's establishment. Their wealth, their connections, and their industrial empire put the Weiss family at the top of the Nazi hit list. After the German invasion of Hungary on 15 March 1944, the Nazis captured several members of the Weiss family, including Baron Eugen Weiss, son of Manfred. On 4 April, the intelligence report says, Baron Eugen was conducted to a meeting with Kurt Becher.

Becher's proposal was simple: freedom for the family and transport to Switzerland and Portugal, in exchange for handing over the Weiss empire to the Nazis. Under great duress, the deal was signed. The Weiss factories on Budapest's Csepel Island were handed over.

"The family bought their way out of Hungary," says historian Marc Masurovsky. "They signed an agreement to release the family on a special train at night, so the other Jews wouldn't know about it. For the Allies the Weiss scenario is a nightmare come true. One year before the end of the war Himmler is holding the most important businessman in Hungary and one of the most powerful businessmen in Europe. The Allies were interested in the Weiss family because the empire spread into twenty-two countries, including the United States. The Allies didn't want to see Himmler taking the Weiss family hostage in order to be able to take over the empire, which he did. The Allies think that if Weiss transfers ownership to the Nazis, then overnight they will have a multinational corporation, with links on three continents, a wonderful cloak. To them, that is the ultimate Safehaven nightmare."

More than that, the Weiss Safehaven files show how skillfully the Nazis exploited the substantial class differences within Hungary's Jewish community to divide and rule. The Weiss family could have exploited their wealth and massive holdings to save other Hungarian Jews, argues Masurovsky. "There is no question about it. The Weiss family had money, tons of money. They could probably have bought every Jew in Hungary. They could have set up a market, just like the Germans were doing with their own Jews, saying, 'You want to go to Switzerland, you pay us.' During the war money talked. When you were a rich Hungarian Jew, your money spoke for you."

Like the Kasztner affair, the flight of the Weiss family still arouses strong emotions in Budapest. Some Hungarian Holocaust survivors agree with Masurovsky that the rich industrialists could have saved more than themselves, instead of abandoning their former coreligionists to the Nazis. In hindsight we can only speculate, for ultimately no group of Jews, no matter how eminent and wealthy, was a match for armed SS soldiers or the Gestapo. What the Nazis wanted, the Nazis took.

But—and it is an important but—Becher expended much effort on ensuring that the agreement to hand over the Weiss economic empire had a veneer of legality. The agreement with the Weisses is packed with clauses, definitions, and caveats, just as one signed freely would be. The Weisses had, perhaps, some room for maneuver. Kasztner, for example—whose organization could have fitted into one room and had virtually no resources—had managed to save 1,685 Jews and helped slow down the final stages of the Holocaust. The Weiss family had many more cards to play than the young Zionist leader, but they saved only themselves. They were extremely rich and powerful, with family connections that stretched to Admiral Horthy. And Becher wanted their signature on his documents so that the deal appeared legal.

Why did Becher take so much trouble with the details of the agreement with the Weiss family? Why did he not take the Einsatzgruppen approach and simply shoot them before taking what he wanted? In part because Hungary, while under German occupation, was not annexed to the Third Reich. At that stage of the war, in early summer of 1944, Becher's boss, Himmler, wanted to maintain reasonable relations with Admiral Horthy. In the event, the Hungarian government was furious that the country's premier industrial combine had been appropriated by the SS, but there was little Horthy's ministers could do about it. More important, though, just as outlined in the economics ministry memo of September 1939, the Nazis could exploit the Weiss empire to camouflage their economic holdings abroad. The Weiss concern, with its links all over the globe, would be the perfect camouflage for Nazi international finances. Even better, in the twisted Nazi scheme of things, it was owned by a family of converted Jews. Nobody could accuse them of being Himmler's stooges.

Surviving Weiss family members who left under Becher's protection, such as Thomas DeKornfeld, grandson of Baron Manfred, deny that the Weisses could have saved anyone else. Now seventy-two and a professor of anesthesiology at Michigan University, DeKornfeld still returns occasionally to the city where his family would socialize with Admiral Horthy, although the old Weiss family apartments are now the French embassy.

"It's nonsense to say we could have helped other people. There weren't any negotiations. We were told, 'You sign this and we will let you go, or we take it anyway.' I know there were considerable hard feelings about this among other people, but there was never one moment to do otherwise," says DeKornfeld, whose polite reserve slips for a moment or two on this touchy subject. "It all happened when our survival was very much in doubt and when many of our colleagues did not survive. I must reemphasize that criticism that we should have done something for other people is wrong. There is nothing we could have done. We were assembled at four P.M., at nine P.M. we signed, and at ten P.M. we were out. There is nothing anybody could have done for, to, or about it."

Like Kasztner, DeKornfeld was quite taken with Kurt Becher. "I met him; he was well educated, courteous, a gentleman who kept his word. He was polite and businesslike." But then the Kurt Becher of 1944 Budapest, who even moved into apartments owned by part of the Weiss family, was a different person from the one serving on the eastern front a few years earlier. Once the deal was signed, the Weiss family members were loaded into a German military vehicle, before being taken to Pukersdorf, outside Vienna. There they spent four weeks, under SS guard. "We were treated with the utmost courtesy and guarded by an SS attachment. They weren't sure who we were, or why we were there, but we were treated as German VIPs," DeKornfeld says.

Over the next few months the various family members made their way to neutral countries, either Switzerland or Portugal. Even now, DeKornfeld finds it hard to understand why Becher kept his word and allowed him to travel to Portugal. "I felt incredibly relieved when we arrived, obviously. We landed in Barcelona to refuel, and that was the first time I truly accepted the fact this was all for real. I thought at any time we might end up in Mauthausen or Dachau. I don't know why the Germans kept their word. I've been wondering ever since. Like most people who survived, my thoughts are of gratitude, amazement, mixed with awe. I still don't know why it happened. It must have been something inside the Third Reich, to do with rivalry between Himmler and Goering. They could have made us sign there and then and made us disappear."

OF ALL those who disappeared in wartime Hungary, the most famous name is that of Raoul Wallenberg, the Swedish diplomat who saved tens of thousands of Budapest Jews in the closing months of the war and perished in the Soviet Gulag. Witnesses recall how he would appear at roundups of Jews and remove as many as possible, right under the guns of the Hungarian Nazi Arrow Cross and their German colleagues.

Ernest Stein worked with Wallenberg. "I met him a number of times. He was a slight man, and you would not expect him to do what he did, or imagine how much courage he had. He was always running, always hiding, and you could never talk to him for more than five minutes. I was with him on the Austrian border. We were typing up people's names and issuing the Swedish passes."

Wallenberg was a scion of one of Sweden's most important families. His father's cousins Jacob and Marcus controlled the Enskilda Bank, and their wartime deals were being closely monitored by Safehaven agents in Washington, D.C. Jacob and Marcus took a more expedient view of wartime opportunities than their nephew, pulling off a series of lucrative wartime deals with both the Allies and the Axis. In 1942 Boris Rybkin, the NKVD (forerunner of the KGB) resident in Stockholm, arranged a deal to supply the Soviet Union with high-tensile Swedish steel for the aviation industry.

"The deal was a gross violation of Swedish neutrality, but the Enskilda Bank, controlled by the Wallenberg family, profited handsomely from the exchange of the steel for Russian platinum," writes Pavel Sudaplatov, a former NKVD officer, in his book *Special Tasks*. (Sudaplatov's tasks were indeed quite special: he is credited with having organized Trotsky's murder in Mexico and running the Soviet atom spy rings in the United States.)

Like Switzerland, Sweden traded profitably with the Third Reich, accepting German gold in exchange for millions of tons of iron ore that were refined into steel to build Panzer tanks and artillery. It was not until March 1944 that the Swedes stopped accepting German gold as payment for the iron. German troops even transited Swedish territory on their way to invade Norway.

Like the Swiss Federal Council, the Swedish government encouraged the country's national bank to accept German gold and not ask too many questions about where it came from. The Swedes received the same assurances as the Swiss from the Reichsbank that the gold paying for iron ore was not looted, but they too were worthless. After the war Sweden returned gold to Belgium and Holland that had been stolen by the Nazis.

In Washington, D.C., Henry Morgenthau wanted action taken against the Wallenberg brothers. A Treasury Department letter signed by Morgenthau, dated 7 February 1945, lists eight points of concern about their activities. They include:

> Jacob Wallenberg recently indicated that he was willing to sell to the Germans a Swedish plant in Hamburg for gold, provided the price was high enough to compensate for possible future complications.
>
> The following facts should be considered in evaluating the impression held in some circles that Marcus Wallenberg is strongly pro-Allied:
>
> a. While Marcus Wallenberg was apparently sympathetic with the Allied cause, Jacob Wallenberg, his brother and partner in the Enskilda Bank, was known to be sympathetic to and working with the Germans.
>
> b. Jacob Wallenberg was the author of the Swedish–German trading agreement.
>
> c. Jacob Wallenberg is a member of the Permanent Joint Swedish–German Trading Commission, and Marcus Wallenberg is a member of the Joint Standing Commission created by the Anglo-Swedish Trading Agreement.
>
> d. Marcus Wallenberg came to the United States in 1940 and attempted to purchase on behalf of German interest an American-held block of German securities.

Enskilda Bank has been repeatedly connected with large black-market operations in foreign currencies, including dollars reported to have been dumped by the Germans.

Why did the powerful Wallenberg family, which had profited handsomely from the war, do so little to secure Raoul's release from the Gulag? After all, his uncles Marcus and Jacob were well connected at the highest levels of the Kremlin. The answer was that Raoul Wallenberg was an embarrassment to some of the Wallenberg family, says his goddaughter, Yvonne Singer. Others theorize that a secret deal—Swedish steel in exchange for Hungarian Jews—allowed him to save so many lives. Ernest Stein agrees: "I heard that his family was cooperating with the Nazis, so the Germans overlooked his role."

Now fifty-one and living in Toronto, Yvonne Singer was born on Raoul Wallenberg's bed in one of his safe houses in Budapest. Her husband is Ron Singer, who has for years been attempting to recover the assets of his uncle Velvel Singer, who deposited substantial funds in a Swiss bank before being killed at Auschwitz (see chapter 1). Yvonne Singer's parents worked with the Swedish diplomat, and when, in the chaos that engulfed Budapest in November 1944, her mother went into labor, Raoul Wallenberg offered them sanctuary.

"Raoul Wallenberg saved my life," Yvonne says, "in that he protected my mother and let her have me in a safe place. My parents knew him well. They were working with him in the underground, to help rescue Jews. He offered his bed in his private apartment for my mother to give birth and helped get a doctor. He slept outside in the corridor. At first my parents went to one of the Swedish safe houses, but he offered his driver and his car and took them to his apartment."

Like many involved in the Wallenberg episode, Yvonne Singer is puzzled by the seemingly less than vigorous attempts by the powerful Wallenberg family made to get Raoul Wallenberg released. "The Wallenberg family did not take advantage of opportunities to save him or to pressure the establishment. There were several. There was an incident off the coast of Sweden and Russia, when some Russian sailors were captured. The Wallenberg family don't seem to be very proactive in terms of pressuring the Swedish government. I think he was an embarrassment to the Wallenberg family. It suited their agenda to have him stay there [in the Gulag]. They may have made some efforts, but it doesn't seem logical to me that a family with that kind of power would not have been able to exert some kind of pressure behind the scenes, to lobby on his behalf."

Singer also believes that Wallenberg was at least an asset, if not an active agent, of Allied intelligence. "I think he did work for the Americans: he passed information along. I know that he was in touch with the Hungarian underground; he was working with them—certainly all of those organizations had contact with the Allies."

It would have been easy to arrange for Wallenberg's death in Budapest in the autumn and winter of 1944, and there was at least one attempt to ram his car. This was a time of total chaos when the streets were ruled by Hungarian Arrow Cross killers. Why wasn't Wallenberg simply "accidentally" shot as he confronted the Arrow Cross and the SS on a daily basis? There were plenty of opportunities. But like the Weiss family, Wallenberg was useful for both the Hungarians and their German allies. The Hungarians did not want to kill a neutral diplomat, and for Kurt Becher, Himmler's emissary in his quest for a separate peace with the western Allies, a Swedish diplomat with links to Washington and the OSS was a potentially useful asset. The OSS ran a network in wartime Budapest, and, whether through an intermediary or directly, Wallenberg's reports back to Stockholm certainly reached the OSS. A declassified copy of Wallenberg's report on the situation of the Hungarian Jews, dated Budapest, 27 September 1944, reached OSS agents soon after and is now available in the U.S. National Archives.

CHARLES LUTZ, Raoul Wallenberg, and Frederick Born had few weapons with which to combat the SS and the Arrow Cross. Their arsenals were immense personal courage, determination, dedicated staffs, a willingness to risk their own lives, and a readiness to break every rule in the book to save Jewish lives. Two Swiss and a Swede, citizens of neutral countries that traded so profitably with the Nazis. The three diplomats' heroic wartime record shames the rest of the world that stood by and ignored the unfolding genocide. A tree stands for each on a quiet hillside in Jerusalem on the grounds of the Yad Vashem Holocaust Memorial Museum, rightly commemorating them as "Righteous Among the Nations."

10

Back to the Future

You should be satisfied now.

Swiss banker, pictured in a cartoon in the Swiss newspaper *Tages-Anzeiger*, shouting as he throws a few coins to a crowd of dormant-account claimants

The Swiss bankers' ombudsman told us that from the twenty-five hundred letters that he got [from claimants], he will have maybe one or two positive answers. I replied, "Can you hear what you are saying? If this is your way of thinking then we have to continue our international activity, until Switzerland understands it is a different world today."

Zvi Barak, of the World Jewish Restitution Organization, in Jerusalem

Among the thousands of claimants applying to Swiss banks to recover their relatives' wartime assets, none, it is safe to say, will be seeking monies held in the name of the leader of the Third Reich. Like many of the Jews whose extermination he oversaw, Adolf Hitler also had a Swiss bank account. The account, at the Bern branch of the Union Bank of Switzerland, one of the country's most powerful financial institutions, was managed by Max Ammann; declassified U.S. intelligence documents describe him as "a close collaborator of Hitler."

Sales of *Mein Kampf* (My Struggle) ran into millions, after it became a school textbook and required reading for a generation of Nazi schoolchildren. Ammann was the owner of the Nazi publishing company that published *Mein Kampf*. U.S. intelligence agents operating in Switzerland believed that the Schweizerische Bangesellschaft (UBS) account held both the foreign royalties for *Mein Kampf* and foreign exchange revenues for the Nazi Party, according to the report, published in late 1944 and headed "Objectionable Activities by Switzerland on Behalf of the Nazis":

> Telegram from Bern reported that information received in Bern indicates that accounts are held for Hitler in the Schweizerische Bangesellschaft (UBS) by a German official named Max Ammann. Ammann replaced Fritz Solm in the Ullstein publishing company in which Hitler has a financial interest. . . . Ammann is a close collaborator of Hitler from his early days. He is the most prominent commercial person for all the publications of the NSDAP [Nazi Party] including *Mein Kampf*. Therefore it is quite possible that Hitler's foreign exchange revenues from his book and foreign exchange revenues of the Nazi Party abroad are held at this Swiss bank in Ammann's name.

Like many of their banking colleagues, UBS representative refuse to talk about this latest revelation, one of the more embarrassing disclosures in a stream of Allied intelligence documents highlighting Swiss economic links with the Third Reich. When the New York–based World Jewish Congress (WJC) passed the documents detailing Hitler's secret bank account to the *Jewish Chronicle*, its reporter Jenni Frazer contacted UBS to get their comments about the reported account in the name of their most notorious customer. But even Adolf Hitler, the man who plotted and implemented the Holocaust from which Swiss banks made such handsome profits, remains protected by client confidentiality and Swiss banking laws. Jenni Frazer wrote: "A spokesman for UBS told the [*Jewish Chronicle*] that it was illegal for the banks to discuss individual accounts, so he could not confirm or deny whether the accounts were extant."

During the war, just as now, Swiss banks were the favorite financial refuge of the world's dictators. Hitler's ally Mussolini also used Swiss banks, according to information in the U.S. National Archives. The Italian fascist leader favored Credit Suisse for his dealings. On 21 January 1941, Credit Suisse in Zürich sent instructions to its branch in New York telling it to pay $5,000 to Mussolini. But a month later, on 21 February, the order was mysteriously canceled, and Credit Suisse in New York was told not to pay anything.

HITLER'S secret Swiss account, OSS agents monitoring a clandestine channel for *Mein Kampf* royalties, a check made out to Mussolini and then suddenly canceled—these historical vignettes are fascinating but did, after all, occur over fifty years ago. Why has it taken so long for the story of Swiss collaboration with the Nazis to finally emerge? The answer lies in part with the macabre scenes played out in Berlin in the death throes of the Nazi regime.

The Third Reich finally ended at 2:41 on the morning of 7 May 1945, in a schoolhouse in Reims, General Dwight D. Eisenhower's headquarters—not with a bang but a signature. Or two, to be precise. The German general Alfred Jodl and admiral Hans von Friedeburg surrendered unconditionally to the Allied forces. Jodl's army had laid waste half a continent, had stolen its wealth, and was the spearhead of the greatest genocide in modern history, but he still asked for lenient treatment, requesting that the Allies treat the Germans with "generosity." As for Mussolini, would-be recipient of Credit Suisse funds, he had been caught by Italian partisans while trying to cross into Switzerland. Together with his mistress he was executed. The bodies of Il Duce and his lover were dumped on a piazza in Milan, before being strung up by their ankles.

Meanwhile, in Berlin, the Red Army advanced through the smoking rubble, battling the pathetic remnants of the German armed forces: a few SS fanatics, pensioners, and terrified teenagers. Anyone refusing to fight the Russians was strung up from a lamppost. Hitler continued issuing a stream of directives and orders to his last remaining functionaries, denouncing his former comrades Himmler and Goering as failures to the German people and traitors. All Himmler's efforts to secure a separate peace with the Allies through Switzerland, via the Nazi spymaster Walter Schellenberg, the OSS station chief Allen Dulles, the Swiss Jewish leader Saly Mayer, or the SS officer Kurt Becher, had failed, and Hitler was furious at Himmler's treachery. Together with Goering, Himmler was fired, and Hitler expelled them from the Nazi Party: "Apart altogether from their disloyalty to me, Goering and Himmler have brought irreparable shame on the whole nation by secretly negotiating with the enemy without my knowledge and against my will, and also by illegally attempting to seize control of the state," Hitler declared.

In the early hours of the morning on 30 April Hitler prepared to die. He assembled his entourage and shuffled down the line of his last loyal staff, shaking hands with each and mumbling to himself. The last survivors of the Third Reich's nerve center then retired to the bunker canteen to dance, drink, and party the night away, fiddling while Berlin burned. The following afternoon Hitler entered his rooms with his wife, Eva Braun. A pistol shot soon sounded while Eva Braun swallowed her poison.

But Himmler, probably the greediest of the Nazi leaders, had no intention of dying in the Berlin bunker. Losing his Nazi Party card was the least of his worries. He wanted to escape and get his hands on his loot, safely stashed in Switzerland. It was not to be. On 21 May Himmler left the Flensburg region and headed south, toward Bavaria and Switzerland, together with eleven SS officers. The once-mighty Reichsführer and SS chief was dressed in an army private's uniform and wore a black eyepatch in a pathetic attempt to disguise himself. The dozen Nazis were arrested on the first day of their journey, at a British military checkpoint.

Himmler's SS interrogators had developed finely honed techniques for obtaining information, but he crumpled at the first questions. He admitted his identity to a British army captain and was immediately taken away to nearby headquarters. He was stripped and searched to check for hidden weapons and poison. None was found. Two days later a British intelligence officer arrived and ordered that Himmler's mouth be examined. The Nazi leader immediately bit into the cyanide capsule he had secreted in his gums. British army doctors frantically administered emetics and pumped his stomach, the war correspondent William Shirer records, but it was too late. After twelve minutes of writhing in his death throes, Himmler finally joined his Führer.

Goering and Goebbels too cheated justice. Sentenced to hang at Nuremberg, Goering died two hours before his appointed time, having taken poison that a Nazi sympathizer had smuggled into his cell. As for Goebbels, together with his wife, Magda, he died at the hands of the SS. On the evening of 1 May, shortly after organizing the death of his six children by lethal injection, he and Frau Goebbels walked into the garden of the bunker. At his request an SS orderly fired two shots, one each into the back of their heads. Their bodies were discovered the next day by Russian troops.

They were ignominious ends, then, for this motley quartet: Hitler, Himmler, Goering, and Goebbels. Many of the Third Reich's secrets died with them, especially the full extent of Nazi looting of occupied Europe and the role of Swiss banks in aiding the Nazi war machine by their supply of foreign currency. Himmler, head of the SS, the Nazis' premier looting force, which signed a deal with the Reichsbank to process looted Jewish gold and valuables, probably knew the most. If the Nazi leaders weren't talking, then the Swiss banks certainly weren't about to reveal anything about their role in funding genocide, the most shameful event in their history.

Over the course of the next few decades, once the war ended, both historians and journalists investigated the fate of the Nazi gold and stolen art treasures. Theories were advanced, rebutted, and reformulated as to where all the gold and valuables went, how much of it there was, and where the Nazis had stolen it from.

The truth was, nobody really knew all the facts. Nazi gold became a modern myth, a legend of Atlantis for the postwar age. It sat at the bottom of a lake in Austria; it was buried on a mountainside in Bavaria; in a basement in Moscow. One theory was that it was used to fund Odessa, the secret postwar network of Nazis. Another held that it financed the clandestine routes for escaping war criminals—run by underground German networks with help from high Vatican officials—that smuggled Nazi leaders to South America. Yet another theory claimed that German gold was used to finance the Marshall Plan to rebuild postwar Europe.

Part of the Nazi gold may have even found its way to Allen Dulles and the OSS in Bern. Dulles remained in contact, whether direct or indirect, with Nazi Germany all through the war, and some analysts believe that he used Nazi loot to finance his networks of anti-Communist agents that stretched across postwar Europe. That once the war was over sections of the American intelligence services recruited Nazi war criminals such as Klaus Barbie, the Butcher of Lyons, is well documented.

All of these theories are possible, some even probable, but one thing is certain: vast amounts of looted Nazi gold and wealth have disappeared for good. Swiss banks were often merely the first staging post for Nazi plunder, says Marc Masurovsky. "If I were a Nazi, I would use Swiss banks as a base, until everything quieted down a little bit. But seeing as how international finance became extremely sophisticated after the war, there is no real reason to keep it there. I could have just as easily sent it to Panama or the Far East."

Some Nazi loot ended up in Argentina, which, under the leadership of fascist dictator Juan Domingo Perón, entered the war on the side of the Allies on 27 March 1945. Why did Perón, admirer of Hitler and Mussolini, wait so long? Perón's aim was to save Nazi lives and bring them to Argentina, according to writer Enrique Krauze. Writing in the *New Republic*, Krauze detailed how in 1947 tens of thousands of Nazis had found sanctuary in Argentina, together with many millions of dollars' worth of stolen loot, works of art, and valuables. Two years before, in 1945, as the Third Reich was collapsing, two German submarines docked and unloaded their cargo. It included tens of millions of dollars in various currencies, 2,511 kilograms of gold, 4,638 karats of diamonds, piles of jewels, and works of art, formerly deposited in the Reichsbank in Berlin.

Juan Perón and his wife, Evita, took charge of the plunder themselves, according to Krauze, with Perón supposedly providing the German military attaché at the embassy in Buenos Aires with 8,000 Argentine passports and 1,100 identity cards to be distributed to arriving Nazis. Perón's reward from his Nazi friends was a mansion in Cairo and a bank account—in, of course, a Swiss bank. When the fascist Perón regime was overthrown in 1955, some of the Peróns' possessions were displayed to the public. They included a storage box containing a set of silver plates. On the lid, set in mother of pearl, was a Star of David.

But if we do not know the whole picture, part, at least, is accurately recorded. In 1946 the Allies and the Swiss negotiated the Washington Agreement, which provided for the distribution of Swiss assets frozen in the United States since June 1941, and German assets blocked in Switzerland, while the United States released to Switzerland frozen assets that did not belong to Nazis or Nazi collaborators. Under the Washington Agreement Switzerland handed over SF250 million ($60 million) worth of gold, but much more was found by Allied troops in Germany and Austria, at sites such as the Merkers salt mine. Restitution payments were handled by the Tripartite Gold Commission, set up in 1946 by Britain, France, and the United States, which oversaw claims from ten countries: Belgium, Holland, Luxembourg, Czechoslovakia, Poland, Austria, Yugoslavia, Italy, Albania, and Greece.

Most of the payments to countries with claims against the Nazis were made in the 1940s and 1950s, but it took until October 1995 for Albania to receive its payment of one and a half metric tons of gold, worth $19 million, from the Bank of England. The claim was delayed after a dispute lasting almost fifty years between Britain and Albania over an incident in 1947 when forty-four British sailors were killed after their ships hit mines off the Albanian coast.

In January 1997 some 5.5 metric tons of gold remained in the vaults of the Bank of England and the Federal Reserve Bank of New York, worth about $70 million.

There is much to examine. The SNB's own 1984 report records that the Reichsbank shipped SF1,638 million ($360 million) worth of gold to Switzerland. It must have been obvious that much of that had been stolen. At the end of 1938 the Reichsbank reported gold holdings of RM70.8 million ($28.3 million). At his trial at Nuremberg, the Reichsbank president, Walther Funk, said its effective holdings were RM500 million ($200 million), barely half of the total shipped to Switzerland. The SNB report says, "Seen from a psychological point of view, these facts were not a very good basis for the Washington negotiations." So why did the Allies let Switzerland get away with handing over only SF250 million ($5.5 million) worth of gold? For the same reason that the Allies kept the Bank for International Settlements, with its American president and Nazi directors, trading all through the war: capital rules *über alles*, and the Allies needed the Swiss banks to rebuild postwar Europe, in particular Germany.

When in August 1945 the three western Allies notified the Swiss government that they were asserting their right over German assets held in Switzerland, Swiss officials responded in classic fashion. They stonewalled, arguing that the Swiss government could not see which laws the claims were based on, claiming that the fact of German occupation by the Allies had "hardly any legal implications beyond Germany's border," as the SNB report details. When the Allies pointed out that their victory had immeasurably strengthened Switzerland's own peace and security, the Swiss agreed to negotiate. For one member of the Swiss team, Herr Alfred Hirs, there were too many Jews to deal with in Washington.

"The members of the U.S. delegation seem exceedingly pleasant although the Jewish element is very strong," he wrote from the American capital on 18 March 1946, according to the SNB report. Hirs also reportedly called Pierre Mendes-France, future French prime minister, a "rich Jew," and again, in a letter of 27 March 1946, he called attention to the number of Jews on the U.S. delegation, particularly "an Austrian Jew from the treasury."

HERR Hirs's anti-Semitism aside, several much deeper issues remained, and remain, unresolved by the Washington Agreement. It failed to cover the ownership and return of nonmonetary gold from melted-down personal possessions such as jewelry and tooth fillings. It also failed to deal with assets held in dormant accounts. In fact, it completely ignored the question of compensation for Holocaust survivors and relatives of victims whose stolen assets had been channeled through Swiss banks. The Washington Agreement was a cynical piece of realpolitik, and fifty years later its shortcomings have returned to plague the Swiss banks, Jewish organizations, and the successors to the Allied governments.

As the torrent of revelations about the Swiss banks' role in aiding the Third Reich pours forth, pressure is growing for the Washington Agreement to be renegotiated. In Britain, the Labor MP Greville Janner, chairman of the Holocaust Educational Trust, had been lobbying Foreign Secretary Malcolm Rifkind on the Swiss issue since the summer of 1996. He was brushed off at first, when on 3 June 1996 he wrote to Rifkind asking for information about reports that British intelligence knew of documents referring to seized funds held in Swiss banks. In a nine-line reply, Rifkind wrote, "None of the intelligence agencies is aware of having such information." This was governmentese for "go away and stop bothering me." But if the OSS and the Treasury Department knew, then so did British intelligence. Unfortunately, as Britain has no Freedom of Information legislation, the evidence remains locked in dusty filing cabinets. When my chief researcher, Barbara Wyllie, was plowing through declassified documents at the British Public Records Office in London, she repeatedly encountered references to relevant documents that were unavailable and, she was told, could not be made available.

Janner did not go away, and kept writing. As even the Foreign Office mandarins slowly realized that Nazi gold was a live political issue, the British government's position shifted. A report was commissioned and published from a historian on looted Nazi assets, and Rifkind himself visited Switzerland in the autumn of 1996, as did Greville Janner, together with the former cabinet minister David Hunt. The visit by the British parliamentarians was instrumental in forcing the Swiss government to realize that they could no longer stonewall on the question of dormant accounts, say Swiss Jews. Once in Bern, Janner called for Swiss banks and the government to pay immediate compensation to Holocaust victims: "If Switzerland wants to be believed that it really intends to make restitution, it will not wait five years, it should make a financial gesture now for the victims of Nazism."

On 14 October Janner wrote to the Foreign Office calling for Britain to renegotiate the Washington Agreement and for the remaining 5.5 metric tons of gold still administered by the Tripartite Commission to be used to pay reparations to victims of the Nazis. Once again, he was brushed off. In his reply of 25 October, Rifkind refused to press Switzerland to renegotiate the Washington Agreement and, firmly in the best traditions of Foreign Office appeasement, spouted the Swiss government line on its wartime dealings with the Nazis: "It is also relevant that the Swiss had little choice in 1940–1945 but to continue to deal with Germany as they did: every other country bordering Germany had been invaded and occupied, and Switzerland was surrounded by Axis-controlled territory."

That after his visit to Switzerland, and pleasant discussions with Swiss officials, the British foreign secretary had been convinced of the terrible difficulties of doing much at all about these complicated issues was perhaps not surprising. That he seemed unaware of existing documentation was. He wrote, "I do not think it has been reliably established how much gold the Swiss National Bank bought from the Reichsbank at various times during World War II." The authoritative SNB report on its dealings with the Reichsbank was written in 1984.

American official Stuart Eizenstat, State Department special envoy on restitution, takes a less emollient line and also argues that the role of the Allies needs to be reexamined. Eizenstat says, "There is another piece to this, which is the U.S. government, and that is something we are just beginning to get into ourselves. If we are going to hold others to high standards of accountability, we are going to have to do the same. There was a 1946 Washington Agreement, in which monies were distributed by the Swiss government . . . to the Allied countries in some proportion. We want to go back and look at this and see if we can piece this together, find out exactly how much was involved, where the funds came from, and what happened to them."

By February 1997 it seemed likely that the last 5.5 metric tons of gold, worth $68 million, still held by the Tripartite Commission would indeed eventually be used to compensate individual Holocaust survivors, instead of being returned to European central banks. The wartime western Allies, the United States, Britain, and France, agreed to freeze the distribution of the gold. Officials had bowed to Jewish groups' arguments that some of the gold held by the Tripartite Commission had come from individuals, rather than national banks, and so an effort should be made to return it to the Jews themselves, or at least Jewish organizations, rather than European national banks. Quite how this immensely complicated question of how looted monetary gold (gold from national treasuries) can be disentangled from looted nonmonetary gold (gold from individuals) remained unclear, but Jewish groups hailed the decision to freeze the distribution of the last 5.5 metric tons as a major step in the right direction, just as Greville Janner had originally suggested.

NEVER before in its history has Switzerland been the focus of so much unwelcome—to the bankers, at least—attention. Commissions and committees to discover the truth about the economic relationship between Switzerland and the Third Reich are springing up like Nazi war criminals in South America.

In May 1996 the Swiss Bankers' Association and Jewish organizations, such as the World Jewish Congress, agreed to set up a joint commission to verify the SBA's search through the banks' records for lost Holocaust accounts. The Volcker Commission is headed by Paul Volcker, a former chairman of the Federal Reserve Bank. Three of its members represent Jewish organizations; the other three, the Swiss banks. The Jewish representatives are Avraham Burg, chairman of the Jerusalem-based Jewish Agency; Rueben Beraja, chairman of the Latin American Jewish Congress; and Ronald Lauder, treasurer of the World Jewish Congress and a former U.S. ambassador to Austria. The Swiss representatives are Klaus Jacobi, former state secretary; Curt Gasteyger, professor of international politics; and Professor Rene Rhinow, a lawyer and politician. There are four alternate members: Zvi Barak, chairman of the World Jewish Restitution Organization; Israel Singer, general secretary of the World Jewish Congress; Hans Baer, of Bank Julius Baer; and Peider Mengiardi, a Swiss accountant. The search for data for the commission is being conducted by the accounting firms Arthur Andersen, KPMG Peat Marwick, and Price Waterhouse. The Volcker Commission's first report is due in mid-1997, and a final version is expected in 1998.

In November 1996 the Swiss parliament passed a bill to create a commission of experts with a much wider and more complicated mandate: to thoroughly examine the tangled network of financial connections that bound the Swiss economy into the Nazi economy. The Experts' Commission, or the Swiss Parliamentary Commission of Inquiry, to give it its full name, will be able to lift the banking secrecy laws—within the historical period covered by its mandate—and examine the wartime dealings of both private Swiss banks and the Swiss National Bank. Most Nazi gold looted from the treasuries of German-occupied countries went to the Swiss National Bank, while private Swiss banks were involved in providing hard currency for the Third Reich to purchase war materials such as tungsten and diamonds. The commission's investigations will cover three areas: assets that belonged to Nazi victims and heirless assets, so far unclaimed; looted assets; and Nazi assets in Switzerland. Any relevant information the Experts' Commission finds on dormant accounts or heirless assets will be passed to the Volcker Commission. The Experts' Commission, headed by Jean-Francois Bergier, consists of five Swiss historians and jurists, as well as four historians from Poland, Israel, America, and Britain. The commission must report back within five years but is likely to complete its investigations in two or three, says Peter Burkhard, a Swiss foreign ministry official working for the specially appointed government task force charged with coordinating Bern's response to the international furor over Nazi–Swiss links. That the bill passed by a vote of thirty-seven in favor, with zero against, shows that across Swiss society there is a genuine desire to discover the truth about the country's wartime history, say many Swiss. According to Burkhard, "The independent commission of experts could turn up some uncomfortable information, but we want a clear picture about what our grandfathers did wrong, and we want transparency."

As well as the Volcker Commission and the Swiss government's Experts' Commission, at least half a dozen other inquiries are being conducted to research everything from dormant Swiss bank accounts that still hold the assets of Holocaust victims to the broader issues of Swiss–Nazi economic cooperation. They include investigations by the Hungarian and Polish governments into secret deals between the former Communist regimes and Switzerland to use Holocaust victims' assets to compensate Swiss citizens for their property being nationalized; an investigation by the U.S. State Department into the retrieval and disposal of looted wartime assets; an interagency U.S. government task force, chaired by Under Secretary of Commerce Stuart Eizenstat, on U.S. knowledge of Swiss–Nazi collaboration, due to report at the end of February 1997; an inquiry by the British Foreign Office on the disposition of gold secreted in Switzerland; and hearings conducted by both the Senate and House banking committees. The Swiss banking ombudsman's office, headed by Hanspeter Haeni, which deals with the individual claims of survivors and victims' heirs, is carrying on its own work, although it has been criticized for its slow pace.

For Switzerland there is now more at stake than discovering how much money lies in dormant accounts or how much looted Nazi gold ended up in the SNB's basements. The end of the Cold War, the collapse of communism, and the globalization of the economy have put the country at a crossroads. Neutrality and isolationism are no longer a practical policy, and as the Swiss economy becomes ever more locked into those of its neighbors, forward-thinking Swiss know that one day Switzerland will have to join both the European Union and the United Nations. Let the historians lance the boil of economic collaboration with the Nazis, they say, and the whole affair will slowly heal up. "We want to establish our honor as honest transparent partners with the international public; that's why we want full transparency. We don't want to say that we behaved badly but the others did as well. We are dealing with our history; other countries are not the issue," Burkhard says. "It's necessary for the Swiss people and Switzerland to clarify their history, to make a clean slate and know what happened, before we enter the next century. Just like a person cannot enter a new stage of his life with unfinished business, neither can a country."

Just as the Swiss parliament was voting through the legislation that would trigger a long bout of national soul-searching, President Bill Clinton too sensed a hot political issue. With Republican senator D'Amato getting all the publicity, Clinton announced that the United States would launch a broad interagency investigation of the U.S. role in seizing Nazi assets after the war's end, under the direction of Stuart Eizenstat. The U.S. government interagency probe will be an extension of the investigative work already being carried out by the State Department and the Holocaust Museum. "I share your view of the importance of an expeditious and thorough review of dormant accounts in Switzerland, and I am pleased that the Swiss government has begun this process," Clinton wrote to WJC president Edgar Bronfman.

Underneath all these revelations, disputes, publicity, committees, commissions, and investigations lies one simple question: why now?

Three major factors combined to suddenly drag Switzerland into the world's spotlight: the end of the Cold War and the fiftieth anniversary of the Allied victory; the American policy of freedom of information; and a U.S. senator, with a large Jewish electorate, who spotted an explosive political issue that he was determined to exploit for maximum effect. That was enough to trigger a feeding frenzy by the world's media, who knew the ingredients of a fabulous story—Jews and Nazis, stone-faced bankers, smug Swiss functionaries, looted gold—when they saw them. This one, as they say in newsrooms, would run and run. So it did, and the more it ran the more the pressure built, in Bern, Washington, D.C., and London.

To start with, the first ingredient in this heady brew: the death of communism. Much of the Nazis' loot was stolen from the now almost eradicated Jewish communities of Central and Eastern Europe. Few Jews remain in the once thriving Jewish centers of Warsaw and (East) Berlin, Vilna and Prague, and the survivors, while living under a Communist dictatorship, had no means of traveling to Switzerland to try to reclaim any family assets. The borders were sealed, and outgoing telephone communication with the West was virtually impossible. Any attempt to contact Switzerland, hub of international capitalism, would only have brought unwelcome attention from the all-pervasive secret police forces that controlled life in the Soviet bloc. Foreign bank accounts were illegal, and most Jews were just glad to have survived the Holocaust and still be alive, without the stress of chasing stonewalling Swiss bankers. But, once the Berlin Wall came down, Europe's Jews could travel where they wanted, write to whomever they liked, and reorganize their communities to press their claims for their vanished assets. They could also contact the bankers their forebears had put their faith in to guard their family assets.

This reopening of half of Europe coincided with the fiftieth anniversary of V-E Day, which triggered a massive bout of national introspection across the continent in several countries about their wartime record and the fate of their Jewish communities. In France and Germany in particular, politicians and opinion makers began to pick at their nation's psychological scars that dated back fifty years. The results were uncomfortable as they questioned whether their nations' wartime regimes had done enough to save their countries'

Jews. In Germany the answer was obvious, but how could things have been different in France, Italy, or Belgium? Could more Jewish lives have been saved? This mood spread to Switzerland, accelerated by the work of Swiss historians such as Jacques Picard. For all its claims of neutrality and isolationism Switzerland, sandwiched between Paris and Bonn, was not immune to this epidemic of historical reflection. At the same time, there was a growing feeling, one that is still strengthening, that Switzerland needs to lay its wartime ghosts to rest before it can properly take its place in a united Europe, as ultimately it hopes to do.

In May 1995 the then Swiss president, Kaspar Villiger, apologized for the 1938 agreement with Germany that the passports of German and Austrian Jews would be stamped with a *J*, a decision that Swiss historian Guido Koller describes as the "national shame of Switzerland." "We made at the time a bad choice in the name of a national interest taken to its narrowest sense," said Villiger. That perceived national interest also led to the Swiss border being virtually sealed against Jewish refugees in August 1942, a policy that was cynically loosened in parallel with the prospects of an Allied victory. Each time the Allied armies advanced a few more miles across the Third Reich, the Swiss border suddenly became more porous to Jews until, by the war's end, it was more or less open, although by then most Eastern European Jews were dead. Even now, many Swiss say that their country's wartime policies were based on the mordant saying, common at the time, "For six days a week Switzerland works for the Nazis, and on the seventh it prays for an Allied victory."

This recognition, that Swiss neutrality was grounded more in national self-interest than in any genuine principle of equal dealing between the Allies and the Axis, is spreading. A month before Villiger's speech, the foreign minister, Flavio Cotti, had used even stronger language in criticizing the policies of the wartime Federal Council: "We cannot and must not deny that Switzerland was implicated in the unspeakable barbarism of the time," he said at a ceremony honoring Charles Lutz, the Swiss consul in wartime Budapest who saved thousands of Jews by issuing them Swiss protection papers. "The very real survival difficulties of a small country surrounded by a Nazi and fascist world should not lead us to excuse serious failures and weaknesses, and I am thinking particularly of our policies against the persecuted Jews."

ONCE the new democracies of Eastern Europe took power, they found themselves confronted by Jewish groups such as the World Jewish Congress, demanding restitution for the assets of Holocaust victims. The WJC is part of the World Jewish Restitution Organization (WJRO), an umbrella grouping of international Jewish agencies seeking restitution for former Jewish property and assets. But the slick PR operation run by the WJC has helped it hog the headlines on the Swiss banks story. In the early 1990s the WJRO began negotiating with the former Eastern bloc countries for the return of Jewish property. School buildings, synagogues, old people's homes, all these had been appropriated by the former Communist governments. The local Jews wanted their property back, and, where there weren't any more local Jews, the WJRO negotiated in their place.

From Eastern Europe it was but a short hop to Switzerland, where for years stories had been circulating about banks holding onto money deposited by Holocaust survivors and refusing to release it to their surviving relatives. As many of the account holders had no surviving relatives, the issue appeared more or less academic. And then the WJRO's researchers went to work, plowing through box after box of musty paper in the U.S. National Archives. They discovered literally thousands of reports from Treasury agents, Safehaven officials, and OSS agents who had been monitoring virtually every franc that was traded by Swiss banks. Thanks to the Freedom of Information Act, this information could be made public. The issue suddenly ballooned from the moral question of dormant accounts into the historical and political one of the extent of Switzerland's and Swiss banks' economic collaboration with the Nazis.

The WJC's researchers were aided in their search for evidence against the banks by staff from the office of Senator Alfonse D'Amato. As the chairman of the Senate Banking Committee, which has piled the pressure on the Swiss Bankers' Association, D'Amato is one of the key figures in this saga. The SBA could deal with protests from Jewish groups, because ultimately they had no immediate sanctions with which to threaten Swiss banks. But Senator D'Amato, the driving force behind the Whitewater investigation that at one stage shook the Clinton administration, was another matter. The whispers that the U.S. government might introduce some kind of legal measures against Swiss banks in the United States if they didn't cooperate had the bankers of Zürich twitch-

ing nervously. Tearful Holocaust survivors would testify at the Senate
Banking Committee's hearings, describing how hard-faced Swiss bank
officials demanded the death certificates of their parents, who had been
killed in the extermination camps, before they would release their
assets. They could not, of course, produce death certificates, as there
were none issued at Auschwitz. This was great copy for newspapers
and gripping footage for television. It was also a total PR disaster for
the Swiss banks.

The lobbyists in Washington helping the Swiss banks fight off the
threat of sanctions are keen to dismiss Senator D'Amato as a cynical
manipulator of the media, acting only in his own electoral self-interest.
Said one, "D'Amato is very contentious and extremely political. He
orchestrated Whitewater—Whitewater and D'Amato are synonymous.
His interest is to exploit issues for his own political gain. There is no
pretense otherwise, and this is a textbook example. Jewish voters vote,
and they make substantial contributions because they are on the more
affluent side of the electorate. D'Amato courted the Jewish vote, especially the religious Orthodox vote."

This may or may not be true, but either way D'Amato's entrance into
the story helped kick it into the headlines, where it has stayed ever
since. Without the senator's efforts it would almost certainly have taken
Jewish groups such as the WJC many more years to get the Swiss banks
to cooperate, if ever. Naturally WJC officials are full of praise for the
senator—although Swiss Jewish leaders accuse him of going over the
top—and even more disinterested figures such as Stuart Eizenstat laud
his work. The U.S. government itself soon joined the fray.

"We have a moral and a political interest in this, as opposed to a
legal interest," said Eizenstat. "As the leader in the Allied effort during
the war, as the liberator of many of the concentration camps, we have
a personal interest in seeing that the last sad chapter of World War II
is closed in a just and fair manner. In addition, many U.S. citizens have
potential claims, and we are interested in being sure that they can
pursue their legal rights as well. Initially the Swiss did not act with
alacrity, but in recent months since the D'Amato hearings, and by our
own intercession, they have acted in a very professional and appropriate way. . . . Senator D'Amato's leadership is to be applauded and con-
gratulated, because by holding hearings he helped focus people's
attention on this."

THE END of communism had also provoked some head-scratching among international Jewish organizations such as the WJC. To put it bluntly, they needed a new cause. For decades Jewish activists had campaigned to free Soviet Jewry and pressed the Soviet Union to let its Jews out. Freedom for Soviet Jewry was a black-and-white humanitarian issue that almost everybody supported, bringing its activists a high media profile as well as plenty of support to carry on their humanitarian work. But by the early 1990s the Soviet Union didn't exist any more, and any Jews remaining on its territories were free to come and go as they liked. A new bête noire was needed. Switzerland, provider of foreign currency to the Nazis, was the perfect candidate: nobody likes bankers, especially smug, secretive Swiss ones. And even worse—or better, depending on how cynical one wishes to be—was the fact that the bankers were refusing to hand over the assets of Holocaust victims. Here was a perfect bandwagon on which to jump, a new raison d'être for the many international Jewish organizations competing for influence, power, and budgets. Evil Soviets out, nasty Swiss bankers in.

For some this analysis will sound unduly cynical, but some Jews too are critical of the way that Jewish organizations have jumped on the restitution bandwagon, creating a media-friendly sound and fury about Swiss banks, while in some cases failing to channel much money back to the most important players in this macabre performance of historical theater: the individual Holocaust victims themselves. For just as the Swiss bankers had failed to deal adequately with the issue of dormant accounts for fifty years, so had most Jewish organizations—although that is partly because Eastern Europe, former home of many Holocaust victims who had deposited money in Swiss banks, had been curtained off under communism.

Writing on the letters page of the *Jewish Chronicle,* Rabbi Thomas Salamon of London quoted the case of his mother, a former slave laborer for the firm of Junkers, which was later absorbed into Mercedes-Benz. Mercedes-Benz refused to pay her any compensation, arguing that it had already paid DM10 million ($6.5 million) to the Conference on Jewish Material Claims Against Germany (CJMC). Rabbi Salamon then wrote to the CJMC. In its reply the CJMC said that the money it received from Mercedes-Benz in 1988 was to be used "for grants to Jewish institutions which provide shelter or home care to aged and infirm former Jewish inmates of concentration camps, forced labor camps or ghettos." The CJMC failed to provide proper details of how the money was spent, according to Rabbi Salamon, who continued in his letter: "When challenged, the CJMC has not provided proof of the use to which the money has been put, nor does it appear to have consulted individuals over the distribution of funds." He also called for "pressure to be put on the CJMC to make at least some payments to the victims of slave labor."

As well as taking on the Swiss bankers, the World Jewish Restitution Organization has also negotiated separate restitution agreements with governments in post-Communist Eastern Europe. But their intervention has not always been welcomed by local Jewish communities, who have complained of high-handedness by the visiting Jewish leaders. "In some cases, particularly the Czech Republic, local Jewish communities in Eastern Europe have been unhappy with what they see as a patronizing attitude, that WJRO officials fly in from New York and Jerusalem, telling them 'Don't worry, we'll negotiate with your government for you and sort everything out,'" says Jenni Frazer of the *Jewish Chronicle*, who has written extensively on postwar Jewish restitution.

As for the CJMC and the question of compensation for slave laborers, the CJMC's regulations are decided by the German government, which also sets its budget. After the war some German companies that used slave labor contributed to a one-time payment fund, but under current German government rules the CJMC cannot make compensation payments to former slave laborers. "We have two hardships funds, one that deals with one-time payments and one for ongoing payments. We do address the question of slave labor, and every year we ask for the rules to be liberalized. But the German government decides the regulations and how much money there is," said a spokesman for the CJMC.

Some Swiss Jews too fear that, when the issue of dormant accounts is eventually solved, Jewish organizations will start arguing over who will actually get their hands on the funds, especially if substantial funds are discovered that cannot be returned to individual heirs because none remain alive or are untraceable. "Where would that money go, and to whom would it belong?" asked one, who preferred to remain anonymous. "We think that once all the claims are processed that money should go into a fund. Then we have to decide where it goes after that, and that's when I am a little bit afraid all the organizations will jump on the Jewish community here and want to have all the money."

THE REEXAMINATION of Switzerland's history and the revelations of the declassified Operation Safehaven and OSS documents are also turning up some unwelcome ghosts for Jewish organizations. Andor Grosz, the Hungarian Jew who worked as an agent for the Abwehr and was sent on a secret mission to buy Swiss goods for the Third Reich, was not the only Jewish black marketeer, says historian Marc Masurovsky. "Holocaust money is a really tricky issue. We have been finding evidence that there are a substantial number of Jewish accounts, possibly, but which kind of Jews? I have to be very explicit about this. There were Jews in Romania—numerically it's impossible to tell—members of the merchant banking class, who engaged in black-market activities. The Germans, particularly in the Abwehr, developed this whole approach toward recruiting Jews who were involved in smuggling and black-market activities. There was a whole section of the Jewish population, small in terms of numbers, but significant in terms of economic and commercial impact, in Romania, Hungary, Bulgaria, France, Belgium, Tangier, everywhere."

Jews profiting from the Holocaust? However minuscule their numbers, this is the crime that dare not speak its name. "This is an issue that has never been really approached. I warned D'Amato's people that some of these accounts will be hard to justify, because it's tainted money. Tainted Jewish money," says Masurovsky. "The Nazis were venal. They are looking for a good deal, at a good price, and if this person is useful to them, they don't care: they will work with that person very actively. They [Jewish organizations] can't just say these were a bunch of bad apples. Of course they were, but since nobody talks about this, it dramatizes it even more. It's a little painful to go through that, but there they are."

And there they were, back in May 1945, American GIs and officers, looting the contents of the Hungarian gold train. Packed with millions of dollars' worth of booty stolen from dead Jews, it had been abandoned in Austria at the war's end. Not just Nazi troops but even some Allied soldiers were ready to profit from the Holocaust, although certainly on a much tinier scale.

Forty-six cars long, the Hungarian gold train that left Budapest at the war's end, jammed with gold, currency, and other valuables looted from dead Jews, was probably the biggest single attempt to transport valuables stolen from Holocaust victims by the Nazis and their allies. But much of the train's wealth was handed over to Jewish groups such as the Jewish Agency in Jerusalem, instead of being returned to the Hungarian Jewish community, documents held in the Central Zionist Archives (CZA) in Jerusalem reveal. About 200,000 Hungarian Jews survived the Holocaust, and they had a stronger moral claim on its contents than the Zionist organizations, although many thousands later settled in Israel. The Jewish Agency also received a proportion of the Becher Deposit, the funds paid by Hungarian Jews who left Budapest in 1944 on the Kasztner train to Switzerland, the CZA documents reveal.

The Hungarian gold train was discovered in late May 1945 by Allied troops not far from Salzburg. Like the loot found at the Merkers salt mine, the gold train's cargo was packed with stolen personal goods and valuables, rather than looted gold from the national treasury. This too the Nazis had attempted to steal, but that train was discovered and returned to the Hungarian authorities.

A detailed intelligence report, unsigned and undated, in the CZA files gives further details of the gold train. Forty-six cars pulled out, while eight were shunted off en route for various reasons such as coupling failures. Various officials and their armed escorts took up fourteen cars, which left a total of twenty-four to be discovered by Allied troops. The report details each car's number and its origin—most were marked "MAV" (Hungarian Railways)—but the train also included cars from French, Italian, and German railways. Each case was numbered, from 1 to 1,560. The loot included gold and silver watches, jewelry, precious stones, antiques, gramophones, cameras, chinaware, typewriters, adding machines, seventeen bundles of walking sticks with silver handles, over 2,700 carpets, many of them Persian, clocks, and the entire stock of the museum of Gyor, a city in the west of Hungary.

It was a massive haul that had been systematically plundered and was all that was left of dozens of Jewish communities that had vanished in the Holocaust. Just as at Merkers, the Nazis had carefully sorted and catalogued their plunder. Case number 2 held mostly wristwatches and clocks, while Cases 251 to 364 contained chinaware. The Allies did not make a complete inventory of the train's contents, but contemporary accounts put its total value at about $30 million.

In Budapest the Hungarian prime minister, Ferenc Nagy, wrote to Moshe Shertok at the Jewish Agency in Jerusalem on 10 May 1945, asking that the agency (or the "Jewish world-organization," as he quaintly referred to it) intervene with the Allied powers who were holding the contents of the gold train and persuade them to release its contents, "so that these assets may serve the purpose of the social and financial restitution of Jews who fell victims to the above [Nazi] persecution."

Shertok was happy to help, as long as the Jewish Agency—which was, more or less, the Israeli government in waiting—obtained a substantial share of the gold train's contents to help pay for the resettlement of Jews in Palestine. The Jewish Agency, he replied on 24 May, would "do everything in its power, by negotiation with the competent Allied authorities, to secure a satisfactory solution of the problem . . . also that an appropriate share of the assets to be realized as a result of the Jewish Agency's efforts will be allocated to the financing of the settlement in Palestine of Jewish victims of Nazi persecution."

After its discovery, the gold train's contents were taken under the aegis of the U.S. and French military authorities. By spring 1947 Allied authorities had charged the Inter-Governmental Committee for Refugees (IGCR) with taking an inventory of the train's contents. American officers helped themselves to its contents, according to a document in the CZA, dated 16 July 1947, a record of a conversation with one Yehuda Gaulan, who was involved in the negotiations with the U.S. military authorities. Gaulan claimed the U.S. military authorities were hindering the IGCR team as much as possible. "The local American military authorities are doing everything to obstruct that work, especially in view of the fact that at the beginning of this work they have lost a source for easily acquiring riches. It is known that top-ranking officers of the American army have pocketed very valuable items. . . . Gualan himself saw strongboxes being broken open and robbed of their contents."

That U.S. officers looted the gold train is apparently confirmed in another CZA document, the record of a meeting in Vienna with Arthur Marget, chief of the Finance and Economic Division of U.S. Forces Austria, and a member of the Allied Control Commission for Austria, dated 16 September 1947. The meeting was attended by Yehuda Gaulan, although the report is unsigned. Marget admitted, the report says, "that it is a well-known fact to him that many officers" had both stolen from the gold train and had looted other property in Austria. One senior officer had even organized his own private gold train. "It was known that a very important general who had recently left Austria had carried with him a whole trainload of 'private property.'" The Becher Deposit was also discussed. "I told him [Marget] that only ten percent of the so-called Becher Deposit was delivered to the JA [Jewish Agency] representative."

Where did the wealth and possessions of Hungary's dead Jews finally end up? A large proportion was forwarded on to the IGCR, which then auctioned it off, with the proceeds going to refugee work. Some found its way into the vaults of the Hungarian National Bank, according to a report in the *New York Times,* dated 29 December 1948. Two years previously the Hungarian government had passed a law that restituted treasure must be put on display so that claimants could repossess it, while unidentified valuables should be turned over to the Hungarian Jewish community. But one shipment of eight freight cars, mostly holding gold and jewelry that had been held by the French and was believed to be the most valuable, was sent back to Hungary. There, much of it was appropriated by the government. Precious stones were removed from the jewelry and the gold was melted down before they were sent on to the national bank, the report says.

French troops had been helping a German officer who had looted the gold train's contents, according to Maurice Boukstein, the Jewish Agency's lawyer in New York. A German colonel who had been attached to the gold train had escaped into the French zone of Austria with two and a half tons of uncut diamonds, Boukstein wrote to the Jewish Agency's London office on 31 January 1947. "He is reported to be free in Innsbruck and on very good terms with the French Military Authorities."

Moshe Shertok got his share of the Hungarian gold train's wealth in the end. About $8 million was sent on to the Joint Distribution Committee and the Jewish Agency in Jerusalem, according to Gideon Rafael, a former Zionist official involved in the affair. As for the rest, "it evaporated into the various pockets of those responsible for guarding it," says Rafael.

FOR ALL the agreements that were signed in 1996 and the commissions that were set up, by early 1997 relations between Jewish organizations and Swiss officials had collapsed into bitter acrimony. They had initially refused Jewish organizations' requests that they set up a $250 million compensation fund for Holocaust survivors, arguing that nothing could be done until the results of the Experts' Commission were finalized, which could take five years.

On top of that brush-off, the outgoing Swiss president, Jean-Pascal Delamuraz, reportedly described the request as "extortion and blackmail" and accused foreign critics of trying to undermine Switzerland's role as an international financial center. "This is nothing less than extortion and blackmail. This fund would make it much more difficult to establish the truth," he told the *Tribune de Genève*. "Such a fund would be considered an admission of guilt."

At this, Jewish organizations went ballistic. Delamuraz's remarks came on top of revelations at the end of 1996 that Switzerland had used unclaimed assets of Holocaust victims to persuade Communist governments in Eastern Europe to pay compensation for nationalizing and confiscating Swiss-owned property.

Delamuraz's remarks were immediately attacked by a chorus of Jewish groups, in both Switzerland and the United States, and even the State Department joined the fray, with its spokesman Nicholas Burns describing his outburst as "ludicrous." Telephone lines buzzed between the WJC office in New York and the Jewish Agency in Jerusalem, and the two groups threatened to organize a mass withdrawal of pensions and investments from Swiss banks and to launch an investigation into Swiss banks' licensing operations in the United States.

For WJRO officials such as Zvi Barak, an international disinvestment campaign against Swiss banks would be a sweet form of revenge, for when the WJRO first began to campaign on the dormant-accounts issue, SBA officials refused even to meet with them. According to Barak: "At first they didn't want to meet with us, they said we didn't represent anything. They said they would meet with the Swiss Jewish community, because they are Swiss. Second, they would not agree to meet in their office, only in our hotel lobby."

Now the meetings are more polite, and the WJRO is admitted to the SBA's offices. But Barak is not impressed with the progress made so far to recover money from dormant accounts. "The Swiss bankers' ombudsman told us that from the twenty-five hundred letters that he got [from claimants], he will have maybe one or two positive answers. I replied, 'Can you hear what you are saying? If this is your way of thinking then we have to continue our international activity, until Switzerland understands it is a different world today.' "

For Barak, who helped organize the airlift of Soviet Jews to Israel via Poland, the Swiss bankers' blend of noncooperation and patronizing indifference held unpleasant memories. "Then the Polish aviation authorities told me there was not enough room at Warsaw airport to transfer Soviet Jews in 1990. They said we had to use another airport, close to the East German border. It took us three months to get permission to use Warsaw, but I insisted the Jews would go through the international airport. When I was sitting in that meeting in the hotel lobby I felt the same."

War, then, was more or less declared between the WJRO and the Swiss bankers. "We cannot control what is going on any more. It's no longer in our hands. The Swiss bankers learned their lesson," says Barak. "We told them that if you don't make an agreement with us it will come to the Senate in the United States, so it came to Mr. D'Amato's banking committee. Then we said if things don't go quickly, then a class action lawsuit would be more dangerous for them. They laughed, and now there is a class action lawsuit. I will not be surprised if the next step is taken not by us, that if they don't do things in the way they have to, then somebody will consider taking away their license to operate."

That would be an economic disaster for Switzerland, which is partly why, soon after the international furor over Delamuraz's accusations of "blackmail and extortion," he apologized for his remarks. In a letter to Edgar Bronfman, head of the World Jewish Congress, Delamuraz said he regretted any offense and said he had been "misinformed" when he gave his now notorious interview. Delamuraz's apology was part of a rapid about-face by the Federal Council, which moved toward agreeing to set up a compensation fund for Holocaust victims. The interior minister, Ruth Dreifuss, said that the government planned to act quickly to aid elderly and destitute Holocaust survivors. "It is now clear that something must happen quickly," she said in a newspaper interview. "We must recognize what has happened and that we cannot keep what does not belong to us."

However much the bankers were squirming under the international spotlight, Swiss Jews suddenly faced a new problem: the furor over dormant accounts and Swiss–Nazi economic collaboration triggered a bout of open anti-Semitism. The claims by former president Jean-Pascal Delamuraz that demands from Jewish groups for a Holocaust compensation fund were "extortion and blackmail" opened the lid on a box of Swiss anti-Semitic hatred and prejudice, long suppressed, but always there, said Jewish leaders. A Jewish community center in Zürich was daubed with a swastika, and hate mail suddenly began arriving at the offices of Jewish organizations. "Hitler's work is not finished," said one letter, while another claimed that "all Jews should be sent to prison." Similar sentiments found a published home in the conservative newspaper *Neue Züricher Zeitung.* "The Jews want to see money from Switzerland. Nothing other than money, money, money. . . . If peace with the Palestinians made money, the Jews would have forced it by now."

"After Delamuraz gave his interview the situation became quite alarming. We received anti-Semitic letters and it was very bad," said Swiss Jewish leader Thomas Lyssy. "There is a lot of latent anti-Semitism in Switzerland, but it was not good to show it. But once a member of the government said that, people thought, now we can say it too." Resentful of Switzerland's bad press over the last year or so, many Swiss said they supported Delamuraz. One opinion poll survey showed that 80 percent of Swiss did not believe that Delamuraz should resign, while another reported that less than a third thought the government should distance itself from the former president's remarks.

But not everyone rallied to his support. "When I hear Minister Delamuraz and his many friends, it sounds as if this were from the Middle Ages: the Jew who claims his basic rights is tiresome and 'extortionist,'" said one commentator in the liberal daily *Tages-Anzeiger.* "The Jew should not be so brazen, but rather remain nice even if Switzerland still hesitates after half a century to own up to its long-established failures and compensate via a fund what can still be compensated."

But no sooner had that soothing PR oil been poured on the troubled waters of Swiss–Jewish relations than another, even worse, blunder by the Swiss bankers filled the world's headlines. This was perhaps the finest example yet of the bankers' "concept deficit" about how to deal with the assets of Holocaust survivors that they still hold. In January 1997 an employee at UBS, Switzerland's biggest bank, whose records will be pored over by both the Volcker Commission and the Swiss government's Experts' Commission, shredded a pile of unique historical documents. Other, saved, papers recorded financial deals dating back to 1875, including loan records to Swiss and German firms and records of properties put under auction in Berlin between 1930 and 1940. Some of those records may have dealt with "forced auctions" of Jewish property in Nazi Germany, when the Third Reich confiscated Jewish land, businesses, and property and put it up for sale.

The remainder of the UBS records were saved from destruction by a conscience-stricken security guard, Christoph Meili, who stuffed them down his shirt and smuggled them out of UBS's headquarters on Bahnhofstrasse in Zürich. The humanitarian traditions of the wartime diplomat Charles Lutz and the border police commander Paul Grueninger, the Swiss saviors, live on. Meili, who handed the papers over to Jewish groups, was fired from his job. But he was hailed as a hero by both Swiss Jews and American Jewish leaders, who presented him with a golden menorah (candelabra) and a check for SF50,000 ($34,000) to cover his legal fees and living expenses. Meili could technically face prosecution for his actions, as they may break Switzerland's bank secrecy laws. So could UBS, if prosecutors decide that the shredding contravened a Swiss government ban on destroying any relevant documents that could help the search for dormant Jewish accounts. UBS denied that the employee who shredded the documents had any intention of destroying any records that could be used by the Experts' Commission and said that no client account records were destroyed. But just how important the documents were will never be known, as they are gone forever.

Barely two weeks had passed since the shredding scandal before Switzerland's battered public image took another pounding. At the end of January 1997, Carlo Jagmetti, Swiss ambassador to the United States, resigned after a Swiss newspaper published his thoughts on the Nazi gold crisis. These included the observations, detailed in a confidential report sent to Switzerland in December 1996, that Switzerland was fighting a "war . . . on two fronts: foreign and domestic." In most undiplomatic language, Jagmetti also spoke of "opponents" who "cannot be trusted." These were widely believed to be Jewish organizations and Senator Alfonse D'Amato. Both welcomed Jagmetti's resignation.

Soon afterward, the Swiss bankers finally surrendered to the inevitable. Three leading Swiss banks, Union Bank of Switzerland, Credit Suisse, and Swiss Bank Corporation, set up a Holocaust Memorial Fund, with an initial contribution of $70 million, to compensate Holocaust victims and their families. The three banks, who paid about one-third each, also encouraged other financial institutions to contribute to the fund, and Rainer Gut, head of Credit Suisse, suggested that other commercial banks, the government, and the Swiss National Bank should contribute the same amount. By mid-February 1997 it was still unclear exactly how the fund would be administered and the monies distributed, but the big three banks emphasized that its work would not prejudice or affect any claims from the Holocaust survivors or victims' relatives on monies in dormant accounts.

This sudden outburst of philanthropy aside, the $70 million donation was a small price for Swiss banks to pay to prevent a move that would have cost them hundreds of millions of dollars' worth of business. Welcoming the news of the Memorial Fund, the World Jewish Congress announced that plans for a worldwide Jewish boycott of Swiss banks were not canceled. Once some money had been laid on the negotiating table there was suddenly a new buzzword in the air: "cooperation." Even Senator D'Amato joined in this sudden outburst of mutual understanding, cautioning against "punitive" steps against the Swiss. The New York state comptroller, Carl McCall, also promised to reconsider his decision to bar deposits of state funds in Swiss banks.

History, it seems, can repeat itself, at least where Swiss banks are concerned. At the end of the Second World War Swiss officials had fobbed off the Allies by returning $60 million worth of German gold from the Swiss National Bank. This time around the big three private banks paid more than the Swiss National Bank, $70 million, but for that they had quieted their former foes at the World Jewish Congress, together with Senator D'Amato, and removed the threat of an international boycott. Quite a bargain.

By March 1997 the Swiss government finally decided that where the private banks go, it too must follow. Just as the furor over Switzerland's wartime record had initially focused on dormant accounts holding the assets of Holocaust victims, and then moved on to wider issues of Swiss economic collaboration with the Nazis, so, too, has the response. The banks, both private and the Swiss National Bank, say they will pay out, and now the Swiss government says it will as well, partly as a means of making amends for its economic links with the Third Reich and also to deflect the barrage of international criticism directed at Bern.

The Swiss National Bank offered to donate about $70 million to the compensation fund originally proposed by the big three banks: the Union Bank of Switzerland, Credit Suisse, and the Swiss Bank Corporation, so immediately doubling the amount available. The Swiss government's proposal is far more radical: to set up a separate $4.7 billion fund and use the interest on the money, which should reach several hundred million dollars a year, to help Holocaust victims, as well as those affected by other disasters, in a "Swiss Foundation for Solidarity." This fund will be paid for by a complicated act of financial juggling, at which Swiss bankers are quite adept.

Swiss gold reserves are currently valued at SF11.9 billion, but their true worth is much more, roughly three times as much. The Swiss still use a bookkeeping price that predates agreements in the 1970s that set up an open market for gold, valuing it at $117 per ounce, the price in 1971, while the market price in March 1997 was $350 per ounce. This valuation is enshrined in Swiss law, and to put it simply, there has not, until now, been any reason to change the status quo. The money for the Swiss Foundation for Solidarity will accrue when Switzerland increases the stated value of its gold reserves to match the current market price, and the difference between the two will make up the new fund.

BUT AMID this ever louder sound and fury, who remembers the individual Holocaust survivors in whose name so many claim to be acting? In Budapest, London, Tel Aviv, and New York, they sit and wait, hoping that somehow something will happen, and one day they might recover something of their family's lost wealth, or use it to aid their fellow Jews. As for Dr. Gyorgy Haraszti, principal of a Jewish school in Budapest, he doesn't want his grandfather's money, deposited in a Swiss bank, for himself, and doesn't really believe that he will ever see it. "It is lost. It is not my money. It belonged to my grandparents and my relatives who were killed. But I think it would be very useful if the Swiss banks would say, 'We are giving ten thousand dollars for community purposes.' It would be a mark of goodwill if the banks gave money for orphanages or the old people's home."

Like other children of Holocaust survivors, Dr. Haraszti could make a formal application to the Swiss Bankers' Association to try to track down his family's assets. He would have to fill out a six-page form giving as many details as possible about his grandfather's account. With the form he would have to enclose a check for SF100.

Over fifty years after the SS boss and chief Nazi looter Heinrich Himmler bit into his cyanide capsule, the Swiss bankers are still profiting from the Holocaust.

DOCUMENTS

Allied Claim Against Swiss for Return of Looted Gold

1. It has been determined from available ledgers of the German Reichsbank that a total of at least 398 million dollars worth of gold was shipped to Switzerland by the German Reichsbank during the war. This figure does not include the following which, when verified and amounts definitely determined, should also be taken up with the Swiss:

(a) one additional shipment known to have taken place after these books were closed and evacuated from Berlin;

(b) other shipments believed to have taken place early in the war and to have been recorded in earlier ledgers of the German Reichsbank which are not now available;

(c) an amount of approximately 12 million dollars worth of gold which the Germans seized when they looted the Italian gold but delivered directly to the Swiss.

2. It is perfectly possible that the entire amount of 398 million dollars (or more) worth of gold received by the Swiss from the German Reichsbank was looted gold because of the following facts:

(a) The large amounts of gold known to have been looted by the Germans from the countries which they occupied in Europe before and during the course of the war. It is known that at least 579 million dollars worth of gold was looted by the Germans and made available to the German Reichsbank. This figure represents a conservative tabulation based upon the estimates of the countries from which gold was looted and upon a careful examination of the records of the Germans.

(b) The relatively small amounts of legitimate gold available to them.

(c) The very small proportion of the looted gold which appears to have remained in Germany at the end of the war or to have been disposed of in countries other than Switzerland. The amount of such looted gold now identified as being in Germany at the end of the war or disposed of to foreign countries other than Switzerland is only 169 million dollars. These figures have been derived from a complete inventory of the gold found in Germany at the end of the war and a thorough examination of the records of the Reichsbank, including a detailed tracing of the processing and disposition of more than half of the gold originally looted.

Subtraction of the loot thus traced to German war-end stocks and to third countries (169) from the total loot (579) leaves 410 million dollars worth of loot or more than the entire amount of the known shipments to Switzerland still to be accounted for.

Allied Policies for Negotiation of Looted Gold Question

It is definitely known that the Swiss received at least 398 million dollars worth of gold from Germany during the course of the war. Of this amount the absolute minimum which is to be classified as loot is 185 million dollars. In arriving at this calculation every doubt has been resolved in favor of the Swiss. A more realistic approach indicates that the amount of looted gold taken by the Swiss is closer to 289 million dollars, and there is a possibility that all gold received by the Swiss from Germany was looted.

With these facts in mind, the Allied Governments should insist that the Swiss hand over immediately 185 million dollars worth of gold. Any bargaining between the Allies and Switzerland should only be with respect to the difference between 185 million and 398 million. As to this, the Allies should take the position that such difference should be turned over unless the Swiss are able to prove that such gold was either included in Germany's non-looted pre-war stocks or legitimately acquired after the beginning of the war.

It is possible that Switzerland will ask to see the data upon which the figure representing the minimum loot was based. If so, the Allied negotiators should agree to this concession upon the condition that the Swiss make available to Allied experts books, records and other documents in their possession relating to their gold stocks acquired from Germany and the disposition of such gold. However to avoid delays, such concessions should only be made after the Swiss have agreed to turn over the initial 185 million dollars worth of gold.

In taking the above position the Allied negotiators should make it clear to the Swiss officials that the fact that specific looted gold is no longer in Swiss possession does not operate to defeat the Allied claim or hinder or impede the handing over of an equivalent amount of gold. The Swiss should be advised that in cases where the original looted gold has passed from Switzerland to another country and the Swiss Government has made the equivalent amount of such gold available to the three named Allied powers, those powers will, insofar as is feasible, lend their assistance to the Swiss in obtaining the return of the specific gold or an equivalent. However, such an offer of assistance is not to be understood or construed as a guarantee on the part of the three governments named.

In the event that the Swiss Government should indicate its preference to settle the gold question by paying over a flat sum rather than assume the burden of proof as is indicated herein above, any compromise figure between 185 and 398 million which is agreed to by all of the Allied negotiators could be accepted. It would seem that 289 million would represent a reasonable settlement.

3. Even if one makes the assumption, which is quite unrealistic but presents the most favorable possible case for the Swiss, that the shipments which they received included all of the non-looted gold available to the Germans during the war, there still remains an absolute minimum of 185 million dollars of the gold taken by the Swiss from the German Reichsbank which must have been looted.

(a) A thorough examination of the records of the German Reichsbank and intensive interrogations in Germany of high Reichsbank officials in a position to know the true facts have determined the amount of hidden reserves of gold held by the Reichsbank before and during the war in addition to the published reserves which were known to the world.

(b) For the purpose at hand June 30, 1940 has been chosen as the base date in order to make the case as favorable as possible to the Swiss and eliminate any uncertainty as to legitimate acquisitions of gold by the Germans prior to their attack on the low countries. The Reichsbank's total gold holdings on that date were 232 million dollars.

(c) From the holdings shown above (232 million dollars), there must be subtracted an amount of 49 million dollars worth of loot accumulated by the Reichsbank in the preceding year, which gives a total of 183 million dollars worth of non-looted gold stocks held on June 30, 1940.

(d) The only significant source of legitimate gold still open to the Germans after June 1940 was Russia. German records show that the total amount of gold received from Russia between the outbreak of war with Poland and the attack on Russia was 23 million dollars. Although it is clear that much of the gold was received prior to June 30, 1940 and, therefore, is undoubtedly included in the German gold reserve figure for that date (183 million dollars), we are making the assumption most favorable to the Swiss and assuming that all 23 million was acquired after June 30, 1940 and is, therefore, to be added to the gold reserve shown on that date as additional legitimate gold. The resultant total of 206 million dollars is the maximum possible amount of non-looted gold available to the German Reichsbank at any time after June 1940.

(e) Subtracting from the total known shipments to Switzerland (398) the portion of those shipments which took place prior to the end of June 1940 (7 million) leaves an amount of at least 391 million dollars worth of gold received by the Swiss thereafter, and the difference between this amount and the maximum possible amount of non-loot available to the German in the same period (206) is 185 million dollars.

4. On the fairest assumptions the amount of loot taken by the Swiss from Germany can be estimated at 289 million dollars.

(a) It is unreal to assume, as was done above, in calculating the absolute minimum figure of looted gold received by the Swiss from Germany that every ounce of non-looted gold available to the Germans was sent to Switzerland.

(b) It is more realistic to assume that the ratio of loot to total gold available to the Germans was reflected in all German gold shipments including those to Switzerland. The total amount of gold available to the Germans after June 30, 1940, as shown above, was 785 million dollars of which 579 million dollars or 74% was loot. Applying this percentage to the total amounts received by the Swiss it would appear likely that at least 289 million thereof was loot.

CONFIDENTIAL

German Gold Movements (Estimate)
From April 1938 to May 1945 (In Millions of U.S. Dollars)

INCOME		OUTGO	
Germany started the war with estimated gold reserves of	100	Sold to Swiss National Bank	275 to 282
(Published gold reserves were only 29)		Possibly sold to Swiss Commercial Banks before 1942.	20
Taken over from Austria	46	Washed through Swiss National Bank depot account and eventually re-	
" " " " " Czechoslovakia	16	exported to Portugal and Spain	
" " " " " Danzig	4	(larger part by far to Portugal)	100
" " " " " Poland	12	Rumania	32.5
" " " " " Holland	168	Sweden	18.5
" " " " " Belgium	223	Found in Germany (including	
" " " " " Yugoslavia	25	64 earmarked for Italy and	
" " " " " Luxembourg	5	32 earmarked for Hungary)	293
" " " " " France	53	Sold to or used in Balkan	
" " " " " Italy	64	countries and Middle East—	
" " " " " Hungary	32	mainly Turkey	10
	748		752

Swiss Gold Movements (Swiss Official Statement)
From January 1, 1939 to June 30, 1945 (In Millions of U.S. Dollars)

Purchased from Germany	282.9	Sold to Germany	4.9
" " " " " Portugal	12.7	" " " Portugal	116.6
" " " " " Sweden	17.0	" " " Spain	42.6
		" " " Turkey	3.5

Conclusions: (1) All gold that Germany sold after a certain date, probably from early 1943 on, was looted gold, since her own reserves, including hidden reserves with which she started the war, were exhausted by that time; (2) out of $278,000,000-worth of gold that Switzerland purchased from Germany, the larger part was looted gold; in addition, Switzerland has taken $100,000,000 looted gold in deposit, which later on was re-exported to Spain and Portugal for German account; (3) among the gold that the Swiss sold during the war to Portugal, Spain, and Turkey, there could have been looted German gold; (4) the gold that Switzerland bought from Sweden during the war could theoretically be German looted gold; monetary experts all over the world (Switzerland has monetary experts at her disposal) knew or ought to have known, roughly the figures and movements as contained in the above estimate—certainly they knew the gold holdings and gold reserves of the German Reichsbank. Switzerland therefore was lacking good faith. In addition, she was warned that all Germany's own pre-war gold stocks had been used up by mid-1943 at the latest and therefore all the gold then in the possession of Germany must be presumed to be looted gold.

ES: CFFletcher:jd
2/5/46

Secret

No. 19,489
BY AIR POUCH   London, November 27, 1944

Economic Warfare (Safehaven) Series: No. 6
Subject: Transmitting Intelligence Report
           No. EW-Pa 188 by G-2 Economic
           Section, SHAEF, regarding plans of
           German industrialists for post-war
           operation.

SECRET
For Department, Treasury and Foreign Economic
   Administration.

The Honorable
   The Secretary of State
      Washington, D.C.

Sir:

   I have the honor to enclose Intelligence Report No. EB-Pa 188 by G-2 Economic
Section. SHAEF, dated November 7, 1944, describing the plans of German industrialists for the post-war resurrection of Germany. Among the topics dealt with in this
report are: patents, financial reserves, exportation of capital, and the strategic placing of
technical personnel.

                                   Respectfully yours,
                                   For the Ambassador:

                                   John W. Easton
                                   Lt. Colonel, P.A.
                                   Economic Warfare Division

Enclosure: Intelligence Report.

(Original and hectograph to Department)
JBW:jme

Enclosure No. 1 to despatch No. 19,489 of
Nov. 27, 1944, from the Embassy at London, England.

S E C R E T

SUPREME HEADQUARTERS
ALLIED EXPEDITIONARY FORCE
Office of Assistant Chief of Staff, G-2

7 November 1944

INTELLIGENCE REPORT NO. EW-Pa 139

SUBJECT: Plans of German industrialists to engage in underground activity after
Germany's defeat; flow of capital to neutral countries.

SOURCE: Agent of French Deuxieme Bureau, recommended by Commandant
Zindel. This agent is regarded as reliable and has worked for the French
on German problems since 1916. He was in close contact with the Germans, particularly industrialists, during the occupation of France and he
visited Germany as late as August, 1944.

1. A meeting of the principal German industrialists with interests in France was
held on August 10, 1944, in the Hotel Rotes Haus in Strasbourg, France, and attended
by the informant indicated above as the source. Among those present were the following:

Dr. Scheid, who presided, holding the rank of S.S. Obergruppenfuhrer and
Director of the Hecho (Hermsdorff & Schonburg) Company
Dr. Kaspar, representing Krupp
Dr. Tolle, representing Rochling
Dr. Sinderen, representing Messerschmitt
Drs. Kopp, Vier and Beerwanger, representing Rheinmetall
Captain Haberkorn and Dr. Ruhe, representing Bussing
Drs. Ellenmayer and Kardos, representing Volkswagonwerk
Engineers Drose, Yanchew and Koppehem, representing various factories in
Posen, Poland (Drose, Yanchew and Co., Brown-Boveri, Herkuleswerke,
Buschwerke, and Stadtwerke)
Captain Dornbusch, head of the Industrial Inspection Section at Posen
Dr. Meyer, an official of the German Naval Ministry in Paris
Dr. Strosener, of the Ministry of Armament, Paris.

2. Dr. Scheid stated that all industrial material in France was to be evacuated to
Germany immediately. The battle of France was lost for Germany and now the defense
of the Siegfried Line was the main problem. From now on also German industry must
realize that the war cannot be won and that it must take steps in preparation for a postwar commercial campaign. Each industrialist must make contacts and alliances with
foreign firms, but this must be done individually and without attracting any suspicion.

Moreover, the ground would have to be laid on the financial level for borrowing considerable sums from foreign countries after the war. As examples of the kind of penetration which had been most useful in the past, Dr. Scheid cited the fact that patents for stainless steel belonged to the Chemical Foundation, Inc., New York, and the Krupp Company of Germany jointly and that the U.S. Steel Corporation, Carnegie Illinois, American Steel and Wire, and National Tube, etc. were thereby under an obligation to work with the Krupp concern. He also cited the Zeiss Company, the Leica Company and the Hamburg-American Line as firms which had been especially effective in protecting German interests abroad and gave their New York addresses to the industrialists at this meeting.

3. Following this meeting a smaller one was held presided over by Dr. Boses of the German Armaments Ministry and attended only by representatives of Hecho, Krupp and Rochling. At this second meeting it was stated that the Nazi Party had informed the industrialists that the war was practically lost but that it would continue until a guarantee of the unity of Germany could be obtained. German industrialists must, it was said, through their exports increase the strength of Germany. They must also prepare themselves to finance the Nazi Party which would be forced to go underground as Maquis (in Gebirgeverteidigungstellen gehen). From now on the government would allocate large sums to industrialists so that each could establish a secure post-war foundation in foreign countries. Existing financial reserves in foreign countries must be placed at the disposal of the Party so that a strong German Empire can be created after the defeat. It is also immediately required that the large factories in Germany create small technical offices or research bureaus which would be absolutely independent and have no known connection with the factory. Those bureaus will receive plans and drawings of new weapons as well as documents which they need to continue their research and which must not be allowed to fall into the hands of the enemy. These offices are to be established in large cities where they can be most successfully hidden as well as in little villages near sources of hydro-electric power where they can pretend to be studying the development of water resources. The existence of these is to be known only by very few people in each industry and by chiefs of the Nazi Party. Each office will have a liaison agent with the Party. As soon as the Party becomes strong enough to re-establish its control over Germany the industrialists will be paid for their effort and cooperation by concessions and orders.

4. These meetings seem to indicate that the prohibition against the export of capital which was rigorously enforced until now has been completely withdrawn and replaced by a new Nazi policy whereby industrialists with government assistance will export as much of their capital as possible. Previously exports of capital by German industrialists to neutral countries had to be accomplished rather surreptitiously and by means of special influence. Now the Nazi party stands behind the industrialists and urges them to save themselves by getting funds outside Germany and at the same time to advance the Party's plans for its post-war operation. This freedom given to the industrialists further cements their relations with the Party by giving them a measure of protection.

5. The German industrialists are not only buying agricultural property in Germany but are placing their funds abroad, particularly in neutral countries. Two main banks through which this export of capital operates are the Basler Handelsbank and the

Schweizerische Kreditanstalt of Zurich. Also there are a number of agencies in Switzerland which for a five per cent commission buy property in Switzerland, using a Swiss cloak.

6. After the defeat of Germany the Nazi Party recognizes that certain of its best known leaders will be condemned as war criminals. However, in cooperation with the industrialists it is arranging to place its less conspicuous but most important members in positions with various German factories as technical experts or members of its research and designing offices.

For the A.C. of S., G-2.

WALTER K. SCHWINN
G-2, Economic Section

Prepared by

MELVIN N. FAGEN

Distribution:

Same as EW-Pa 1.
U.S. Political Adviser, SHAEF
British Political Adviser, SHAEF

NOTES

Abbreviations refer to these archives:

CZA   Central Zionist Archives,
Jerusalem
HNA   Hungarian National Archive,
Budapest
IWM   Imperial War Museum,
London
NA   U.S. National Archives,
Washington, D.C.
PRO   British Public Records Office,
London
SFA   Swiss Federal Archives,
Bern
YV   Yad Vashem Holocaust
Memorial Museum,
Jerusalem

All interviews listed in these notes were conducted personally by the author unless otherwise stated.

Chapter 1: A Trust Betrayed

3   Opening epigraph: Interview with Dr. Zoltan and Katalin Csillag, Budapest, October 1996.

3   Second epigraph: Press reports, November 1996.

6   Auschwitz preparations for extermination of Hungarian Jewry: Randolph Braham, *The Politics of Genocide* (New York: Columbia University Press, 1981), p. 674.

7   Letter to Ben-Gurion, 12 July 1944: CZA, record group S25.

7   Auschwitz operating at full capacity: Braham, p. 676.

8   Dr. Zoltan and Katalin Csillag interview, Budadest, October 1996.

9   Dr. Gyorgy Haraszti interview, Budapest, June 1996.

11   Sergio Karas interview, Toronto, July 1996.

11   Aide to Senator D'Amato interview, Washington, D.C., July 1996.

13   Testimony of Hans Baer to Senate Banking Committee, 23 April 1996: Available from Bank Julius Baer.

19   Jack Weisblack telephone interview, New York, July 1996.

21   Ron Singer interview, Toronto, July 1996.

24   Seymour Rubin interview, Washington, D.C., July 1996.

25   Peter Hug quotes: Press reports, October 1996.

25   Gisela Blau interview, Zürich, December 1996.

Chapter 2: Looting a Continent

27   Opening epigraph: Account of the torture of Alexander Leitner's mother, quoted in "The Tragedy of the Jews in Nagyrad (Oradea): Memoirs of Alexander Leitner," Hungary files, CZA.

27   Second epigraph: Account of the activities of the Devisenschutzkommando, Report E 259, 29 May 1945. FO 1046/763, PRO.

28   Yehuda Bauer interview, Jerusalem, November 1996.

28   Swiss National Bank legal office report, 1943–1950: Quoted in Robert Vogler, *The Swiss National Bank's Gold Transaction With the German Reichsbank* (Bern: Swiss National Bank, 1985), p 8.

28   Gerhard Riegner telegram on Nazi plans for extermination of Jewry: *Encyclopedia of the Holocaust*, Israel Gutman, ed. (New York: Macmillan, 1990), p. 1275.

31   Nazi occupation payment figures and U.S. Strategic Bombing Survey study:

Quoted in William Shirer, *The Rise and Fall of the Third Reich* (New York: Simon & Schuster, 1990), p. 943. Cited hereafter as Shirer.

31 Art treasures collected for Goering by Miedl: Information extracted from Safehaven file, included in report from U.S. Embassy in London, 22 September 1945, NA. Declassification authority NND 765055, 6 February 1996, NA.

31 Goering's secret order of 5 November 1940: Ibid., p. 945.

32 Details of bids for Auschwitz crematoria: Shirer, p. 971.

33 Nazi looting of Vienna: Shirer, p. 351.

34 Devisenschutzkommando, *op. cit.*

36 Leitner, "Tragedy of the Jews in Nagyvarad (Oradea)," *op. cit.*

41 Description of Merkers valuables included in "Disposition of Loot by Reichsbank", 8 May 1945. German Loot-FO 1046/763, PRO.

42 Eisenhower telegram, 6 May 1945. German Gold Hoards—FO 1046/267. PRO.

43 Albert Thoms interrogation report: Included in "Disposition of SS Loot by Reichsbank," *op. cit.*

45 Reichsbank memo on Melmer, 31 March 1944: FO 1046/763, PRO.

46 Letter from Reichsbank to Berlin Municipal Pawnshop: Shirer, p. 974.

47 Oswald Pohl's conversation with Emil Puhl: Shirer, p. 973.

47 Reichsbank official on dental gold: Shirer, p. 974.

47 Czechoslovak Finance Ministry memo, 23 September 1945: Declassification authority NND 775059, 10 April 1996, NA.

48 WJC official interview, New York, June 1996.

47 Livingston T. Merchant letter, U.S. Embassy, Paris, 19, July 1946: RG 59 1945–49, Box 4211, NA.

Chapter 3: The Financiers of Genocide

49 Opening epigraph: Quoted in Robert Vogler, *The Swiss National Bank's Gold Transactions With German Reichsbank From 1939 to 1945* (Zürich: Swiss National Bank, 1985). Cited hereafter as Vogler, *Swiss National Bank's Gold Transactions.*

49 Second epigraph: Marc Masurovsky interview, Washington, D.C., July 1996.

50 Allied Claims Against Swiss for Return of Looted Gold, 5 February 1946. Declassification authority NND 959150, June 11, 1996.

52 Paul Einzig's article: Quoted in Vogler, *Swiss National Bank's Gold Transactions.*

56 Masurovsky interview.

57 Robert Vogler interview, Zürich, December 1996.

58 "Red House" report on plans of German industrialists for postwar operations. Economic Warfare (Safehaven) series no. 6, London, 27 November 1945. Declassification authority NND 765055, 6 May 1996, NA.

63 Memo 2694, enclosing report entitled "Objectionable Activities of Two Leading Swiss Banks During 1944," on Credit Suisse, Zürich, and Union Bank of Switzerland. Declassification authority NND 968103, 16 April 1996, NA.

64 Sofindus intercepts, FO 115/4149, FO.

69 U.S. State Department, memo on Portugal and looted gold, 6 December 1946: Quoted by Reuters, 29 October 1996.

Chapter 4: Capital *über Alles*: The Bank for International Settlements

70 Opening epigraph: Piet Clement interview, Basel, December 1996.

70 Second epigraph: Michael Hirsch and Christopher Dickey, "A Global Trail of Gold," *Newsweek*, 4 November 1996.

71 Gian Trepp interview, Zürich, December 1996.

72 Auboin's description of the Bank for International Settlements: In "The Bank for International Settlements," *Essays in International Finance*, no. 22, May 1955 (International Finance Section,

Department of Economics and Sociology, Princeton University).

74   Gian Trepp interview.

75   Piet Clement interview.

75   Emil Puhl interrogation report: FO 1046/24, PRO.

77   Walther Funk testimony at Nuremburg: Quoted in Charles Higham, *Trading With the Enemy* (New York, 1984), p. 17.

78   Piet Clement interview.

80   Merle Cochrane letter to Henry Morgenthau, 9 May 1938: Quoted in Higham, p. 6.

81   Gian Trepp interview.

82   Marc Masurovsky interview.

83   Letter from British Embassy in Washington, D.C., to State Department, 2 November 1942, PRO.

83   Andrew Crockett interview, Basel, December 1996.

87   Thomas McKittrick letter to Clifford Norton, 2 May 1945: FO 1046/267, PRO.

89   U.S. government study of the activities of the BIS: Hirsch and Dickey, *op. cit.*

Chapter 5: Whose Safehaven?

91   Opening epigraph: In note by Swiss Banking Society official, dated 5 March 1941, translated by Congressional Research Service, Library of Congress, Washington, D.C.

91   Second epigraph: In Safehaven report 11902, on Johann Wehrli & Co., Zürich, dated 12 June 1945, NA.

94   Foley memo to Morgenthau on placing of Treasury agents in New York branches of Swiss banks, 2 June 1942: Declassification authority NDD 968103, 16 April 1996, NA.

95   Seymour Rubin interview, Washington, D.C., July 1996.

98   Role of Johann Wehrli bank, Zürich: Safehaven Report 11902.

99   Maj. Gen. Georg Thomas, Chief of the Nazi Military Economic Staff: Shirer, p. 259.

99   Hjalmar Schacht's reports and memos to Hitler: Shirer, pp. 259–60.

100   U.S. military official interview

with Dr. Landwehr: Undated attachment to report. Declassification authority NND 897171, 1 April 1996.

102   U.S. official on Johann Wehrli & Co.: Quoted in Nicholas Faith, *Safety in Numbers* (London: Hamish Hamilton, 1982), p. 106.

103   Eric Cable letter: Ibid.

103   Safehaven report 11902 on Johann Wehrli & Co., Zürich.

104   Safehaven report 12179 on Bally Shoe Factories, dated 26 July 1945. Declassification authority NND 735027, 28 March 1996.

105   Nazi participation in 358 Swiss economic enterprises: Safehaven report 2969, included in telegram from American Legation, Bern, 31 May 1945. Declassificiation authority NND 968/03, 22 April 1996, NA.

107   Correspondence on Kurt and Anny Kadisch, RG 59 Department of State, file 1930–1939 from 354.113T to 354.117/162, box 1529, NA.

Chapter 6: The Art of Economic Camouflage

109   Opening epigraph: In memo from German Economics Minister, Berlin, September 1939, on camouflaging Nazi foreign assets, in Control Commission for Germany (British Element), Dusseldorf 1945, report dated 27 November 1945, entitled "Reichs Economic Ministry—Secret Instructions for Camouflage of External German Assets. Germany 1945—Assets and Neutrals," FO 371/46767, PRO.

109   Second epigraph: In report to Royal Society on 7 February 1945, London, by Brig. N. Hamilton Fairley. Germany 1945 FO 371/46765, PRO.

110   Memo on camouflaging Nazi economic assets, German Economics Minister, 9 September 1939.

114   Nazi activities in Davos-Dorf and Davos-Platz, 5 September 1945: Record Group 59, NA.

121   W. A. Brandt letter to Lt. Col. Dendy, 19 December 1945: "Germany

1945—Germany and Neutrals," FO 371/46766, PRO.

122   Letter from Commercial Secretariat of the British Legation in Bern, re: Moser: Ibid.

122   Gian Trepp interview, Zürich, December 1996.

123   Brandt letter to Vyvyan, 15 September 1945, "Germany 1945—Germany and Neutrals," FO 371/46766, PRO.

124   Safehaven Report, Istanbul, 21 May 1945, on Swiss diplomats and Red Cross. Declassification authority NND 907172, 4 February 1996, NA.

125   U.S. Intelligence Report, Enemy Agents and the Red Cross, 4 February 1944.

127   *The ICRC Infiltrated by the Nazis?* Geneva, International Committee of the Red Cross, 15 September 1996.

129   Edward Reichmann telephone interview, Budapest, 4 December 1996; personal interview, Budapest, 16 December 1996.

131   U.S. memo to American embassy in Madrid on Iberia passenger air certificates, Tangier 18 October 1945, NA.

132   J. Rives Child letter to Renee Reichmann, Tangier, 13 June 1945. Copy given to author by Edward Reichmann.

132   Report of Brig. N. Hamilton Fairley to Royal Society, *op. cit.*

133   Lord Winster letter to Lord Hankey, 16 February 1945: "Germany 1945. FO 371/46765, PRO.

133   Marc Masurovsky interview, Washington, D.C., July 1996.

133   IG Farben as metaphor: Shirer, p. 665.

135   Allen and John Foster Dulles and IG Farben: Quoted in Mark Aarons and John Loftus, *The Secret War Against the Jews* (New York: St. Martin's Press, 1994), p. 66.

Chapter 7: The Boat Is Full

136   Opening epigraph: In A. A. Haesler, *The Lifeboat Is Full: Switzerland and the Refugees, 1933–1945* (New York: Funk & Wagnalls, 1969), p. 53.

136   Second epigraph: Ibid., p. 49.

142   Letter from Federal Department of Police and Justice to Swiss legation in Berlin on limiting German immigration, 13 April 1938: Ibid., p.31.

142   Guido Koller interview, Zürich, December 1996.

143   Discussions between German diplomat Roediger and Swiss ambassador to Germany Paul Dinichert, in Haesler, *Lifeboat,* p. 32.

143   Dinichert's report on Jewish immigration discussions: Ibid.

145   Report of Dr. Franz Kappeler on J-stamp proposal: Ibid., p. 40.

147   Thomas Lyssy interview, Bern, December 1996.

148   Isabelle Silberg interview, London, October 1996.

156   Betty Bloom interview, London, October, 1996.

157   Albert Goering's Swiss bank account: HO 4/101 SOE Hungary no. 17, PRO.

Chapter 8: A Nest of Spies

161   Opening epigraph: Col. Roger Masson letter to Karl Kobelt, Masson file group E27, files 10019, 10025, 10027, SFA.

162   Second epigraph: Gen. Walter Schellenberg interrogation report, undated, Masson files, SFA.

164   Guido Koller interview, Bern, December 1996.

166   Dispatch of SF3,000 to *L'Action Nationale*, letter dated 7 August 1940. "Documents sur la subversion nazie en Suisse pendant l'été et l'automne 1940," *Relations internationales,* 1975, no. 3, pp. 107–32, Paris, Swiss files, YV.

167   David Whipple interview, McLean, Va., July 1996.

170   Gisela Blau interview, Zürich, December 1996.

172   General Guisan letter to Gen. Walter Schellenberg, 6 March 1943: In Jozef Garlinski, *The Swiss Corridor* (London: Dent, 1981), p. 115.

173   Masson's reaction to the March Alert: Ibid., p. 117.

173   Masson letter to Karl Kobelt, 3 October 1945: Masson files, SFA.

175   [Second] Allied Intelligence Interrogation Report on General Walter Schellenberg: Interrogation Summaries, no. 733 Schellenberg, 13 December 1946, IWM.

176   Masson to Kobelt: *Op. cit.,* SFA.

176   Jacques Picard interview.

176   Marc Masurovsky interview.

Chapter 9: Dealing With the Devil

181   Opening epigraph: Report of Dr. J. Goldin, Istanbul Office of the Jewish Agency, 16 May 1945, Charles Lutz files, YV.

181   Second epigraph: Extract from *Das Bericht des judischen Rettungskomitees aus Budapest, 1942–1945,* by Dr. Reszo Kasztner, Kasztner files, CZA.

185   Hungarian police raid on Budapest's international ghetto: Goldin report, *op. cit.*

186   Extracts from Swiss collective passports: Charles Lutz files, SFA and YV.

188   Eichmann interview: *Life,* 5 December 1960.

189   Yehuda Bauer interview, Jerusalem, November 1996.

190   Katalin Csillag interview, Budapest, October 1996.

191   Ernest Stein telephone interview, New York, July 1996.

192   Eichmann on Kurt Becher: *Life,* 5 December 1960.

192   OSS report on Obergruppenführer Becher, Germany and Hungary, Nazi Financial Operations, Switzerland, 6 April 1945. Declassification authority NND 877183, 25 January 1992, NA.

193   Hungarian Holocaust survivor's view of Reszo Kasztner: Dora Czuk interview, Budapest, November 1996.

194   British interrogation report of Andor Grosz: FO 371/42711, Brand—German interrogations, PRO.

197   Bank Intercommerz AG's offer to wipe out Hungarian debts: Protocol of the Hungarian Government, 2 August 1944/25, HNA.

198   Saly Mayer's dispute with Recha Sternbuch: Joseph Friedenson and David Kranzler, *Heroine to the Rescue: The Incredible Story of Recha Sternbuch* (New York: Mesorah Publications, 1984), p. 34.

200   Himmler's note to himself: Quoted in Bauer, *Jews for Sale,* p. 231.

200   Becher and the war refugee telegram: Kasztner *Bericht,* Kasztner files, CZA.

200   Meeting on 5 November at Hotel Baur, Zürich: Bauer, *op. cit.,* p. 205.

201   Roswell McClelland's statement on Mayer and Kasztner negotiations with the SS, Bern, 6 February 1945: Kasztner files, CZA.

201   U.S. intelligence report on the Weiss family, Lisbon, 23 May 1945: Safehaven Hungary files, NA.

202   Marc Masurovsky interview, Washington, D.C., July 1996.

204   Thomas DeKornfeld interview, Budapest, October 1996.

205   Ernest Stein telephone interview, New York, July 1996.

205   Enskilda Bank and the Soviet Union: Pavel Sudaplatov, *Special Tasks* (Boston: Little Brown, 1995), p. 203.

206   Morgenthau memo on the Wallenberg brothers: U.S. Treasury, 7 February 1945. Declassification authority NND 760050, NA.

207   Ernest Stein interview.

207   Yvonne Singer interview, Toronto, July 1996.

208   Raoul Wallenberg report on Hungarian Jews, September 1944: OSS Jewish Desk files. Declassification authority NND 907191, 8 May 1996, NA.

Chapter 10: Back to the Future

209   Opening epigraph: *Tages-Anzeiger* cartoon, 13 November 1996.

209   Second epigraph: Zvi Barak interview, Jerusalem, November 1996.

210   Hitler's bank account: U.S. intelligence report, "Objectionable Activities by Switzerland on Behalf of the Nazis." Declassification authority NND 968103,

15 July 1996. Reported in *Jewish Chronicle,* 6 September 1996.

211   Hitler's expulsion of Himmler and Goering from the Nazi party: Shirer, p. 1126.

212   Himmler's death by cyanide capsule: Shirer, p. 1141.

213   Masurovsky interview.

214   Juan and Eva Perón and Nazi loot: Enrique Krauze, "The Blonde Leading the Blind: Evita," *New Republic,* 10 February 1997.

215   Swiss National Bank report on Washington negotiations: Vogler, *Swiss National Bank's Gold Transactions.*

215   Hirs on the Washington negotiations: Vogler, ibid., p. 12.

216   Correspondence between Malcolm Rifkin and Greville Janner: Made available to author.

217   Stuart Eizenstat interview, Washington, D.C., July 1996.

219   Peter Burkhard interview, Bern, December 1996.

220   President Clinton's letter to World Jewish Congress president Edgar Bronfman: Press reports, November 1996.

222   Former Swiss president Kaspar Villiger on the J-stamp: Press reports, May 1995.

222   Swiss foreign minister Flavio Cotti on Switzerland and the Holocaust: Press reports, October 1996.

224   Washington lobbyist interview, on Senator D'Amato, Washington, D.C., July 1996.

224   Stuart Eizenstat interview.

225   Rabbi Thomas Salamon letter to *Jewish Chronicle,* January 1996.

226   CJMC spokesman telephone interview, February 1997.

226   Swiss Jews' fears of competing Jewish claims for money: background interview, Bern, December 1996.

227   Marc Masurovsky interview.

228   Hungarian Gold Train document: itemized contents list; Ferenc Nagy letter, Budapest, 10 May 1945; Moshe Shertok letter, 24 May 1945; record of conversation with Yehuda Gaulan, 16 July 1945; record of meeting with Arthur Marget, 16 September 1947; *New York Times* report, 29 December 1948; correspondence from Maurice Boukstein: All in file S25/10719, CZA.

230   Gideon Rafael telephone interview, January 1997.

230   Scandal over former Swiss president Jean-Pascal Delamuraz: Press reports, January 1997.

231   Zvi Barak interview, Jerusalem, November 1996.

232   Swiss interior minister Ruth Dreifuss quotes: press reports, January 1997.

236   Gyorgy Haraszti interview, Budapest, June 1996.

BIBLIOGRAPHY

Auboin, Roger. "The Bank for International Settlements, 1930–1955." *Essays in International Finance*, no. 22, May 1955. Princeton University, International Finance Section.

Bank for International Settlements. *The Bank for International Settlements and the Basle Meeting*. Basle: 1980.

Bauer, Yehuda. *Jews for Sale? Nazi-Jewish Negotiations, 1933–1945*. New Haven: Yale University Press, 1994.

Ben-Tov, Arieh. *Facing the Holocaust in Hungary*. Henri Dunant Institute, Geneva; Dordrecht, Boston and London: Martinus Nijoff, 1988.

Braham, Randoph L. *The Politics of Genocide: The Holocaust in Hungary*. New York: Columbia University Press, 1981.

Craig, Gordon A. *Germany, 1866–1945. The Oxford History of Modern Europe*. New York: Oxford University Press, 1980.

Dawidowicz, Lucy S. *The War Against the Jews: 1933–45*. New York: Bantam, 1986.

Dobroszycki, Lucian, ed. *The Chronicle of the Lodz Ghetto, 1941–1944*. New Haven: Yale University Press, 1984.

"Documents sur la subversion nazie en Suisse pendant l'été et l'automne, 1940," *Relations Internationales*, 1975, no. 3, pp. 107–32.

Faith, Nicholas. *Safety in Numbers: The Mysterious World of Swiss Banking*. London: Hamish Hamilton, 1982.

Garlinski, Jozef. *The Swiss Corridor*. London, Melbourne, and Toronto: J. M. Dent & Sons, 1981.

Gilbert, Martin. *Auschwitz and the Allies*. London: Mandarin, 1991.

Goldhagen, Daniel Jonah. *Hitler's Willing Executioners: Ordinary Germans and the Holocaust*. New York: Knopf, 1996.

Gutman, Israel, ed. *Encyclopedia of the Holocaust*. New York: Macmillan, 1989.

Haesler, A. A. *The Lifeboat Is Full: Switzerland and the Refugees, 1933–1945*. New York: Funk and Wagnalls, 1969.

Hitler, Adolf. *Hitler's Secret Conversations, 1941–1944*. New York: Signet, 1961

Jacobs, Gerald. *Sacred Games*. London: Penguin, 1995.

Kahn, David. *Hitler's Spies*. New York: Macmillan, 1978.

Levy, Alan. *The Wiesenthal File*. Grand Rapids, Mich.: William B. Eerdmans, 1994.

Linklater, Magnus, Isobel Hilton, and Neal Ascherson. *Klaus Barbie, the Fourth Reich, and the Neo-Fascist Connection*. London: Coronet Books, 1985.

Loftus, John and Mark Aarons. *The Secret War Against the Jews*. New York: St. Martin's Press, 1994.

Marton, Kati. *Wallenberg: Missing Hero*. New York: Arcade, 1995.

Perrault, Giles. *The Red Orchestra*. New York: Pocket Books, 1970.

Picard, Jacques. *Switzerland and the Assets of the Missing Victims of the Nazis.* Zürich: Bank Julius Baer, 1996.

Red Cross, International Committee of. *The ICRC Infiltrated by the Nazis?* Geneva: 1CRC, 1996.

Segev, Tom. *The Seventh Million: The Israelis and the Holocaust.* New York: Hill and Wang, 1994.

Shirer, William L. *The Rise and Fall of the Third Reich: A History of Nazi Germany* 20th ed. New York: Simon & Schuster, 1990.

Sudoplatov, Pavel. *Special Tasks.* Boston: Little, Brown, 1995.

Trepp, Gian. *Bankgeschäfte mit dem Feind.* Zürich: Rotpunktverlag, 1996.

Turner, Henry Ashby, Jr. *German Big Business and the Rise of Hitler.* New York: Oxford University Press, 1985.

Vogler, Robert. *The Swiss National Bank's Gold Transactions With the German Reichsbank From 1939 to 1945.* Zürich: Swiss National Bank, 1984.

Wallenberg, Raoul. *Letters and Dispatches, 1924–1944.* New York: Arcade, 1995.

Waters, Donald Arthur. *Hitler's Secret Ally, Switzerland.* La Mesa, Calif.: Pertinent Publications, 1994.

Wyman, David S. *The Abandonment of the Jews.* New York: Pantheon Books, 1985.

INDEX